THE LONG LETTERS HOME

THE LONG LETTERS HOME

THE COLOR OF MORNING

1990

To Gaby with love and gratitude for your friendship
Ralph

Ralph Alpert

Published by Rach Mi El Press, Santa Cruz, California
PO Box 8288, Santa Cruz, CA 95061.

Photo editing and design of book interior, cover and maps
by Rebecca Barnes.

Drawing on back cover by Rich Mick.

Typefaces used are Century Schoolbook, Minion Pro,
Calibri, and Optima.

ISBN-13: 978-0692819562 (Custom Universal)
ISBN-10: 0692819568

to the saints among us

Contents

A Brief Introduction

In the 1980s I started writing long letters home, when traveling, to several friends. Later, I saved the originals and mailed copies. When I returned from the trips I put the originals of the Long Letters Home in a cabinet and never looked at them until last year when I happened to pick up one (Jerusalem, 1995) and began to read it.

Hey, I said to myself, this is interesting stuff. I began to type them up on my computer.

About this particular 1990 letter: I went to Spain in 1983 with a group from Santa Cruz to study Spanish for the month of August at the University in Salamanca. Afterwards, in September, I traveled about Spain. In Madrid, I met Pepin, a remarkable guy doing remarkable work with "marginados" (poor people on the margin of society) with some help from the new Socialist government.

In 1984, I came to Europe again with two ideas – first, to be in Spain in August, where Pepin was conducting a camp (in the Sierra de Guaderrama, near Madrid) for kids from the poor South side of Madrid, and then to go to France in September where I and six friends from Sacramento had rented a house for a month in the village of Venasque, near Avignon. Between Madrid and Venasque, I wanted to learn some more French and I found a little school in a village (La Petite Eguille) 90 miles north of Bordeaux.

I loved La Petite Eguille and La Ferme (the school) and I came back three more times (1986, 1990 and 1992).

In Madrid, I became very involved with Pepin, the people around him, and the work. In 1987, I helped find an isolated former dairy farm five miles from the small town of Huete, some 75 miles east of Madrid, for a farm-school (la granja-escuela) for Escuelas para la Vida (Schools for Living). Escuelas para la Vida, which is still going in 2016, is a place where ex-drug addicts and other marginados can learn a different way of living, one where they can see and value themselves as the subjects of their own life and not as objects of a consumer society, and can help to create a fairer society. I came back to Madrid and Escuelas para la Vida some dozen times over the years.

THANKS to Joyce Michaelson, for appreciating this disjointed scribbling; to Marilyn Bosworth, the distinguished reader of the letters to the Tuesday Pizza and Literary Society; and to Sunshine Gibbs and the other intrepid members of the Society. And to Diana Rose, Marty Stevens, and especially Rebecca Barnes, for help in translating scribbles to book.

~

San Francisco to Paris

A great gray airplane flying across the turning world

San Francisco Thursday, March 15, 1990, 7:58 AM
Well. There are two old people in the seats in back of
me. The old man has an oxygen bottle and the steward
is standing there in a dark-blue golden-wings uniform –
stern and official and officious. Beside him the daughter.
No, they don't speak English, she says. Only Spanish.
Oldness and age. It comes, it comes. Day by day and
the flowers wilt and stone buildings crumble and bodies
stumble. And yet, the sky shows baby blue with grey
wisps floating above the dark green hills.

This letter is starting late – usually it begins itself at
4:30 AM, in the Denny-ness of the very early morning –
waiting for the airport bus. But this time Janine came to
my house at 5:19 AM – she was eleven minutes early and
I chose a sweater from the blue and gray – I chose Union
blue and not the dignified old Confederacy gray – but not
to choose ancient sides and old griefs – no – not at all – it
was for Paris I chose – the blue is warmer. Ah, choices
and Paris – there was a famous choice and an ancient
grief. Paris chose Helen and the strife began.

Well my my my – I only have 13 hours to Paris and it will not be enough time. Enough time to finish reading *Little Dorrit* and *Where Are We? – The Inner Life of America's Jews* and two Economist magazine and the San Francisco Chronicle, and to scribble in this letter and to write two checks and to read three grant proposals from the American Friends Service Committee and to sleep and to look out the little window and ahead of the great grey wing to the snowy mountains and the dry mountains and the great flat plains, the lakes and the ever-blue sky.

There is hustle and bustle and rattle and announcements. They say the airplane is about to move. We cannot leave the gate until all passengers are seated with seatbelts fastened, he says once more – the father steward to the wayward children passengers. Okay – Now the plane is backing out. Four hours and 35 minutes to New York, he says – at 37,000 feet. And I feel warm – maybe I should have gone with the Confederacy. He now gives all the instructions and I look at the plastic card for where the exits are – this is a Lockheed 1011. Golly, I think I must take off my sweater.

I did and I am still warm. So. Shall I read my morning Chronicle now? Maybe I should help lift this plane from the ground first.

I look out the window and I see the big fat gray and red TWA plane ahead of us moving up to the takeoff runway. There is green grass of California winter between the runways. The plane ahead runs down the runway – smaller and smaller and I see it turn its nose up and lift just before our plane turns onto the runway. I tighten my seatbelt a little more. Here we go – rumble and roar and slick we slide along. Faster and bumpier and up. Goodbye Momma Earth. Hello Zeus and blue heaven's host.

We are out over the gray blue bay and off the wing is gray white San Francisco. And the bridge and now Oakland rising. California here I go – we will meet another Springtime, California. The hills are green and comfortably folded – the rumpled green hills of California Spring. There is Carquinez Straits – the wing dips north and then rises south.

Oh, I have a tiredness in my bones – I have been a long time tiring. What can I make of all this? The great grey airplane, the green hills below, the misty stained air, the muffled roar of the great engines, the confusion of California and vast America, the tightness at my temples, all my going and coming and being and tiring? Where shall I find reason and reasons, sense, meaning, purpose, serenity? There are the square fields, green and brown, of the Central Valley. We move quickly – the plane flies back across the turning world, which spins and loops through dark space and everything is turning, moving – this around that and that around the other and all rushing outward to the end of time.

Oh, the man in back has started taking the oxygen. The steward – who has the accent and the portliness and the gray mustache to be a Swiss maitre d' (what do I know from maitre d's?), says to the middle-aged stewardess handing out headphones "This bottle lasts one hour and 35 minutes." She says, "That is 9:30 so I will write it on this envelope." She looks at me and says – "I'll wonder what that 9:30 means when I see it." I have 8:40 – so how does she add one and 35 and get 9:30? Maybe her watch is set to Mongolian Central Time.

Ah – the snow-capped mountains approach. Lovely. Mighty. The wings rise to South and I no longer see the mountains. Dip down again. There is dense fog among the mountains in places. Ah – the navy blue winter lakes. I went this way – over the high mountains – not long ago – to Phoenix. My, the engines are bouncing – ball-like – is that right? proper? mechanical? And the cabin wall at my elbow bounces also – this is a twitchy airplane. That, I don't like. I like serene airplanes, sedate airplanes, gracious old-lady-from-Pasadena airplanes. Shape up and simmer down, Airplane 1011! Maybe there are down drafts and up drafts and crosswinds over these icy mountains. Ah, there is a pale blue lake among pale brown hills. I would say Pyramid Lake. No, not pale brown – I'd call it iron-brown hills.

To eat an apple – an organic Santa Cruz apple? To eat a peach? What is his name? Yes, J. Alfred. J. Alfred Prufrock. Let us go then, you and I / when the evening is spread out across the sky / like a patient etherized upon a table. I'm not sure of that last line – did he say "etherized"?   I yawn. I slept only four or six hours last night, depending on when I woke – I woke at 3:30 but then I woke again at 4:45.

And the world turns and the waking is done and the packing is done and the driving and arriving is done, and Janine is gone, the plane rises and it moves against the turning world. And what is my part, my place, that is not motion? Because the motion will go on – I have no choice on that. Is there a way to stop the motion? To be blue sky and faint white moon? Ah, there ahead are more snowy mountains. The desert mountains, bright white atop the iron-brown slopes. My, I look out and I see several white mountain islands floating in the misty stained air.

10:31 AM   Below there are gray clouds. I was up walking about for 10 minutes. The small gray man in back of me breathes from the oxygen bottle. I didn't look closely as I walked by – I didn't want to stare. I saw the green plastic bag just below his chin and a white plastic bottle below that.

I think about when we will arrive in New York. We left at 8:15 – I think my ticket says we arrive at 4:35 PM. It is now 10:35 AM on my watch (California time). The pilot said the flight would take four hours and 35 minutes. Now. We put all those numbers together and what have we? Bingo? No. 8:15 plus 4 hours is 12:15 plus 35 minutes is 12:50 plus 3 hours time difference is 3:50 – that is an hour earlier than my ticket says. Well, we shall see what happens in the event. Now I will read *Little Dorrit*.

12:17 PM (3:17 PM New York time)   Well, I see an ocean out there, I think. So we must be around New York. I just woke from an hour's nap. So maybe we will indeed arrive an hour earlier than my ticket says.

12:24 PM   No, I am a mistaken – the stewardesses are passing out drinks. Maybe that great water down below was one of the Great Lakes. Now we fly through a white mist – dim sunlight wavers on the wing.

12:57 PM   We are circling and below is a great wide river. The whole continent this day carries a dull misty overlay – the ground appears but dimly, there is no clarity. Is it winter? Or is it pollution?

1:22 PM   Circling over the water and gliding over

the rows of buildings. There on the horizon are the tall buildings of lower Manhattan, ghostly ghastly in the yellow-brown air.

2:24 PM (5:24 PM New York time)   I was so concerned about taking warm clothes. And. here at gate 29, TWA is doing a sauna at no extra charge. It must be in the high 80s. Flight 804 to Paris, the young woman announces over the speaker system, is overbooked – if you give up your seat, TWA will give you a $300 travel voucher.

4:25 PM (7:25 New York time) Over   the   white   and yellow lights of Long Island streets – and now the dark night sea is below.

Friday 7:17 AM French time.   Below us is the sunrise, a bright orange-rose blush across the white clouds and, above, a fresh blue morning sky. Below the clouds is still the ocean, I think. A new day for the old world.

7:22 AM   Now the coastline – white surf outlining the brown land – it is a lovely sight below the brilliant clouds of dawn.

~

Paris

When anyone asks me hereafter "Do you speak French?" I will tell them: "I ordered carrot juice in Paris"

Paris Friday, March 16, 6:22 PM
Sitting at a café table at Place des Vosges, drinking cider – I didn't know it had 4% alcohol. It is dusk – the Place des Vosges has seen dusk and night, now it is come to renaissance. I am tired in the bones. And learning about life. I spent so much time buying a right jacket – a navy blue windbreaker – that was then; this morning – now – I left it on a counter at De Gaulle airport. My little Paris hotel – when I arrived, they told me the room was being painted so they couldn't honor the reservation. But they got me a room at another small hotel. No choice but to surf the way the waves go.

Paris Saturday, March 17, 9:32 AM
So. Another kind of day. A Paris day. Which begins at a café with the newspapers. I managed to spend 30 francs on newspapers this morning at a news shop on Blvd. St. Honoré. Now I am at a table just inside the corner windows of Café de l'Epoque on Rue aux Croix-des-Petits-Champs. I saw this café yesterday evening while

walking about. I like it because the street is a by-way unfrequented much by autos. Most streets of Paris are horrendously dominated by ever-passing autos and ever-present auto exhaust fumes. I think I have now become a European – biological-time-clock-wise speaking. That is to say, in the short space of 24 hours I have achieved that basic skill of falling asleep at 10 or 11 PM and waking at 6 or 7 AM.

And The Sun Also Rises. But these days the Sun of Paris rises within the envelope of auto exhaust. Paris has thrown a petrol curtain between its ornate buildings and le soleil royal. Ah, there walk by in front of the café – two gendarmes in the traditional dark blue uniform with the round kepi hat. I thought they had changed years ago to the kind of soft hat worn by American police.

I still feel somewhat tired this morning – which is okay, I guess, since it is now almost one in the morning in California. Yesterday I was very tired and had no desire to write. I had many things I wanted to say about myself and I thought – Well, I will write them tomorrow. But now I cannot remember what they were. One thing is that I now feel a good deal older. Older than what? Older than when I was younger. Older. Now – I think that in order to make the transition to older one must latch on to a different energy. The younger energy is basically sexual – an older energy is awareness – the sense of oneself, being within one's body, being quiet and knowing how the inside feels and how it moves – the muscles, the thoughts, the breathing, the sensation. Something like that. If one cannot achieve, cannot access, that energy of age, then (perhaps) one dies when the fundamental sexual energy is finally all used up. That is a hypothesis. So far, I have not been successful in making the transition. And thus there is that re-current anxiety – angst – that occurs in me.

My other thesis has something to do with metabolism. Animals – little animals – with rapid metabolism, don't live long – squirrels rabbits etc. There is wild fire burning up the cells. The tortoises survive longer – elephants and whales. Do I know what I am talking of? No. But –

Oh wow – magic. The waiter just pulled away the table next to me and then the floor under the table began to split open before my very eyes. No. Not the Great Paris Earthquake of 1990 – but rather the way the café disposes of its refuse. Two sections of the café floor opened on hinges and up came a platform on a hydraulic lift. The garçon put a gray plastic trash barrel on the platform and the platform descended, the floor folded back to horizontal and the garçon replaced the table. The Paris café meets the 21st century.

Well, it is 10:05 AM. What shall I do? I think I shall take the train to the Gare d'Austerlitz and buy my train ticket for tomorrow. I regret, right now, that I am leaving Paris tomorrow. But that is something about how I structured this trip. For, this trip is now almost completely structured, don't you see? And that is not by chance. One structures when one does not want to take risks. Unstructured time means wandering at risk in a wide wild world. And, isn't that what travel is about? Being on adventure. Which means being spontaneous, free, able to improvise, on a different trajectory from the everyday? But the sense of being older – Ah, Madame brushes by me to the corner window, where she hangs today's lunch menu. – So – yes, the sense of being older – oh, I have forgotten what I was saying. Anyway, I am committed and have paid to go to La Petite Eguille tomorrow.

Now both Madame and the garçon are in the corner. Madame is standing on a chair – she is consulting with the garçon. Perhaps they are changing the menu. Pardon, says Madame, pour vous deranger. Something like that. By God, I am beginning to comprehend the French as she is spoken – by real people on the Rue aux Croix-des-Petits-Champs. I look up as Madame departs and she bows her head gravely to me and says Pardon, Monsieur. I nod my head to her. I look up at what she has wrought on the corner window. It is the little placard with the list and price of the drinks. This hangs above the placard with the lunch menu. All is now in readiness for the day.

So. Let the day begin! By golly, it feels good. Sitting here in a café and scribbling. Even now – 1990 under the petrol-hazed sky. The fantasies begin. Rent an apartment in the Marais, close to Place des Vosges, sit every morning in a café, scribbling – in a year I would have a novel completed: *Paris in the Kishkas*. (For the non-Yiddish speaker, Kishkas means Intestines.)

Well now – at 10:24 AM your Paris-in-the-kishkas correspondent begins to leave the Café de l'Epoque on Rue aux Croix-des-Petits-Champs and to proceed via the Metro to Gare d'Austerlitz. It is written: Ye shall, on the morrow, the Lord's day, take thyself to La Petite Eguille. No, no, says the spirit – I want to stay in Paris. It is written – comes the Voice from out gasoline Heaven above.

10:48 AM On a bench made of clear plastic slabs at the Metro stop Louvre-Rivoli on the line to Vincennes.

Ah, here is the train. And I find a seat. How very lucky
– at first I am too bashful to write – but then I begin to
scribble. The noise of the train. The two girls besides me
are speaking German. I think – even in Spring – there
are but a minority of French in Paris. At least, so it
seems. Maybe the French are still in bed – on Saturday
morning. I think I shall go to the stop at the Gare de
Lyon and walk across the bridge over the river to the
Gare d'Austerlitz. My handwriting is, I think, getting
worse and worse. Here we are at the Bastille station. The
line comes up to daylight here. What a treat it is for the
Metro passenger to see the light of the sun – even the
sunlight filtered by gasoline haze.

10:58 AM   I sit on one of the yellow plastic seats on
the platform at the Gare de Lyon station to scribble a
few more words. The old man who got off with me here
was wearing a black fur cap – was he Iranian? The two
men seated beside me here on the platform are Arabs. A
tremor in my mind. Is this a rough Arab neighborhood
I plan to walk through to the Gare d'Austerlitz? I am
timid. One of the Arab men stands and stoops to kiss
the other. On one cheek, and the other cheek. Even here
– particularly here? – there is the strong, unpleasant,
smell of gasoline fumes. Well, I shall try the air outside
and above ground. The other Arab leaves – he is an old
man and he carries two straw baskets – one seems full of
ears of corn. Is that possible in March? Who knows?

12:01 PM   My, the time passes. I walked across the
bridge. Just as I did so, a young man, his arm about
his girlfriend, asked me something. I looked blank,
so he asked again. Je ne comprend pas, I said. He said
Do you have two francs? No, said I, and walked on. To
his exact question, a lie. But the No meant and we both

understood: No, I do not wish to help you.

Anyway. I am now sitting on the access quai to the trains. I bought my ticket. All in French. I started talking to the woman at the information booth in French. Then when I wanted to ask her: Can you use the ticket any time or is it only for one particular time? – I said to her Est-ce que vous parlez anglais? And she said – No, but go on, you are doing well in French – I understand you. So I went on. A fellow sits down now in the next seat and he is smoking. I must go.

12:40 PM   On the Metro – line 1 – leaving the Bastille station. There is a mural on the wall of the Bastille station depicting the events of 1789 – one of the women in the mural wears a pair of 1989 spectacles colored red, white and blue – it is a nice funny touch.

12:44 PM   Now I am on a seat on the platform of the Hotel de Ville station – one must be alert – I almost missed getting off at this station. I am on my way back to my favorite Paris restaurant – the vegetarian one on Rue Catherine Bretonnerie – near the Pompidou Center. Or the street may be Croix Bretonnerie. The street signs have it one way, my map the other.

1:06 PM   In my restaurant, on a bench, my back against the rough textured wall (textured – not spelled right? – The first thing that goes when one gets into a foreign language is the crazy English spelling.) It smells very good in here – onions and spices and good things nices. I am quite hungry. Bread and tea in the morning does not make a breakfast for me. I am not sure of the name of this place – I look in the menu – it does not give the name there. I think it is Aquitaine. It is run by a group, I think. A religious group? They sell books here also – and raisin rolls. There are notices posted in the windows on meetings of a group – *the* group? Croix of something.

I wonder if the waiter understood me – I ordered carrot juice and the plat du jour. At first he thought I wanted a tarte de carrote. I didn't pronounce the S in jus. I think that's right. Ah, here is the carrot juice. Another linguistic triumph! When anyone asks me hereafter Do you speak French?, I will tell them: I ordered carrot juice in Paris. My plat du jour has arrived and I eat with my left hand and write with my right. It is a pretty plate – of things I like to eat. Lentils, millet, cooked carrots and anise and raw grated carrots and beets. Not many people would come to Paris to eat this, but for me it is the best meal in the world. Across from me is a blue suited fellow eating the same thing. I am trying if I can use the fork and the pen at the same moment, but I fear I have not the brainpower for both of these – although I can walk and chew gum at the same time, thereby at least qualifying myself to be President of the United States.

1:34 PM   I have eaten everything on my plate, so not only can I be president, I also qualify for dessert. – Ah, I get a restaurant plus in language today. I asked the waiter for yogurt *and* I said Can I have a little fruit compote on top? – Now I am again eating with my left hand and writing with the right. Perhaps I shall devote my stay in France to learning to eat with my left hand. Pourquoi pas? People do stranger things – like play golf. I wonder if I could learn to write with my left hand? My sister and several of my cousins are left-handed. The yogurt was quite good – though I think it had sugar or honey in it. So it goes – perfection is not of this world. I certainly prefer this place to where I had lunch yesterday – I ate yesterday at a workingman's restaurant on a small street somewhere around here and I had an awful omelette with fried potatoes in it. The fellow across from me was eating sliced beef heart – it looked raw to me. Do they eat raw beef heart in Paris?

4:04 PM   Going home. Hotel home. On the Metro. I left from the station Les Filles Calvaires – something like that. I'll look it up. Filles du Calvaire – that's it – on Blvd. du Temple. I have been walking about the Marais. It is quite a warm Spring day – shirtsleeve weather. The Marais is becoming very chic – new shops and new buildings are sprouting. When I came up to the Metro entrance, I stopped to look at the Metro system map posted there. A portly old man came over and asked me if I needed information. I know this district, he said. No, I said, I just want to go to Concorde. Ah, he said, yes, here below, this line goes to Opera, Madelaine, Concorde. Merci bien, Monsieur I said. I think he came over because I had been looking about in all directions for the entrance to the Metro – my map showed it a block away from where it now is.

7:42 PM   Here is something. Quite by chance. I was walking about Montparnasse. I came to Blvd. Edgar Quinet and then I walked up Rue Gaiety. That's its name. On Rue Gaiety are half dozen sex shops that show pornographic video. I didn't come to Montparnasse to walk up Rue Gaiety, but once I came to it, I thought of the sex shops. So I walked up the street and looked at the stores and looked at the sex shops. Didn't go in any of them, walked to the end of the street, turned down another street, then down another street. And then, I felt confused. That feeling of not knowing what to do, not

knowing what I wanted to do. That is a familiar feeling
for me. Not as much now as earlier when I was younger.
A sense of wandering at a loss. And it struck me – this
feeling seems to be related to the sex shops. So there is
something about sex equaling confusion or bringing on
confusion. Confusion in the sense of not knowing – not
being able to choose, without direction. Now, I have not
felt 100% the last several days – so very tired yesterday
and so on and so on. But not this feeling – of the many
ways of not being at peace, this feeling is a particular
feeling. And it is one that has been a major motif in my
life. That sense of being at a loss. How does it relate to
sex? Does it relate to an early sexual incident? I don't
know – but it interests me that it came on at that point.

Wow. Now I am sitting at the Café Liberté – Is it Liberté
– now I am not sure. I am sitting at an outside table. A
family sat down at the next table shortly after I arrived.
The man is smoking. I absolutely hate cigarettes. What
an awful awful smell. It is death – if death has a smell.
Ah, they are leaving. I didn't want to move because I
didn't want to offend them. They had a little boy who is
running about and I thought that if I moved they would
think it was because I was irritated by the kid.

So. I know this café well. When I was in Paris in 1956,
I stayed for three weeks in at hotel a block away and I
would come here every morning with the Herald Tribune
and sit and eat my petit dejeuner. Now I am drinking a
beer. I don't know what to order at cafes. I don't want
caffeine and I don't want sugar and I don't want alcohol.
That leaves water. So I got beer. Pression? he asked
and I said Oui. I was looking up biere in my paperback
dictionary to see whether it is une biere or un biere – the
articles are very important in French. One time long ago

I ordered beer and got a liqueur, maybe because I used the wrong article. Last time I was here – in 1986 – I had lunch at the Chinese restaurant a few doors down from here. It was an awful lunch. I think that after I finish my beer I shall walk down toward Blvd. Monparnasse and have supper. I passed several little restaurants as I walked here.

I am doing remarkably well on the old biological clock – I am quite firmly European. Or maybe not – it is after 11 AM in California – almost lunchtime – maybe that is why I am hungry.

Oh. I just checked my map. The street is not Rue Gaiety, it is Rue de la Gaite. Rue Delambre is where my hotel was in 1956. I thought it was Rue de la Bain. Maybe it was Hotel de la Bain. So. It is unbelievably pleasant this evening in Paris – leaving aside the gasoline fumes. The temperature is best imaginable. It is now 8:17 PM, I am wearing a sleeveless sweater and sitting comfortably outdoors. Why, Santa Cruz is almost never this warm at eight in the evening. Obviously, the song should have been March in Paris.

I also feel good about my French. I feel on the very verge of speaking – like a fledgling bird about to flutter from the nest I am about to flutter into French – mais oui, bien sur. My mind turns back to sex. What an interesting thing it is. So life-like and lively. And the social order is both built on sex and opposed to sex. The tension between social order and sex. That is interesting. I really have little idea of what I am writing. I finished my beer and my mind is somewhat set free from order. I am now the only person at the tables outside the Café Liberté, all the others have left. Perhaps for supper. The man at the newspaper kiosk on the sidewalk in front of me may be closing up. If I remember correctly, it was at this very kiosk that I bought my Herald Tribune about 35 years ago. It was not the same proprietor – he looks about 45 years old.

My goodness – it is amazing what a night's rest will do. I just felt the back of my neck – the muscles are relaxed – I am relaxed – yesterday I was a bound bundle of taut muscles. So. The autos of Paris – those horrible mechanical monsters – have one redeeming feature. They have muted yellow headlights in lieu of the blazing white American lamps. You know, I could easily spend my four weeks in France wandering about Paris and scribbling. I feel good doing this – I am a born café person. Although the gasoline impregnated air of Paris would be a strong negative. I wonder how the auto exhaust standards of France compare with those of United States?

8:50 PM   Here I am at the Vietnamese restaurant that has no name, that has no menu posted in the window, that is all but invisible from the street – and for all that, has only 10 diners right now – at the Saturday night supper hour. The waitress handed me the menu – four pages of densely packed writing – and a little slip of paper. The menu asks that one write the number of the dishes – just a number, not the name – on the slip of paper. I suspect the waitress may not speak French. Or maybe they find that the customers do not speak French. I like the sense of this room. It is quiet – the loudest noise is the hum of a fan somewhere overhead. There are two rows of tables – one against each wall. I am sitting at the table closest to the street. There are long padded benches against the walls and on the other side of the tables are a miscellany of metal chairs. The whole front of the

restaurant is made up of what I think is a folding door –
panels that go from floor to ceiling and are glass within a
wood frame.

Here is my shrimp soup. It is rather sweet – there are
chunks of pineapple in it. Well, that was good. Sort
of sweet and sour soup. The next dish is squid and
vegetables. I didn't want pork or beef and the soup had
shrimp. So – squid. I hope that it is a familiar, rather
than a strange, squid.

Gee, I am feeling a bit tired – which is a good sign, since
it is now almost noon in California. Now the fan overhead
is rattling and grinding, thus cracking the tranquility
of this room. I shade my eyes against the overhead
fluorescent light and look for the fan. Yes, it is a square
portable fan set up against the ceiling. There is, in front
of me on the table, a little aluminum tray with a round
loop of a handle. In it are a little jar of what looks like
red chili sauce, a bottle of soy sauce and a bottle of what
looks like vinegar, and salt and pepper shakers.

Oh, about the doors in the front of the restaurant – they
are I think – appropriately – no more, no less, than –
French doors. Voila.

9:21 PM   And now – enter a musician. He is playing
a guitar and singing a booming baritone. He has
quite overcome the rattling fan. I pointed to the fan
when he pulled out the guitar from its case. It is an
accompaniment, he said. Of the songs I catch only a word
here and there that I know. He played three songs, then
went about the tables with a small wooden cup. I gave
him 5 francs. And he has left – it was a good 10 minute
interval. And the waitress then went over and turned off

the fan. There was a murmur of approval. I said Merci in my best French, keeping the R down in my throat. Ah. Voila. The squid and rice.

9:41 PM   The dish is not bad, but what I like least about it is the squid. Given the language and the elan, I would have said: Give me the squid and vegetables, and hold the squid.

10:44 PM   On the Metro – this is line 12 and has the modern cars. Inside this car, the walls are scribbled up with slogans and names – reminiscent of the New York subway – although not as bad. There are only about 10 people in the car now. Half of us got in at Montparnasse-Bienvenue, the rest are a group of noisy boys. There is also the faint but pervading smell of urine in the car. Can there be a society people don't want to rebel against? Can there be satisfied people? Even at 15 years old? I would like to read something about primitive society.   A drunk guy has gotten on the train. The kids are giving him a hard time.

∿

Paris to La Ferme

Past fields glowing green in the sunlight,
past rows of bare grape vines,
past young trees now showing
the green beginning of Spring leaves

Paris, Gare d'Austerlitz   Sunday,   March   18,
11:20 AM
So much for gastronomy. I have had my lunch – a
sandwich de crudités and an Orangina, both bought at a
kiosk in the rail station. The sandwich de crudités was
not bad – a salad sandwich. Although the train does not
leave until noon, I – and some half, I would guess, of the
passengers – are already aboard. This is a modern car –
it has two long rows of two by two seats rather than the
compartments of four and four facing seats.

12:01 PM   At exactly 12 noon the train begins to roll
– past old Austerlitz, rails, backs of buildings – under a
lazy hazy sky.

12:48 PM   I just had a nap attack. When the train
began to roll I literally could not keep my eyes open and
I fell asleep for 45 minutes. It was California calling me

at three in the morning and it said sleep.   Many
bushes along the track are full of bright white blossoms.
The train is moving as silk over still water – French
railroad beds are taken-care-of things. There is an
incomprehensible announcement over the speaker and
the train slows. We are arriving somewhere. Many people
are up in the aisles ready to leave. Well, it is Orleans.
Joan d'Arc, nous sommes arrivés. When I was out
walking this morning I passed an ancient statue of Joan
of Arc near the Louvre. This station here is called Les
Aubrais-Orleans – I see as we roll out and away. There
are so many places I have not explored. Once I know
French, I would like to do a trip on the intercity buses
about France – like I did in southern Spain in 1986. Ah,
in the yards of the houses we pass, there are the white
blossomed trees. Spring Sprang Sprung Blossom Bliss-
um. We pass a large village – French houses have a stout
stable air about them – these are the houses built by the
third pig – that the wolf could not blow over, huff and
puff as he might. What a marvelous track this is – not a
ripple, not a rut. France, a train rider salutes you.

1:42 PM   About 10 minutes ago we stopped at
Blois, which is, I believe, on the Loire. I am not an avid
traveler this afternoon. I don't even have my map out. I
am reading a Simenon book with the aid of my French-
English dictionary.

 2:12 PM   The train stands at the station of Tours,
where it and we have stood for some 15 minutes now.
It is interesting – the book I am reading is called *Tante
Jeanne* (Aunt Jeanne), and it opens with a described
elderly woman on a train – she has changed trains at
Poitiers, so if she came from Paris, she came the same
way I am now traveling. She is afraid of something, very

conscious of her age. On page 11, when she checks into the hotel, her age is given as 57. Well, Tante Jeanne, I have a few years on you. And I am going past Poitiers today, to the next town, Angouleme, to change trains. And it is 1990, 40 years on from 1950 of the book. But I, too, am vaguely afraid, conscious of age. And the white blossoms go by. And there is a pink blooming tree. The train crosses over two rivers. And that is the Loire – both Tours and Blois are on the Loire.

2:59 PM   A thought while reading Simenon. One reason we may thrill to travel in a far land is that, often, what we know of that far land we have learned through artists – And what is an artist? An artist is one who sees, senses, feels *better* than most of us, and is able to convey to others that acuity of perception. So I read Simenon and I see, through him, a Paris seen better than I see Paris – and reading Dickens I see the people of London better than I alone would see them. So, in traveling, we are in one sense exchanging our manner of sensing – that is, from our every day unaided mode of seeing the daily things and places and people in our accustomed habitual manner – to seeing some place and people we are not habituated to *and* seeing that new place partly through the eyes and senses of a remarkably good see-er (or seer). That is just one idea. But. Being able to see and sense is so important. I read once that an old fisherman claimed that he had told Hemingway the story of the old man and the sea – that it was *his* story, not Hemingway's. But – it is not the story. Every day every one of us passes through and alongside greatly moving exciting sensational events – and do not know that anything is happening – or more, cannot express what has happened. Dickens' London is Dickens, not London, Simenon's Paris is Simenon, not Paris. So forth.

Now – 3:11 PM – the train is stopped in Poitiers station. In 1975, I was sitting at a table on the terrace cafe on the other side of this station building – and *there* is a Hemingway-esque story, if I could but write it. I think I wrote about it in a letter I wrote when stopped in a train in Poitiers station in 1986. And so the years go round and round. Back to Simenon.

5:21 PM   On the small train from Angouleme to Royan – past fields glowing green in the sunlight, past rows of bare grape vines, past stands of young trees now just showing the green beginning of Spring leaves. I have taken off my vest sweater and the train window is opened a couple inches at the top. It is a warm day. The conductor just announced we are arriving in Cognac and here is a big new factory. No, I don't think it's a brandy factory. The six young girls who have been in this compartment since Angouleme are leaving.

5:35 PM   I am feeling rather tired and flat – unexcited. And I say to myself What! We spent all this money and time and trouble to bring you over here, we spread all France at your feet, we bring out the best March weather in 80 years, and you say you feel flat?! I look at a 16th-century farmhouse going by. Hey man, I continue, you better shape up or we are going to ship you out. Maybe – maybe it is because I really haven't eaten all day – I had a cup of yogurt and a banana when I woke and then that salad sandwich and orangeade at Austerlitz station.

5:47 PM   We are arriving in Saintes. In 1986 I spent a day in Saintes between trains – it was a Roman town and has an ancient church. I see the church towers from here.

~

La Ferme

Birds singing as the night sky darkens. I begin to talk le vrai francais – a word, a phrase, a stumble, a mumble, mais il arrive.

7:32 PM   La Petite Eguille

Well, I am as happy as a clam. I have the same pleasant room on the second floor of the converted barn at La Ferme. And it is so tranquil here, the birds are singing as the night sky darkens, the air clean and fresh. There are three other students here. One came on the train with me, although I didn't know it at the time. She is a woman who was born in New Zealand and married an Italian and now lives in Rome. I am so happy to be in a quiet, pleasant place. And this Spring weather is absolutely perfect. We are going to have the grand opening of the week of study in 10 minutes when we all gather for aperitifs and then we will have supper. Yea supper. It is for me a supper much looked forward to.

Circumstances *are* important. There are times when I say I am up, I am down, I am depressed, I am happy – and I think, well, I should be this way or the other way. But, very often I am in a setting that is depressing.

A pleasant place to be is something important for me to provide for myself. As I write I munch on a few almonds that I bought at a little grocery store near Blvd. Montparnasse last night. Ah, Blvd. Montparnasse – it is a very distant place from here and now. I thought I would have liked to spend another week in Paris. And yes, Paris is a fascinating city. But so inhospitable now to the human – the air, the noise, the traffic – it is all very difficult to support, to cope with. Well – it is 7:45 – off to the Grand Opening.

La Ferme (at La Petite Eguille)

10:16 PM   A very pleasant supper. Pleasant is the describing word here at La Ferme. The four students this week are me, the woman from Rome and an English couple who live in Brussels (the husband works there – I suppose for the European community). And then Mirielle, our teacher, and Farrar, her husband. Farrar is American and an excellent cook – he prepares the meals. We talk French at meals, of course, so it is a continuation of the classes. I am pretty much of a mind to give up reading English while I am here, so I will set aside the three English books and two English magazines I brought with me, and I shall continue reading Simenon and follow the adventures of Tante Jeanne.

L'Eguille Monday, March 19, 4:53 PM
Well, what you gonna do? The inn is closed. No way am I going to get a cold drink after walking 2 miles on a warmish afternoon. So I content myself with sitting at one of the tables under the awning over the terrace in front and scribbling a bit. What I will do in a bit is walk to a grocery store – there used to be one in the village – and buy something there to drink. Otherwise, I can report on the white flowers of yesterday – the ones growing, springing in the Spring – along the railroad tracks. They also grow and blossom along the little roadways here and they are berry flowers – blackberry or raspberry or other berry. Along with the berry blossoms, sweet Spring is called forth by green shoots unfurling of the reeds of the marsh canals that runs through this countryside. For this is a watery land – estuaries of the sea and oyster farms. L'Eguille is the bigger village – the one with a port and two restaurants, a post office, a church and a grocery store – it is a few miles from La Petite Eguille where stands La Ferme, my alma mater.

I sat in almost 6 hours of classes today – from 9:15 to 12:45 and from 2 to 4. A bit too much, I think. I am in a class with the two women in the morning – Diane and – is it Jenny? I felt at first that I was ahead of them in French and I didn't like that. Now I am not sure I am ahead – but I am willing to talk more. I have gotten my

French in rather unorthodox schooling – so I don't have the grammar well, but I talk more. Well, I shall read Simenon – that is an important, and enjoyable, part of my education. But. First I will describe. The terrace is concrete, the chairs white plastic.   Say, an enormous brown and black German shepherd just came trotting up onto the terrace – I don't think he likes me sitting here

There is a little wall, say 18 inches high, along the edge of the terrace, brown steel poles are set in the wall and they support the great orange canvas awning. In front of the terrace is a narrow asphalted roadway and beyond the roadway is the port, which is a channel about 100 feet wide and 20 feet deep with stone walls. Right now the tide is out so the mud bottom is exposed in some places, and the boats lie grounded – small motor boats. On the far side of the channel there is a line of small sheds – I suppose they are used for preparing and storing the oysters and the gear.

Here – a small auto has stopped in front of the terrace, two fellows get out and come up to read the sign that says Open Friday Saturday and Sunday – in French of course. And they read the menu posted on the wall beside the door.

9:43 PM   Le repose apres le diner. That may mean I am resting after dinner. We have long dinners – about three courses and two hours – French cooking and French speaking. Tonight we talked of the new buildings of Paris, among other things: the glass pyramid in the courtyard of the Louvre, the Pompidou Museum, the buildings of Les Halle, the new arch at La Defense, the rehabilitation of the house of Madame de Severny, and so forth. Mireille does most of the talking since she knows a great deal and also she is the only one at the table who really knows French well. Outside it is a starry bright night, a rather damp-feeling night and with the high squeaking chirps of the frogs – perhaps they are crickets – these are marshlands that merge to the sea.

La Petite Eguille Tuesday, March 20   10:16 PM
And so to bed. This is a day in which the ordered pattern took hold and Zip Away went the Day. Up at 7 AM and I did 10 minutes of mild yoga. Down and over to the living room of the house just after eight and I called Pepin. He says I will be surprised when I see the farm. I wonder what it looks like now. I was certainly surprised in October 1988 when I saw what they had accomplished since we bought the place in February 1987. What have they done now – in the last year and a half?

So – Breakfast, le petit dejeuner, at 8:30 – there is the ubiquitous Kellogg's, in several different boxes, on the table and the coffee and hot milk and bread, jam and butter. I have Kellogg's and tea and bread. And the French begins. We chatter, as best we can, in our fractured French – the seven of us – five students and Mirielle and Farrar. Carolyn, the fifth student, who returned from a weekend in London on Monday morning, is the other American at La Ferme. She is a tallish woman of about 35, of Korean background I think. She lives in New York, but she attended UC Berkeley where she studied journalism. She seems quite a nice person but I have hardly talked with her because she knows scarcely any French and I don't want to talk English.

Breakfast finishes shortly after 9 AM and the morning classes begin almost immediately. Annique is my teacher and the class is me and Jennie, the English woman who lives in Brussels, and Diana, who is married to an Italian

and lives in Rome, but was born in New Zealand. We sit
about a small table and talk and do grammar exercises
and read – until about 11 AM, when we go over to the
kitchen for a short coffee break and then we re-group and
go on to 12:45 PM. Lunch, which is a light meal – a salad
and some cold cuts and cheeses or some such thing – is
at 1 PM and again we sit about the table and converse
in French. Mirielle leads the talk – she is very good –
she always has interesting things to say and everyone
feels very comfortable. Mirielle gives little corrections
from time to time, so we are learning still. I and Diana
do an afternoon class from 2 to 4. Yesterday it was with
Annique, today with – oh my, I forget her name. An older
woman, very elegant and gracious – oh yes, Arlette. And
today we went until 4:30 PM. I was quite tired by that
time.

Farrar drove me to Le Eguille and we went to the
post office where I rented a bicycle from the village
postmaster. He was very solicitous as I am his first
client. He likes to repair bikes and he is going to begin
renting them to students at La Ferme. I rode the bike the
mile back to La Ferme and then I rode to Saujon, about
three miles in the other direction. At Saujon, I went into
the supermarché and bought a windbreaker jacket to
replace the one that I left at DeGaulle airport. It cost me
70 francs, about $13 – in Paris the windbreakers I looked
at ranged from 200 francs to 1200 francs – incredibly
expensive. I came back from Saujon at about 6:45 – just
at dusk – and I did my homework in an hour.

Then dinner at 8 PM – this is the big meal. Tonight we
had cold beets to start with and then fish with caper
sauce and boiled potatoes and then Charlotte mousse.
We left the table early – at about 9:15 – to take coffee

and tea watching a program from East Berlin on what is happening in East Germany. The Germans were speaking French, since this program was for French television, and I understood a good deal of it. That is satisfying – when you begin to understand things.

Somehow, I think that French is a language that comes easier to English speakers than Spanish. Once you get past the pronunciation, which is a *vital* part of knowing French, the French rhythm and vocabulary is closer to English. And, at 10 PM, up to my room and so to bed. I like to read my Simenon novel a bit before I go to sleep. I really like that book, but I don't have much time to read it.

La Petite Eguille   Wednesday, March 21, 8:25 AM
Morning and birds a-twitter and far off the distant roar of the tractor is heard in the land. For lo, the Springtime of the year has arrived and all manner of good things are showered upon us – sunlight and good air, a smiling Sun and a rising Earth, the Birds of the field and the breakfast of cool morning. And it is to thence I hence haste from my hayloft bedroom above the ancient barn.

6:44 PM   Well my, I have been interacting with the inhabitants hereof. I asked Diana, the woman from Rome, if she wanted to go for a bicycle ride and we rode off toward Mediz, (is that the way it is spelled?), the next town west from Saujon – and never got there because I got lost. So we went into Saujon and I bought Le Monde and Le Figaro and bananas and apples. Then we rode back and just as we arrived in La Petite Eguille, there was Carolyn, the woman from New York. She wanted to find a little store, so Diana turned over her bike to Carolyn and we rode down the back road winding to L'Eguille and to the little store there. To Carolyn I talked English because she hasn't enough French for conversation. She works as an editor for the *Wall Street Journal* in New York and before that she worked for the Associated Press. The people here at La Ferme always seem to be quite accomplished. Carolyn told me that Alan, the English fellow, is the manager of the IBM office in Brussels. Well, I must do my homework now.

7:52 PM   Well I finished mes devoirs – the verb "devoir" means "to owe" –– so it is an interesting derivation for the word "homework". And the grand dinner is in a few minutes, so I will scribble awhile. One experiment I have underway now is what effect a change of diet will have on me. I am now eating meat and sugar and white bread and all those un-SantaCruzian things.

10:09 PM   And so to bed. The days pass very quickly here – and I enjoy being here. There is just about nothing I enjoy more than studying and living in a quiet country place.

La Petite Eguille   Thursday, March 22, 8:26 AM
The birds twitter and flit over the moss-covered red tile roof I see from my window. An airplane drones overhead – there is a gray sea mist over the sky. To le petit dejeuner.

9 AM   Et maintenant apres le petit dejeuner. My mind is like the morning air – it started off covered with morning's gray mist and now there is a lightening, a warming – great Father Sun arrives. I am beginning to talk le vrai francais – a little, a bit, a word and a phrase and a stumble and a mumble, mais il arrive, il arrive.

1:52 PM   Just had a stirring luncheon conversation.

We talked about what is happening in East Europe, about religion in France, about the First World War – and all in French. And I was right there, expressing ideas – maybe having a glass of wine helped. I almost believe I can talk French. Almost, almost. I sure wish I were going to stay here 4 weeks instead of two. Because after a month here, I'd come out speaking like Louis the Sixteenth (before he parted from his head).

Saujon   5:35 PM
First I will write a few lines and then, maybe, I will begin to read. Right now? Seated. At a little table on the glassed-in front terrace of Cafe Thermalia, behind the church and the Square – what would one call it in French? Not a plaza. Anyway, the Square is not French. No – not so as to be recognized by any of the Kings Louis, or Manet or Monet or Balzac or etc. By a 20th Century American? Mais, bien sur – for the old square is no more, no less, than a parking lot. Saujon approaches Gopher Prairie, USA – Carol, the doctor's wife, wouldn't like it at all, nor do I. The church is, I think, a 19th Century creation. Many of the towns and villages around here have 12th Century churches. Pauvre Saujon – it must do with a 19th Century church festooned with 20th Century automobiles. This café doesn't belong to Balzac either. It is mostly pinball machines, television and linoleum floor. Saujon is mostly a tourist town – now bare of tourists – except one fellow in blue sitting at a small table on the glassed-in front terrace of the Cafe Thermalia.

La Petite Eguille   7:19 PM
So. It is darkening into obscured night. I bicycled back from Saujon about an hour ago. From the café, I went to the market on the other side of the church and bought three bananas and two pears and one pair of wool socks

and a partridge in a pear tree. The socks were a great bargain at 21 francs, marked down from 42. When I came out of the market, a light rain had begun. I wiped the water from the bike seat, and pedaled under grayness and wetness and the fresh smell of Spring rain. My new windbreaker (blouson) and my gray felt hat (from out of a Raymond Chandler novel) served me well as I biked along the country road to La Petite Eguille – a picturesque sight for any passing tourist – a modern French peasant on his way back from market and une biere at the Cafe Thermalia – although, untypically, I was singing Over The Rainbow as I pedaled past field and farm house. Once arrived, I went out back to the clotheslines and confirmed that the three shirts, five undershirts, five undershorts, four pairs of socks and one handkerchief I had washed before I bicycled to town were good and wet and must hang yet many an hour before they may be worn. You may wonder why there were only four pairs of socks – and the answer is – if there were five there would be none on my feet. So it goes.

10:08 PM   What fun. We have lively dinners. Tonight I told Mirielle that I wanted to learn the words to La Marseillaise and she brought down a placard of the 200th anniversary with all seven verses on it and we sang a rousing rendition. Then the English couple sang God Save the Queen. And some of Land of Hope and Glory. A satisfyingly chauvinistic time was had by all.

Little-known fact: God Save the Queen is sung at the end of English cinema showings. La Marseillaise was written in 1788? by a fellow named Lisle – who wrote it in 15 minutes at a gathering – it was written for the army of people from Marseille who were marching to Paris to save the republic. So there, Mr. Dickens – it wasn't all guillotine and blood. However – it probably was. The Tree of Liberty irrigated with blood, as Jefferson would have it. There is hardly a song more stirring than La Marseillaise – it sets the table dishes rattling. And then – God Save the Queen – now that is a conservative song – no street revolutionaries digging up paving stones singing God Save the Queen.

My my – it makes one want to read history. It all started, as I now recall, with the English couple telling of their visit to Cognac this afternoon – and to the Hennessy establishment, which was founded in the 18th century by an Irish officer who served Louis XIV. Then we talked of how the idea of nationalism didn't develop until after – with the French Revolution. That is why Napoleon's armies were so powerful – because in it were the French fighting for their own France and their own republic and spreading the idea of republicanism to other countries.

La Petite Eguille   Friday, March 23, 8:22 AM
Up in the morning, out on the job, work like the Devil for my pay – but that Lucky Old Sun – got nothing to do, but to roll around Heaven all day. That is the situation – that Lucky Old Sun is rolling about this morning and there are the Winter trees, patterns of black branches against the pale blue morning sky. And the birds? – they squeak, squawk, twitter, twit and embroider the sounds of the morning across the wet red tile roofs. It is Spring, it is arriving, it is the Coming. He is risen – the Earth God. Or a goddess? Or both?

1:46 PM   Apres le dejeuner, I sit on my bed in my above-the-barn room and look out the window, past the old red tile roof to the advance of Spring – the white-flowered tree that rises just beyond the roof, and beyond it, still-bare branches. Today is a beauty of a day. I look forward to bicycling after the lesson ends at 4 PM. I told Mirielle I did not want to take afternoon lessons next week. I want to be outdoors in the afternoon.

5:26 PM   Saujon
The sunlight is on my back, the sunlight is in my eyes, the sunlight reflects off the red metal table, the sunlight puts a brilliant charge over the facade of the Bar-Hotel le Terminus across the street and over the bright blue van parked in front of it and over the black roadway and over tables, chairs, umbrellas and all across the vast blue sky. There is sunlight uber alles this bright Spring afternoon in a small town near the Atlantic coast of France. So what? So what, he asks. Why, there is nothing more important. From sunlight comes bright fish and green grass, yellow flowers, blue vans, brick hotels, red metal table, and thee and me.

I am sitting at the café-restaurant which is across the street from Bar-Hotel le Terminus and is either named Adelshoffen Restaurant or Aldeshoffen Biere d'Alsace has pulled a fast one on the proprietor and named his restaurant while he thought it was just another advertising sign.

The Adels-etc is also across the street from la gare, which sits in 19th century dignity besides its tracks.   That is how I come to be here. I went to la gare to find out about the train schedule to Madrid. But, said the fellow at the window, you must go to Royan to buy tickets for the international and the schedule I have (said he) may not be right also. Therefore I must go to Royan. By bicycle or by train. So, walking out of the station, I was in sunlight and across the street there were the mellow red – not bright red – mellow red metal tables and chairs of the Adel-etc.

So, I am here, with my citron-pressé before me and two dogs – a big brown and white one and a little black one – lying at my feet and a little dark-haired boy sitting in the doorway. It is that kind of afternoon. The world has turned to Spring – it is at the mid-point, the resting place, the sweet time – a time to lie in sunlight and let the gentle breeze blow.

Across the road, in front (Ah, there, the bright blue van has driven off – and the dogs are gone, the little boy is walking about in front of the door – the world keeps right on turning) Across the road, in front of the station are five trees. Important-looking trees, street trees, trees that make a statement to an arriving world. They are as tall as the roof of the Hotel le Terminus and they would be taller were they not cut off at the top. For these are not trees that grow every which way with time and tide and wind and rain and sunlight. No, these are civilized trees. They show ordered grace in the French manner. So they are cropped at the top – all at the same height, and their main branches are cropped at six or 8 feet out, so that there is pattern of the small branches reaching out to a uniform invisible line around the trees. All the branches are bare and maybe it is my imagination that I see a reddish greenish hue of life on the branches. Maybe not, for I think in not many days, maybe before I leave this area for Spain, these tall civilized trees will have the green leaves of 1990. The 1990th year of He is Risen. And maybe what once rose will rise again in the five formal trees in front of Saujon rail station, a place in a town near the Atlantic coast of France. We shall see.

So. Well. It is now 6 PM and I think about returning – it takes about 20 minutes to ride my bike to La Petite Eguille and dusk begins to set in about 6:30. And yet – there is a never dying Sun in the Spring sky. Who could believe that this Sun will set? My God – there are sounds like a fellow choking inside the café. I guess it is part of the conversation, for he stopped his strangling noise and the conversation continues. I see my shadow stretches now halfway across the street to the Hotel le Terminus, and the shadow of the furled umbrella that is set through the table has almost reached the curb opposite. So the world is still turning.

10:21 PM La Petite Eguille
I feel tired. A week of coping with another language and the bike rides. Tiring but enjoyable.

A village lunch . . . cold salmon vinaigrette
on butter lettuce, with quartered boiled eggs and fat
tomato slices

La Petite Eguille   Saturday, March 24, 7:37 AM
It is a beautiful morning. I know that because I hear the birds a-chatter and because a moment ago I looked out the window of my bathroom at the sunlit green grass white house red roof. Here, as I lie in bed, I still have the curtains drawn across my bedroom windows. The weather report on television last night predicted 4° for the low temperature this morning, rising to 18° – I translate that into Fahrenheit as 37° and 65°. So. Not bad at all – a little cooler than it has been but still pleasant. Today, vast possibility stretches before me. For, after breakfast, the day is all mine to fashion. I, on my trusty bicycle, can wander across farm, field, forest and

marsh.

Meursac   1 PM

Well, the cat is in the pigeons. I have in front of me a quart (quarter of a liter) of vin rouge. Here at what I believe is the Restaurant Eugene in the faraway village of Meursac. Oh, the other people – the only other people – the four people at the far table – have had a platter of oysters delivered. Ah, would that I had the savoir-faire to order oysters. I plod the – Ah, here is my cold salmon vinaigrette. In a small metal serving tray – on a bed of butter lettuce, with quartered boiled eggs and fat tomato slices around. It is a goodly plate. A meal in itself. I picked the salmon (saumon) for the first course because I recognized it. I come to timidity when I enter the small restaurant in the far village in the gourmet land with the imperfectly known language. Madame the proprietress came to take away the emptied platter of oysters. Délicieuse, said the four people. So now I know what to say when asked. In Spanish, one can say sabroso or muy rico.

Meursac is a gathering of buildings on a low hill that rises past the valley of the river Seudre – which here is but a riverlet. The Seudre is the river that goes through L'Eguille and Saujon. Meursac must be some 15 km from Saujon. So. I have had a couple – here is my veal steak and haricots vert. More meat than I eat in 6 years in Santa Cruz – but I have determined to eat in France a la mode francaise. I would have liked more time between the salmon and the veal to scribble. My, I am becoming full quickly. This is very substantial fare. It is good I did a couple hours bicycling to arrive here. I may have to be taken back in a wheelbarrow.

I started off about 10 in the morning to one of three
destinations – to the sea at St. George Didonne near
Royan, or to Pont l'Abbey, a small town to the northeast,
or to Meursac. Ah, ah – I just noticed how difficult it is for
me to be true to myself. I was eating the last of the green
beans directly from the metal serving dish. And then
(Here is a woman in a green sweater and gray slacks
who comes through the front door – oh my, the events are
piling up as I write. This is why Proust shut himself up
in a soundproof room.) Madame just came to take away
my dishes. You are finished? she asked. Oui, I said. And
she took away the metal platter and my plate – and also
the bowl of butter lettuce. Ah, ah – I called after her –
la salade. Oh, she said, you have not finished the salad?
No, I said. She brought it back and gave me a new plate,
a new fork, a new knife. I stumbled on dessert. She said
glace or fruit or creme caramel. Now, naturally I would
order fruit, but I heard myself say "creme caramel". I
hear them getting the wheelbarrow ready.

To go back to the woman in the green sweater: She came
in and advanced to the open door to the kitchen (open
because one walks through there to arrive at the toilet).
Est-ce que vous servez le petit dejeuner? she asked. My
goodness, it is almost 2 PM – breakfast at 2 PM? How
many are you, asked Madame. Two. Oui. But this is not
a French breakfast they are eating. As far as I can make
out in the dimness and the distance, they are sharing an
omelette. But how did they get an omelette so quickly?
I lose the time when I scribble – perhaps more time has
passed than I am aware of.

Now – what was I talking of when the woman in the
green sweater and grey slacks walked in? I must look
back. No, I remember. How I am not true to myself – in

the little things, in the moments that are the stuff of a
life. What happened was that I was eating the last of
the haricots verts from the serving platter and then I
thought – well I had ought to transfer them to my plate.
Actually the previous action was also acting out for the
others – I was being the casual carefree diner. I am so
often doing what I am doing – I mean in the gestures and
the manners as well as the substance – for the spectators
– the others – and it doesn't come from within me. It
bounces out and comes back in an unreal way. I pause
and lay down the pen, I take the first spoonful of the
creme caramel.

I do feel the wine – I feel a distance, as if I am floating
a little bit apart from what I hear and what I do. A bit
earlier there was jazz music on the radio off somewhere
beyond the kitchen door. Now a woman is talking. The
four people in the corner are talking. Earlier they were
talking about routes – I heard words for road and Paris
and Royan. Now it is something about family – I hear
grandmere, les femmes. Now I hear bourgeois, grand
bourgeois, petit bourgeois. They look like country people
– two older men, one older woman and one younger
woman, dressed in comfortable everyday shirts blouses
sweaters. Yet they seem to be talking, in a relaxed, quiet,
post-dinner way of some interesting, rather intellectual,
things. Maybe they are only trading old histories. If I had
the French I could hear the whole conversation, for they
are talking clearly and this is a small room. On the other
hand, the women in gray slacks and her companion are
talking in a way that hides even one word from my ears,
even though they are only half the distance from me of
the four people. Hey listen, people who eat breakfast at 2
PM – although they are both middle aged.

Oh boy, I am coming into complete, C-O-M-P-L-E-T-E, disintegration. Madame just came to take the plate of the creme caramel and she asked me Voulez vous du cafe? and me, instead of saying No – I heard myself say Avez-vous du cafe decafine? She is going to look. And I am not going to sleep for four nights. Ralph boy, take hold – you are walking the Primrose Path – they will never let you re-enter Santa Cruz if you acquire these spectacularly bad habits. Here it is – Nescafé. I am putting <u>sugar</u> in the coffee – it is obvious that I am more than learning French, I have dropped down the rabbit hole and I am now in French land, and becoming a French-land-er. Hey, this coffee and sugar is good stuff. I am making myself another cup. I now feel the wine-bred distance disappearing.   I am beginning to TWANG. Twwwwwaaaaaannnng. I hope I don't forget my hat. It is sitting on the big wood hat rack, near the kitchen door. Actually, I couldn't forget my hat. As soon as I get out into the sun I will think Hat.

Something I didn't know until now – the little restaurant sugar packets have divided themselves into 3 little cubes – instead of two. Although now they are no longer cubes – they are mere rectangles. Yes, I definitely judge the lady in grey and green and her companion, middle aged though they may be, engaged in what they see as a liaison dangereuse – this is what whispering over the 2 PM breakfast table signifies.

2:31 PM   I am finished with dinner – salmon, veal, beans, salad, creme caramel, wine and coffee. But. Am I in shape to bicycle back? No. I shall go out and sit in the little grassed square beside the 12th-century church before I start off again on my bicycle. Interesting, as I was going through Corme Ecluse, the next large village over, I saw that the church door was open and I went in and looked about. It, too, is a 12th century church – I think the plaque on the wall said that construction began in 1104. The floor of the church is some 5 feet below the level of the ground outside and there is a worn set of stone stairs inside the church door leading down to the floor level. Now, I imagine that the church floor would have been at ground level when it was built. So that means that the ground about the church has gone up 5 feet over the almost 900 years. That is buildings being built and destroyed and rebuilt and falling down and all the garbage and broken pottery and broken chairs and so forth. And the ground slowly rises. This is a fascinating countryside. Saintes, the large town east of Saujon, was a Roman town, with a Roman bridge and arch and arena.

2:42 PM   Well, the four people just left – the two late-breakfasters left some minutes before – and when I catch Madame's attention, I too shall depart. It has been a pleasant lunch – although not my usual fare. My – what do I see out the window? Is it a palm tree, dimly seen through the lace curtains? I shall have to check when I go out.

3:16 PM   Oh, I just remembered the palm tree. I forgot to look. I'll look when I go to get my bike, which stands opposite the restaurant. Right now I am sitting on a bench on the grassy square next to the church. I just went in the church, another of the 12th century I think. This is a larger church than the one at Corme Ecluse. When I came in a woman was playing the small organ and two women standing alongside were singing. They were practicing. There was a little printed sign near the entrance that said: Tourists, don't miss seeing the crypt. So I went to where the stairs were, but there was no light. Then I saw a sign that said: Look on the other side of the pillar for the light meter. And there, on the other side, was a long instruction. Put three one-franc coins in the grey box, one at a time, slowly – then push the button – when you want to come up, push the button in the crypt. I looked, but I only had two one-franc pieces. I asked one of the women practicing if she could change a two-franc piece. No, she said, I have no change. So I walked to the door. A minute later a little energetic woman came hurrying after me. Wait, she said, I have change in the house. She went out and returned in a minute with change. So I put the coins in the meter, pushed the button, lo, there was light on the stairs and I went down. I had to squeeze around the circular stone stairs which went down, I would say, a good 20 feet – to several chambers cut into the living rock below the church. Was this used for burial? I shall have to investigate. Put it on the list, after the palm tree.

It is getting colder – now at 3:31 PM – and gray clouds cover much of the sky. Is rain possible? The grassy square just outside of which I am now seated, is marked out by a double row of formally cut trees – all topped at the same height, about 15 feet. From the cut tops grows an electric band of twigs. I say electric because the twigs stand on end reaching fiercely for the sky like iron filings standing on a magnet and also because when the sunlight struck them a few minutes ago they had a very alive reddish glow. That is the red glow of life – they are pregnant with green leaves. The Resurrection certainly has meaning, especially in the lands of barren bare-tree Winter.

There are two cars parked next to my bench. Now people are getting into them – they are the people who were

practicing in the ancient church. I was thinking as I was walking about the church that it was not these old stones that survived – it was the culture, the religious belief. There are wooden temples in Japan many centuries old. The wood does not survive– the temples are completely rebuilt every certain number of years in the same form and manner. So it is with these churches. You see here a patch of new stones, there a re-carved portion of the facade. The strongest and most lasting things are intangible, I think. This makes me think of the personal, psychological phenomenon –   Ah, an owl hoots from somewhere about the church. I think it is an owl, though I look up and see flying by what looks like a dove.   Anyway. Psychologically, change happens with awareness. There is an adaptation to present conditions if there is awareness   Three   kids roller skate by – the wheels are plastic, for they make no metallic sound on the asphalt walk behind me
Now, the question is – what does that psychological fact have to do with the cultural phenomenon of the 900 year old church? I sneeze. It is becoming quite chilly. I think of the persistence of the cultural artifact as good but the persistence of psychological personal artifacts as bad. Artifacts is not a good word for the second thing. What shall I call it?

There is the bird again. Maybe it is a dove. Yes, we'll call it a dove – though it is certainly a strong, loud call. Whoo Whoo Wok Whoo Whoo Wok. Something like that. And there is also a twitter of birds – very much like the twitter outside my windows at La Petite Eguille each morning. It has been going on all the while I have been sitting here, I think. But I just noticed it. Another look at these trees. I am not sure –   There is the church bell above me One Two Three Four – 4 PM, although my

watch has it at 3:58.   I am not sure how old
these trees are. 40 years? 50? The trunks are not very
big.   There is the dove again. The trunks are about a
foot in diameter. The trunks are dark gray brown with
splotches of white, light grey and yellow.   There   are
the church bells again. One Two Three Four – and this
time we agree: 4 PM. I think the splotches on the trees
are – what do you call it? – the same as on rocks. There
are the doves – and I hear the twitter again. The gray
clouds are solid across the sky behind me now – I think
that is North. In front of me I still see patches of electric
blue. I had better be on my way

9:44 PM La Petite Eguille
And so to sleep. I have been in bed ever since I arrived
back about 6:30. I rode the bike against a wind all the
way back and I was very tired when I arrived. I had two
large glasses of orange juice and water and a banana.
That was all the supper I wanted after that enormous
lunch.

Bicycle to the sea at Royan.
boules courts . . .an eruption of voices

La Petite Eguille   Sunday, March 25, 11:26 AM
I still feel rather tired from yesterday. I woke this
morning at 8:15 AM – that is, I thought it was 8:15 AM
– but the hours were advanced in France yesterday, so it
was 9:15 AM. I am thinking now of riding over to Royan
today – it would not be as far as Meursac.

2:25 PM   Royan
A word or two before le dejeuner. I have bicycled to
Royan and the great Atlantic. Behind me are the red-

roofed villages, the green fields, the yellow flowers of Springtime, the white-blossomed apple trees – I have done my dozen kilometers of bicycling across field and marsh, little hills and little valleys. Now the ocean is in front of me, though I see it not from this place. This place is a concrete bench in a green park by the railroad station. It is a chilly, mostly cloudy, day. I have on sweater and windbreaker and I would put on my wool mittens were I not about to eat my cheese and bread and pear. A spare and spartan lunch after the Dionysian orgy of yesterday's lunch.

2:38 PM   I sit here on my bench eating from the loaf of bread I bought yesterday morning in Saujon and from a tranche of cheese I bought yesterday afternoon in Meursac. And I thought – I would never eat cheese if I were at home. But, I answered, I am on vacation. On vacation I can eat cheese and meat and wine and coffee. So that is what I am on vacation from. I am vacationing from myself – my usual habitual everyday self. It is a good thing to do. And that is, perhaps, what vacations are becoming more like as people work less. Not to rest in a cottage by the sea, but to canoe in the Amazon, climb the Himalayas. Am I making a point? Or is it all scribble-mania?

2:55 PM   I have finished all my little lunch except the end of the little loaf of bread. The sky has cleared considerably and a March sun shines over Royan. Royan is a resort town – it lives off summer vacationers, so today, in late March, Royan is tranquil, there are few cars in the streets, most shops are closed (of course, today is also Sunday). This park has several boules courts and over at my left, several middle-aged men are playing a vociferous game. There is quiet, the clunk of the balls and then, suddenly, an eruption of voices – it is not Apres vous, mon cher Andre – but rather   What the hell do you mean, I didn't hit that ball? – etc. Alors, I must find a place out of this chill breeze to sit and write. I shall search out a cozy café.

3:35 PM   The café is a grand bar on the promenade of the sea. Royan was destroyed during the war and so its buildings are modern. But the buildings along the central promenade are arranged in a formal pattern. There is here a wide cove of seashore, something like the Santa Cruz shore at the pier and boardwalk. There is a wide white beach reaching to four or five wide concrete ledges that rise to the promenade walk. Beyond the walk there is grass and flower beds, then a narrow motorway and then the façade of uniform, rectilinear, modern buildings, five stories high, with stores on the ground floor and hotel rooms on the upper floors.

4:35 PM   Still in the café – I confess that I have been sitting here for ye entire hour writing postcards. Trying to help poor old Royan – it has great need for a tourist-type Tourist – someone who will sit at the table in front of the corner window looking out at the Promenade and write picture postcards. That's me. And it has worked. When I came in, there was not another soul at a table in this place. Now the tables are full and the clatter of dishes is heard in the land. Saint Ralph – he brought back the tourists to Royan. Or?   Could it be something like the swallows at Capistrano?

12:11 AM (technically Monday)   I can't believe it – but I just had a two-hour long conversation with Mirielle on abstract intellectual subjects – mostly the nature of the film industry and European politics – all in French –

always almost on the edge of not quite understanding or not quite being able to express myself clearly – but I did understand and I did express myself, My, my, my. And so to bed.

La Petite Eguille   Monday, March 26, 8:29 AM
Since I went to bed so late last night I set my wristwatch alarm (did Dick Tracy have a wristwatch alarm as well as a wristwatch TV?) – I set my wristwatch alarm for 8 AM. And it so occurred. The morning is quite cold. March 26 leans to the Winter side of the family. So to breakfast.

10:33 PM   This has been something of a recuperative day for me. I didn't go to the afternoon class. Instead I slept for two hours after lunch – then I bicycled to Saujon for an hour, mailed some postcards, bought some fruit at the market.

La Petite Eguille   Tuesday, March 27, 10:33 PM
Once again 10:33 PM.   24 hours have passed.
Sleep Breakfast Class Lunch Class Do Laundry Bicycle to Saujon Do Homework Dinner Talk Watch Television. And it is 10:33 PM again. On the evening of a cold March day, a grey Spring day. What are the little touches? Oh, there were lots of them but I will be long before I go to sleep if I write them all. There is the brown colt in the green field that I walked by in my 10 minute walk between the end of the morning class and lunch. He came running over to the fence and I gave him some green grass I picked from along the roadside and patted his head. He did the same thing yesterday. At the same time. There was this evening during dinner – talking about computers and I went blank – it would take a long time to write that all out.

La Petite Eguille   Wednesday, March 28, 7:58 AM
The truth of the matter – true true – is that I woke this morning with this sentence in my head: Quel domage! Si je restais quatre semaines, je parlerais un bon francais! What a shame! If I stayed four weeks, I would speak a good French! Thinking it that way makes it true, I am practically dreaming in French.

3:49 PM   Just a minute or two or three to scribble – because at 4 PM I am going to Royan with Mirielle and Ferrar – I want to buy my rail ticket to Madrid. That is the main purpose of my journey. Right now I sit at the little white desk in my room. But – I think I shall go downstairs and scribble sitting on the couch in the living room.

3:58 PM   So. Here I sit – not on the couch but on a dark brown bamboo-framed armchair with rough-textured off-white seat cushions – a country kind of furniture for a country kind of place. It is cozy warm in here but I keep on my green and blue nylon windbreaker – the one I bought last week at the Intermarche supermarket in Saujon – and my long-lasting cashmere scarf – the one I bought in 1979 at the little mill in western Connecticut – they have since moved the little mill to western Massachusetts – the Berkshires. Must go.

10:29 PM   My – we had an animated conversation over dinner tonight. Mostly about history. Mirielle used to be a history teacher and is passionately interested in history, especially French history. So. What else about today? It was another cold day – although along about early afternoon it looked like it was going to be warmer – a promise that was not realized. We made the trip to Royan – the entire present populace of La Ferme, which

is Mirielle and Farrar and me and Diane, the woman
from Rome. My errand in Royan was to buy the ticket
for the train trip to Madrid – which I did. It will be
during the night of next Thursday, April 5. I leave here
sometime about 8 PM. Catch a train in Bordeaux about
10:30 PM and arrive in Madrid about 10 AM.

Today I got the least exercise of any day since I came
here. All I did was bicycle for about 10 minutes   One
thing I have been thinking of lately is how important it
is for me to always be letting go of the past, including the
childhood past, and being where I am when I am – now
and here. Not a facile thing – but thinking of it is helpful
– I become aware that my shoulders are hunched up and
my face screwed tight because I am protecting something
in me which there is – now and here – no apparent
reason to protect. I notice now the quietness of the
country night – as a dog barks from faintly away and that
is the only sound and it is gone. I like the country. But
here it is a country place with other people and that is
important. I do want to explore some such situation for
myself on a permanent basis.

La Petite Eguille   Thursday, March 29, 8:14 AM
Morning. A cold wintry-white haze lies over the field
beyond the red roof and beyond the trees. The birds
sound distant and subdued. King Winter stalks the land,
white icicles, white beard, woolen robes and all. The
television people promise warming for the weekend. Do
I have time to write about last night's discussion? Well,
I shall begin. Mirielle was talking of the French kings
and their endeavors to gather together the territory of
France through war and more war. I said – It is a sad
history. Mirielle was stung by this characterization of
French history. I said, We should not glorify these men –

they were for the most part pursuing petty vicious selfish and cruel goals, destroying etc. I think this is something of an American criticism of Europe. But I think it has validity. There should be a standard of morality to which we should subject historical figures and not glorify bloody deeds. Nor should we justify by saying – But look here at Country X, they were doing worse. The Americans, too, have a horrible bloody selfish history. And it should be recognized as such. One of my points is that one must be suspicious of the writers of history. The people in power most often govern how history is written and they guard against history in which they appear as ignoble, as they mostly are. And so to breakfast.

7:34 PM   Dinner is in the wings or on the stove or in the air. It hovers. I sit before the little white desk in my room. I finished my homework exercises and I went down to see if I could copy my first 11 pages of this letter on La Ferme's photocopy machine, but both Farrar and Mirielle were on the telephone. I sat down in one of the rattan armchairs of the living room to read the new book I have started, *L'Orme du Mail* (*The Elm on the Mall*, as far as I can figure out) by Anatole France. But, I found I did not have my reading glasses with me. So out I went, back into the cold gray evening air, and around to the entrance to this far end of the rambling farm building, up the stairs to my room, and to the seat before the little white desk.

I am thinking of sending the first 11 pages of this letter to five people: Joanna, and copies to Rita, Willie, Pratt and John. And then I have questions of trust and revelation coming up because I am writing about some things I don't talk freely about and I think I am something of a secretive person. And also having the letter copied. The copying itself.

So. I did the afternoon class today, which means I didn't finish lessons until after four in the afternoon. Then I bicycled with Diana to Mornac, which is a well-worn tourist village about 5 miles away. Part of this trip is not very pleasant because one must go along the high-speed highway between Saujon and Royan. I preferred not to try riding my bike there, but instead walked with the bike on the grass verge along the road. The cars and trucks roared by in terrifying flurries.

Mornac is a place where there is sold nougat candy and paintings painted by the dozen and silk scarves and ceramic plates and etc. I was there the last time I was here – when it was August – and the streets were adrift and afoul of ice cream-eating, sandal-wearing tourists. This time we were the only visitors walking the streets of the village. There is a nice 12th-century church which we went into. Went <u>down</u> into – because the church at Mornac, like the church at Corme Ecluse, has a stairway inside the front door that leads down some 4 feet from street level to the level of the church's floor.

So. 7:51 PM – I shall go down to catch the last of the evening news on television before dinner.

10:34 PM   I seem to arrive in bed at the same minute each night. I am stuffed to the gills, having eaten and eaten, and finished by taking a full quarter of a large apple tart. After dinner we watched on French television an interview from Bonn of Chancellor Kohl of West Germany. I could understand only a small fraction of what was being said. Over dinner this evening we talked of dreams and Esalen, of our bicycle trip to Mornac this afternoon.

I am not sure what I want to do over the weekend. I had called Plum Village, which is the place in the Dordogne where Thich Nhat Hanh teaches. I called again this evening to check how they felt about a visitor. The woman I talked with said they weren't really set up now to receive visitors – for one thing it has been cold and they don't have heating. Also T N H is probably going to be in retreat this weekend. But she said it would be okay for me to drop in. I can rent a car at Royan. Plum Village is about 100 miles from Royan, I calculate. I enjoy just being quiet on the weekend and bicycling about the countryside – so to what avail renting a car and driving hither and yon? Then again, I have never seen the Dordogne. I am sure that if I were with someone I would do it. Two people energize each other.

La Petite Eguille   Friday, March 30, 7:36 AM
I had a most marvelous dream just before 7:11 AM. Strange – I often wake at 7:11 AM. Marvelous is not quite the word. Interesting? No. Too banal a word. Anyway. I am in a traveling city. I am traveling, not the city – but I didn't want to write *strange* or *foreign*, because it didn't feel (to me) strange or foreign. And I want to have a haircut. Even though I am not staying in this large, elegant hotel, I go to the concierge and I ask where is the coiffeur. He says – go through that entry and go straight ahead and there is the coiffeur. At first I go the wrong way and then I go through the right entry and walk right to the place where are the barbers. It is a bit confusing, with the barber chairs set in what is a large elegant public place. One barber motions me to sit off to one side. I am a little concerned that I will miss my turn. I turn and ask, How long will it be? Oh, she says,

with a nonchalant gesture and holding up the fingers of one hand – five minutes, ten minutes. So I am soon called and I am attended by two young women, one the barber, the other the assistant. Oh, I forgot to mention, I noticed Michael G. came into the barbershop after I did – I was somewhat concerned that the haircuts there cost a lot and he would find it too expensive.

It is 7:48 now – I want to rise – me leve – so I shall continue this later – although I fear I may forget some of it.

7:28 PM   At my little white desk, the little black desk lamp shining bravely with the daylight. Because, of course, the sun is still hanging golden bright in the sky on the other side of the house. This I can personally attest because I just came in, after washing three undershirts, three undershorts, three pairs of socks and two shirts in the laundry basin near the kitchen. Rub-a-dub-dub with a bar of soap and a basin of water and then hang outside on the line where a brisk wind has them all streaming flat out, as if to carry it all, line and clothes and pole, away to Royan and out to sea.

This morning we – Diana and I – had our class with Annique and it was spent mostly by talking of the countryside about here – and also I talked about the work of my friends in Spain.

After lunch I bicycled to Saujon. It was sometimes slow going because of the sweeping wind – that came and went and came again. In Saujon I went to the newspaper store and had the first 11 pages of this letter copied – at great expense. It cost 33 francs for the 11 pages (both sides) or 1 1/2 francs per page – that is something like 25¢ – 30¢

per page. What Saujon needs is a Kinko's copy center.

Then I went to what I call Café du Mairie – because it is across the street from the Mairie (City Hall). An old-fashioned, 19th-century kind of place, with marble-top wrought-iron tables, a tile floor, the toilettes a half city block walk through the buildings and the men's urinal screened by a wooden half partition from the women's toilet, and the washbasin back halfway to the café – shining brightly under daylight from a skylight – and alongside a long blue towel sewn to itself, end to end, so it is a continuous, forever, blue towel. Altogether, a charming place – straight out of a 19th-century novel. There, in the café, I put together my letters (and later mailed them).

Diana came by the café at about a 4:45 and later we bicycled back together, exploring a new route which didn't follow the main auto road, but went along a narrow paved road and then along a dirt track alongside the River Seudre – it was a bit muddy at places, but we got through without too much difficulty.

Now. Unfinished business. Do I have time to talk about my dream of last night? Well, not really. Because it is now 7:49 and dinner is at 8 and I want to be a bit early to watch the news and weather prediction for tomorrow. Well, I'll go down and take this with me. Maybe write in the living room. Allons -y.

7:57 PM   Watching the weather: 21° in the Bordeaux region. A nice day for all.

11:12 PM   So. We watched tonight the very good discussion program on books which is on French television for an hour and a half, from 9:30 to 11, every Friday. I saw it, by chance, on the TV in my hotel room in Paris the first day I arrived in France and I have seen two subsequent programs. Tonight's program was on new books about nutrition and eating. There was a couple who have written a book on Chinese diet and eating habits; a man who wrote a detective novel based upon a murder by poisoning of cognac, wherein he talks much of how cognac is produced; a man who wrote a book on the restaurants of Paris; a man who wrote a book on the way the industrial producers of food products are taking over French cuisine; a fat man who wrote a book on fat people; and a man who wrote a book on nutrition for the brain. Not the same kind of group you might gather for an American program of this kind – very French, very interesting. Of course, I far from understood it all, but I caught the drift of it. I certainly would like to see a program like that on American TV.

Now, another good thing about French television is that the advertisements never interrupt the programs. All the ads are grouped together and only shown between the programs. We have done ourselves horrible harm in allowing our television to be dominated and destroyed by advertising. We have sold ourselves into 70 years of bondage.

Overnight in Marennes. A contented mind arises from simple things.

La Petite Eguille   Saturday, March 31, 9:42 AM
My Oh Wow. The gods are smiling this morning. It is warm, it is still, the sun shines and the grass glows. Le bon temps for the Weekend. And off I go on my bicycle. I

won't write more now because I am all a-flutter to get on my trusty bicycle and go. Where? We shall see.

10:46 AM   Here I am, stopped on the little road between St. Martin de Gua and St. Sornin. Why? To note the first dog. Of all the fierce looking German Shepherds that run wildly along the fences and leap and bark and snarl. This one was just past the field with all the fat white sheep. And a breeze whistles past my ears and the green grass bends before it.

11:22 AM St. Sornin
Well, we make our choices. I was going to go into the café, as I did in 1986 when I was bicycling back from Pont l'Abbe d'Arnoult late on an August day. But after I went in the church, now completely restored, I saw the neat little boulangerie, so I went in there and bought a little apple turnover. The boulanger was just right – a black-haired, rosy-faced man with a neat black mustache. As I remember from 1986 in the café, I felt the other patrons of the café had been sent out by central casting. So too with le boulanger. Maybe this is a set for *Hollywood visits Provincial France: Part II: The Village.* The 12th century church sits in an expansive grassy square – the square and its paths lined by the evenly-cropped ornamental trees that are the French manner. Around the square are neat stone two-story buildings. A block off the square is the café and the boulangerie.

When I was here in 1986, the interior of the old church was being reconstructed. Now the work is done and the church is a neat amalgam of old stones and new stones. Merielle said she had read an article about St. Sornin. Apparently an immensely rich but modest man lived here and he was the Maire of the village. And it was he,

I believe, who gave the money to rebuild the church. And he has since died – in his late 50s, I think. So it may happen with the rich and modest.

Well. I shall push on. I am bound, more or less, for the town of Marennes. I think I shall stay there overnight, for it would be a tough ride back and forth in one day. And there is a nearby town which was a port and still has its city walls. It is called – and I look for my map – Brouage. Brouage is now quite a way from the sea. Mirielle said that it was a Protestant city and Richelieu had a ship sunk to block the channel to its port, the channel silted up and now Brouage is no more a port than Watsonville. Mount up – and onward into the sunlit day.

1:33 PM   Here I am. In Brouage. In a restaurant. At table. A basket full of bread, a glassful of wine. And I have ordered the menu at 76 francs, which begins with a terrine of the country and then a plate of the sea – oysters, mussels. My, here is the terrine – a huge casserole filled with paté – with a large knife stuck in the middle. I serve myself. And alongside is a large earthenware jar. Mustard? No – pickles. I cut myself what I think is a small slice of paté. But on my plate it is a great slab. So, I plunge into excess. I have earned excess. I have pedaled cross farm, field and forest – what? 30 kilometers? Three hours and 20 minutes. Oh my faith and oh my liver. They sound the same in French: Foi and Foix. The French go on faith when it comes to the liver. A slice of pate, a buttered croissant, a cream sauce here and a butter sauce there, a white wine, a red wine, a glass of cognac – one has faith that the liver will not take it badly.

Ah, the waitress just came over (I have a waitress <u>and</u> a waiter – hey, listen – for someone who has bicycled 30 kilometers – you understand? – one is entitled.)   And she said – You have served yourself, Monsieur? And I said Oui, Oui. So she took away the great terrine of paté and the great stone jar of pickles. And I?   I am well and truly launched on The Lunch At Brouage – a drama in six acts. I can see I was hopelessly improvident in ordering only one glass of wine. I went through <u>that</u> with the paté.

Ah – the plate of the sea – 3 oysters. 30 or 40 little sea snails, 3 crayfish. Here we go. It is Me against the Sea. It is Carnivoreism gone mad. Picking little worms out of shells with an oversized needle. Eating incredibly shaped raw animals. To be frank: no one would do it sober. Like the fellow who bites the heads off the chickens in the Carnival – one must have the wine. And the bread – that helps too. I wouldn't do it if I weren't French. I am French, aren't I? God – you'd swear the little worms are alive. If you don't catch them with the needle the first time, they retreat inside the shell and it is impossible to extricate them.

There is a German Shepherd in here – the size of a horse. He came over when the great terrine was on the table, but he doesn't seem interested in the worms – probably hasn't had enough to drink yet. The carnage on my plate now is incredible. *The dead and the dying, the wrecked shells.* Perhaps I need another glass of wine. It is white Muscatel, you know. Some of the worms are escaping, I know that. They will have to be buried by their relatives. The whole thing is on a bed of seaweed. I eat a shred of it. Hey, not bad. The French would be astonished. You don't eat the seaweed, they would say, you eat the worms.

Well, it is done – it is over. But. Now – the fricassee of eel. There is a packet of finger wipes on the plate. Is that for before or after eel? Maybe I should order another wine. The eel is crunchy. That is because the spine is still inside. So I try to cut out the spine. Fortunately it is covered with something and fried. It might be chocolate nougat without the sugar.

Will they allow me back in the Santa Cruz if they know I ate the spine? I am running out of wine and bread. If they go before the eel, it is all over for me. I am rationing. A sip of wine, two bites of eel, a morsel of bread. Oh Susanna, don't you cry for me. Think of all the calcium in those spines. Actually, fish don't have spines, do they? Vertebrates and invertebrates. 7 days. The Creation. All that. Yeh, but fish are vertebrates – didn't you ever de-bone a fish? The eels have a lot of garlic going for them. Add that to the wine and bread. I didn't mention the little cubed french-fried potatoes. Yes, next to the eels. The eels are gone. Rather, the eels and I have merged. I am now part eel. Part eel, part oyster, part sea worm – and all the other stuff. I have merged with the Sea.

Now is the time for the finger wipes. Hello America. Finger Wipe Welcomes You. Also Modern Plumbing. Hey the toilets here don't flush – they simply open. And there is only one sip of the white Muscatel left. And all the other diners have left. Except the two old ladies in the corner. And they have stood up and are adjusting their clothing. It is only Finger Wipe Me, eel-inside Me. And yes. Toothpick. I need a toothpick, there is a worm between my teeth.

There are some lovely Spring tulips in a little brass vase

on the next table – solid red and solid yellow and pale green leaves – the life comes forward from out of dark Winter's earth. It is – once again – the Resurrection.

The waitress came over – for dessert, she says you wish the crepe? Which are the other choices? I say. And now I forget the other choices – but she said the crepe with Grand Marnier – with sugar or chocolate. Ah – said I – with chocolate.

And – I have found the packet of little orange toothpicks I put in my shoulder bag back at La Petite Eguille. Blessed relief. I can now eat the crepe with relaxed teeth. But – on writing that while picking my teeth at the same time, I swallow air in the wrong lung tube – something like that – and I begin to cough. It seems I can't write and pick my teeth at the same time. And breathe. I forgot to mention that. Three things. My brain simply can't tackle it all. Here is the crepe. No Grand Marnier, only the chocolate inside. The Grand Marnier comes only with the sugar. No mind – no matter. I am surfeit, I am satisfied. A nice, rather light dessert. Vive la France!

Ah – a tragedy. When she brought the crepe, I took the toothpick out from my mouth and set it on my napkin. But I moved the napkin and the orange toothpick now lies par terre – on the ground. So it goes. Well – it is 2:54 PM. Maybe I shall pay and go outside and sit in the sunlit afternoon and digest – incorporate eel and chocolate and muscatel. Ah – my future, my near future, le proche avenir – is settled. You will have coffee, Monsieur, asked the waitress. Is it that you have infusion? I asked in return – a question for a question – a Jewishness. Oui, she said – tilleul. Oui, I said – it is some kind of herb.

And here is the brown pottery pot of the tea and a big white cup with two packets of sugar cubes. I shall take them with me. I fed sugar cubes to the colt in the field near La Ferme at La Petite Eguille. This place is signed outside as Hotel-Restaurant. Do I want to stay here tonight? Not sure.

There – a young woman peers through the glass door. There is a whole party of young people. And now they enter. Seven of them. They are motorcyclists – for they wear the black leather jackets and carry the Star Wars helmets. Four young men and three young women. They sit together at a long table – the men at one end and the women together at the other. They are a club or a class – they are not of Noah's Ark – two by two. Actually there are only three helmets on the table – on the women's side. Do only women wear helmets? At first I thought they were speaking German. But no – it is French.   This herb tea is good – nice and soothing. The only, unique and sole part of the meal related to my previous life – as a Santa Cruz vegetarian.

There are two parts of this large room – divided by an arch, which I think can be closed with sliding wooden panels that hide in the wall. On the one side, where I am – and just me alone right now – the tables are covered with dark-flowered cloths. On the other side – where are the Seven Motorcyclists – the tables are bare. That is the café part of the room, I think. I am in the restaurant part.

I look through the glass door into the street. Across the little street, standing in her doorway, is a woman wearing a light blue smock over a white blouse. A little earlier she was sweeping the sidewalk in front of her door. And now – she has disappeared and the white door is closed. So it goes in a changing world.

There are – in my part of the room – three vases of red and yellow tulips. The tulips are Spring but not subtle. They are flat: we are here, we are red and we are yellow. Spots of bright color but no nuance. Tulips are for reaffirming life, not for speaking subtility. Personally, I would put different tablecloths in this room – brighter, free-er, sunnier. I think it is a northern kind of room; the tulips, the dark cloths, and there is a Dutch kind of painting over the fireplace in the corner.

3:23 PM   I have well and truly finished lunch – and – I don't want to bicycle right now. I think I shall go out and wander about Brouage – it is actually just a large village but it has these formidable walls all about it – in the midst of a green grass sea. And maybe later I shall bike down to Marennes, which is something of a town (towards the size of Saujon, I think) and maybe stay the night there. Actually here in Bouage, I am only about 15 kilometers from Rochfort – which is a large town (besides a cheese). That is one thing about French towns: many of them can be eaten or drunk – Rochfort, Cognac etc.

3:41 PM   Well, here we have it – for, you know, Brouage was the birthplace of Samuel de Champlain – the founder of New France. So here is a little park with a bronze plaque, which says, "1570: Ici s'elevait la maison ou naquit et vecut toute son enfance Samuel de Champlain, pere de la Nouvelle France et fondateur de Quebec – Homage du Gouvernement du Quebec, 29 Aout 1970". And, behind, there is a pink flowering tree and on either side a large pot of – yes – red and yellow tulips. And the wind whistles in the trees and over all there is sunshine. It doesn't look to me like much is left of old Brouage but the outer walls. Most of the buildings seem fairly recent.

5:58 PM   Marennes
I am tired – bien fatigue. The ride from Brouage to Marennes, while not very long, went up a couple slopes and was against the wind. I am now sitting on a rush-seat chair in my room at the Cheval Blanc – which is restaurant, bar and hotel. Mostly a bar right now. What it lacks in elegance it makes up in quiet. I want to put my bicycle in some safe place in the hotel property for the night – the propriétaire, who is tending the bar, says it cannot be done, for some reason, until 6 PM. Or something like that. I asked him when I took the room – about 5 PM – and he said: in a half hour. I went out and bought a bar of soap and a liter of orange juice at an épicerie. I asked again when I came in about 10 minutes ago and he said: in 10 minutes.

I am going to have mainly a liquid supper. I have a liter and a half of water and liter of orange juice, an apple, a banana and some crackers. When I came in, the propriétaire asked me if I wanted supper with the room. No, I said. Then, he said, you must pay immediately for the room. The room is 100 francs, which seems a bit high – but then I have no idea what things cost here.

8:56 PM   I lie on the bed reading Le Monde of yesterday. Le Monde is a good and interesting newspaper but it takes all day to read it – even for the French. I feel quite at home here in my room. As long as a hotel room is quiet and clean, I feel at home in it. In Le Monde, the second section, I just read a long article about the superior of a prestigious abbey – at Bec – who (at 50) fell in love with the mother-superior of the nearby convent (55 years old). They made a public confession of their attachment and then gave up their posts and then separated and went to other religious houses. Now I am reading a book review of recent biographies of Truman Capote and William Burroughs.

9:52 PM   I just finished reading a Home Series letter I wrote from August to October last year. I like it. It encourages me to continue to express myself. Because I find myself interesting. Now isn't that a happy occurrence? – to find oneself interesting. And here – the night goes on a-pace – every so often there is a click or a cluck from the little hot-water radiator in front of the window. How very kind, how very generous of M. le Propriétaire to turn on the radiator. Because he really didn't have to – it is a warmish evening. (I think – for I have now lost contact with the outside.)

I am now a hotel room habitant, enclosed by the dull-red curtains and the rose-flowered wallpaper and the green and white abstract flower pattern of the screen set on the floor in front of the bidet and the sink. This is a very French, very 19th-century, little room. In the corner is a tall wood armoire with a long mirror on its front. The little table covered by a red and white cloth, the rush-bottom chair, a little shag throw-rug over the pine wood floor beside the bed. And the large double bed with the immoveable long round French pillow all the way across the head of it. The single light hanging from the ceiling with its bell-shaped, red and white, fringed shade. And on a little shelf on the wall beside the bed, a tiny lamp with a tiny lamp-bulb and a tiny red shade. And me, lying on the bed, my left elbow on the pillow, my legs crouched up, as I write this on the top of my dark green plastic letter case, which is on top of several spread-out sections of yesterday's Le Monde.

And so now it is 10:05 – I don't feel very sleepy, I am gradually recovering my energy from the great fatigue I felt earlier this evening.

10:16 PM   I just went down the hall to pee. I am quite sure that I am the only guest at the Cheval Blanc tonight. There is no sound of movement in any other part of the little inn. When I went outside the door of my room, the hall was quite dark. I felt my way to the toilet – outside the toilet door there were two lighted switches – one for the light in the toilet compartment and the other a timed switch for the hall light. A timed switch, meaning that when you press the switch the light goes on for about a minute and then goes out automatically. A thrifty old European device that would be well to introduce to the United States. Now I just brushed my teeth. I use the water from my liter and a half bottle. I may be overcautious but I don't know whether to trust the sink water in a far-off French provincial town. I probably am mistaken. At La Ferme I use the sink water – which comes from a well, I think.

Marennes   Sunday, April 1, 9:26 AM

A bright sun-filled morning, the clutter cluck of birds. I am up but not out. Dressed and packing my little into my shoulder bag. Whether one gets a cup of tea with the chambre at Cheval Blanc is not yet known.

10:28 AM   Luzac

Sitting on a concrete terrazzo bench in a public square in the village of Luzac, which is, perhaps, some 8 kilometers from Marennes. It is a bright charming morning but the brisk wind makes bicycling difficult. And my direction is just about full against the wind. So I am resting before setting sail once again. It appears that Luzac does not have a café, so I sit in this open-air, bare-ground square next to the road. It may be that this is used as a playfield, for I think a school is the next building back up the road. Around the periphery of the square there are the usual row of cropped ornamental trees, just now faintly budding forth in April sunlight and April wind. Oooh – I must go on – with the wind whipping about me and the cold of the concrete bench coming through, it is too chilly to sit still.

Bicycling back from Marennes

11:30 AM   Nieulle-sur-Seudre

My, here is a pleasant and well-tended village. It may well be the Marin County of the region. I just stopped at a pretty little boulangerie/épicerie and bought some fruit and a baguette. (I think the bread was called a fiselle.)

I am now not too far from La Petite Eguille – maybe 8 or 9 kilometers – although one stretch of 3 kilometers I have to go along the main auto road to Rochfort. Though I wish I had pee-ed somewhere back there along the uninhabited part of the road. Then I could sit here on this bench (which is a brother-bench to the one I sat on an hour ago in Luzac) with a contented mind. For you know, a contented mind does not – as many think – arise from problems resolved, obligations fulfilled, relations established – no – it arises much more from emptying the bladder, breathing simply and well – and such other simple things. Such is my belief on April First in Nieulle-sur-Seudre, the Marin of the marais (marsh).

Aperitifs and courteous discourse
in the language of the Sun King

1:31 PM La Petite Eguille
I have arrived. Moderately tired. I shall lie down for a bit and then take a shower.

3:54 PM   I did. I lay myself down a bit and then I took a shower. In the shower I started singing and I went through my limited repertoire. Old Man River. Oklahoma. Swing Low, Sweet Chariot. Sentimental Journey. We Shall Overcome. When I dressed, I remembered the Donut songbook I had brought with me and I took it out and went over the songs. The songbook only has the words – no music – so I didn't know how to sing many of the songs. I would like to teach some songs in Spain. I wonder if I can do that?

Right now, I am sitting on a white plastic garden armchair in back of the house of La Ferme. It must be something like an acre or more of land here and it is now all covered with mowed green grass. (Is there other than *green* grass? – probably – somewhere – anyway, let the record show that the grass here is green.) There is a stone wall at the far end in the direction I'm now facing – which is with my back to the sun. There is a twitter fritter of unseen birds and here the wind is gentle, it ruffles this page and gently rocks the tree branches. Everything is French here. Well, not everything – the grass could be in Santa Cruz, the birds probably go to Florida every Winter. But the old man who just walked to the yard of the neighbor house – he was wearing the royal blue cotton jacket and pants of the working person here. He could only be French. And the neighboring house itself – the little round windows in the garage door, the neat blue trim, the red tile roof, the square green hedge in front – it is French in the marrow and in the twig and in the hang of the cloth. The French style is studied, careful, neat, rather formal and has a solid lasting look. It is a reassuring, pleasing style.

There is now a high white cloud layer moving in over the sky and King Sun can no longer be seen, but His warmth abides over the land and the birds still twitter and I still sit here with but a sleeveless sweater over my shirt. It is a good deal warmer today than it was last week. The temperature has returned to the balmy days of my arrival. Here comes a buzzing large black bumblebee, hovering and flitting and humming just over the lawn. And a little black fly sits on the edge of this page, then goes away, then returns. Springtime and the living is becoming easy for the beasts. Or is it? Is living ever easy? What a question. Everything is relative.

So maybe we should always talk in comparatives. Easier

instead of easy. We are adapted to comparatives. Our senses and our sense is directed toward: What was it that just changed? and What was the change? – Instead of   What is? It may be that we miss a good deal by that way of being. But that is the way of survival – keep looking for the change.

Now I am becoming confused by the seeming clash of two of my clichés. What are the two cliches? Well – one is that one should be with what IS – so that one is not looking for the differences but for the essentials. That is not very clear. What I mean is that one shouldn't be all taken up with change, but be aware of basic securities and harmonies. That is still not clear – not because it is not explained thoroughly, but because I don't have it clearly in mind. Anyway. The second cliché is that one should be aware that everything is changing all the time; that we live in change, that nothing is constant and that any sense of permanence is only illusion. So. How do these two ideas fit together?

Maybe the first idea is that one is looking at change and disturbed by change because one thinks things are permanent.   Over behind me a chicken is clucking in a loud voice. Do chickens have voices? It is a triumphant kind of cluck – you know, the I've got an egg cluck.   So. Anyway. Is it that if one understands that everything is changing, one then gets in touch with the essential? I am not sure what I am talking about. Maybe I shall come back to it sometime.

4:32 PM now. I shall read a bit in my Anatole France novel. So far – I'm at about page 20 – it is about events in a seminary.

7:11 PM   A lucky time. I am again sitting out here on the vast green lawn in my white plastic armchair. Two new students arrived a half hour ago in the white Volkswagen van, driven by Farrar from the rail station at Saujon. They are an older couple. (We near-60-year-olds no longer use the word elderly – nor, yet, do we say senior citizen – older will do.) They look English and naturally I forgot their names as soon as introduced. The only name I usually remember after an introduction is my own. Then, a minute ago, Mirielle came by. I asked her how many students there would be next week. She said three, you and the couple.

There was to be another, she said, mais il est mort. I didn't quite catch it the first time but when she said it again I got it: but he is dead. I remember her talking of him last week – a retired English professor. I was looking forward to meeting him. Actually, I think Mirielle said something about him not coming at dinner on Friday, but the information I get from French conversation often lacks precision, so I had thought he was still coming. Mirielle said just now that he had been here last September and at that time he had some cold or flu and had been sick in bed for 10 days. And he had invited them to his house but when they were in California apparently he had not been there.

Mirielle said – it was a heart attack; he was tres gros – very fat, with a large stomach. One always wants to have an explanation for death – an explanation that fixes it on some peculiarity of the one who died – particularly a fault. So that death becomes a consequence of a lack of will or an unusual characteristic. We the living don't like to think of ourselves as like those – the dead. We are different – so what happened to them is not something that we too are subject to. Of course, there is a great difference between us and them. Namely and precisely, they are dead and we are not. The mere-est of us, the least able and the most backward, has greater possibilities than Dante or Alexander. Something to think on.

Well – now it is 7:28 – at 7:45 there is the grand social occasion of the week at La Ferme – that is the aperitifs before Sunday dinner. On the other days there are no aperitifs – only on Sunday when the new arrivals gather for courteous discourse in the language of the Sun King and Edith Piaf. Well, now the shadows are cast long over the green grass. The fellow in the sun hat sitting in the plastic chair casts a shadow almost past the house.

And old man Sun is resting on the bare tops of the trees behind me at the other end of the yard.

The question of the hour is whether I can get by this evening wearing a sleeveless sweater or whether I must change to my blue pullover. Prudence says change and – what? I have forgotten the English word – when you want to look good – well, anyway, that word, that characteristic, says no, don't change, you can get by in your smart looking sleeveless sweater. Not exactly smart looking – but I have worn that blue pullover to dinner every night for the 14 days I have been here and I want to prove that I am a versatile dresser, that I have two sweaters. Shouldn't one be willing to suffer a little for *that*, for fashion – in *France*?   So. Now it is 7:36 PM. I am determined not to go up to my room, but to proceed directly from here – where I was just wracked by a slight shiver – to the dining room. Can I do it?

7:39 PM   The answer is No. Prudence wins. Hurrah. Old faithful blue sweater.   And I have the word opposed to Prudence: VANITY.

10:31 PM   And so to bed. The new people, Michael and Lucy, are from Portland, Oregon. She has a pretty good French already, he has just a rudimentary level. She is small and a rather gathered-together person – she doesn't flow outside herself freely and seems to be holding herself tightly against a threatening world – she may have been ill. He is a tall man with a good-humored face – he wasn't able to talk much.

La Petite Eguille   Monday, April 2, 3:44 AM
Just to record the fact. The fact is that I woke up in this earliest of the morning a couple minutes ago. Something I rarely do. And I switched on the bedside lamp to see what time my watch had. It was exactly 3:33. What does that mean? Nothing, but it is now recorded.

7:08 PM   My, I haven't written much today. A day of class in the morning, then lunch, and in the afternoon, after 3:00, I bicycled down to Saujon and mailed off the 11 page Home Series letter to Joanna and a copy to John. I looked for the barber and the bank – alas, both closed on Monday. I sat in Café Thermalia because Café Plai . . . (can't remember the whole name now – the one across from the Mairie) was closed, its iron shutter all rolled down – a true 19th century café – always ready for the next revolution – the shutter protects against the cobblestones torn from the pavement. I have been reading the *seven* verses and the refrain of La Marseillaise: Allons enfants de la Patrie . . . Aux armes citoyens! Formez vos bataillons!

11:02 PM   After dinner, Mirielle showed me a video
tape of the bicentenary celebrations in Paris on July 14,
1989. The moving part was the American opera singer –
(I have forgotten her name, to be later added) – singing
La Marseillaise. She was on the monument at Place de la
Concorde – it was midnight. The spotlights shone on her,
she wore a billowing cape-dress, blue at the top with the
cowl over her head, white in the middle, and a red train.
She strode around the monument and the wind caught
the cape and it billowed about her – Allons enfants de la
Patrie / Le jour de gloire est arrivé – Aux armes citoyens!
  The great mass of people sang with her – at the end she
strode onto a platform, a chariot carried along by dozens
of men.

La Petite Eguille   Tuesday, April 3, 8:03 AM
No, it did not rain during the night. I just put aside the
curtains and looked out on the morning world. There
is a wide band of black cloud lying against the horizon,
but above, into the zenith, there is the pale soft barely-
lit innocent blue of young morning. And one bird sings
outside. Aux armes citoyens – Up and to breakfast.

1:03 PM   My, I had a great conversation in French
with Mirielle all morning – from 9:30 to now – my, I
hate to leave now – two more weeks here and I would be
speaking a darn good French. At least that is how I feel
in the enthusiasm of the moment. And so to lunch.

5:14 PM   Saujon
Well, it has been an adventure. A little, everyday, my
kind of, adventure. Getting to the bank on time. That
meant I clipped my bike to the railings of the bridge over
the River Seudre – right there on the main street which
is now being constructed and re-constructed, dug in,

filled in, piped, boxed, tractored, dumped on, pounded down – and God only knows what a main street goes through to be à la mode.

And at the bank no problem, the young fellow with the Alexander Dumas beard called on the telephone and gave the card number, put the slip of paper into the square box and it rose through the top, and then gave me the 500 francs. So then I went to the Maison de la Presse, bought today's Le Monde and a roll of scotch tape – not too difficult, although I misunderstood the price of the big roll and settled for the small roll. Oh oh, the barber is ready for me.

5:54 PM   I just left chez le coiffeur and I have walked across the street to the old Café Plaisance, where I sit in lonely splendor at the marble-topped table nearest the door. I felt I had to come in here to explain myself. Explain yourself Alpert, I said to myself – you can't simply walk on, walk on to the bicycle on the bridge. So. Where was I?   Yes – I look up above and see the *small* roll. I got the small roll of scotch tape, went across the street – for everything is across the street from everything else here. That is because the clever gens de Saujon have a five point intersection, here, near the Mairie. The Mairie sits on one point, la Poste on another, one door down from another point is la Maison de la Presse, crossing the street and up two doors is Cafe Plaisance, and if you cross the point on which stands la Mairie and then cross the second street you come to chez le coiffeur, where I just got my haircut. There you have it – we have the whole world in our hand. Whatever you want – it is there. Even Citron-Pressé, which I have before me now on the marble-topped table.

Well, anyway, I crossed the street to la Poste with the box of books I am sending back to California: *Little Dorrit*; *Where Are We?*, the book on American Jews; the street guide to Paris – the little brown book I have had for 20 or 30 years; my French grammar book I have had since 1975 – and my long underwear. I have decided, April having arrived and mildness over the land, to do without the security blanket of long underwear – this is just the lowers and in cotton. I still have my navy blue cotton long-sleeve turtleneck shirt.

I gave the box to the clerk at the post office. This, I told him, I wish to send by boat. He gave me three forms to fill out. Books (livres) I wrote – value 100 francs. I brought the forms up to the window. He weighed and calculated and stamped and affixed. Cinquante-quatre francs, he said. So I put 54 francs under the glass. No, he said, Cent trente-quatre. Oh, I said and I added a 100 franc note. So it cost about $23 to send the package. Probably I should have given the books to La Ferme. But then – there is sentimentality. And also the holding-on syndrome. I find it particularly hard to let go of books and papers. I must practice abandoning books. But, I haven't finished reading these books.

I haven't wanted to read anything in English while I am here in France. In fact the only contact I had with this, my native language, is via this longest of letters. So. Now I look up and out the open door of the café. The strong sunlight lights white the fronts of the buildings across the street, and above the buildings there is a brightness, a blue brightness that speaks openness, sparkle, good times, warm times, a vast expanse of life and time and possibility.

Oh, I should mention that I had a nice conversation with the barber as he cut my hair. We talked of how he would cut my hair and then he said, You are English? No, I said, American; I am studying French. Oh, he said, at La Petite Eguille? Yes, I said. Yes, he said, what is his name – Richardson – he comes here. Yes, I said, it was he. He recommended me? Yes. He cooks there, no? Yes, I said, he is a good chef. And then he asked me how long I had studied French and I said I took the first course in 1975 but then I studied Spanish and I had feared to mix the French with the Spanish so I didn't start seriously again until last year when I was in Québec. But I have been here twice before for short times. And we talked of the pronunciation of French and the pronunciation of Spanish and how there were words alike in each language. And he said, Yes – we say prochement and the Spanish word is like that. Cerca, I think is the Spanish word, I said, but I don't know all of Spanish. Ah, he said, maybe it is Italian.

When I paid he asked, And how much is a haircut in United States? They do not give you a shampoo in the United States, I said. No, he said, not shampoo, we say shampooing. Oh, I said, they do not shampooing. I think it is like eight dollars. That is much, he said, like 48 francs. We shook hands when I left.

10:39 PM   My, the days pass so quickly. In two days I depart La Petite Eguile. I have enjoyed my stay here a lot – I love learning something in a relaxed way in quiet surroundings.

La Petite Eguille   **Wednesday, April 4, 8:27 AM**
One word before breakfast. Bright morning, grey morning. Blackbird against the sky morning. White

flowers against the earth morning.   *The Earth is our mother/ We must take care of her/ Hey yunga, ho yunga/ Hey yung yung.* And I have also been singing to myself this morning *Wearing my long-winged feathers as I fly* and *Tis a gift to be simple, tis a gift to be free.* And the ever-popular *Allons enfants de la Patrie.*

To breakfast.

9:20 AM   After breakfast and before class, back in my room, sitting on the bed, the window now wide open and the fresh cool morning air coming in. Out across the red tile roof, beyond the tree all in white flower, stands the tall tree – its branches still black and bare. But the little trees have green sprouting leaves now. Just this week have come the leaves.

6:55 PM   Of final things. Of the little white shoe that rests on the red tiles of the roof I see from my window as I now sit at the white desk. Of the great gray and white heron that flapped from the salt pool aside the little road as I bicycled past 20 minutes ago.

As one of the last things, I had bicycled over to L'Eguille to return my bike. The bike was rented to me by none other than the young postmaster of L'Eguille, and I was his first client. I went today to give back the bike and get my 200 franc deposit. And the afternoon is pretty and fresh – the gray clouds of earlier in the day have all cleared away. So I rode to L'Eguille and then through the village and kept going on the little paved road that goes out to the salt marshes and the ponds where they raise the oysters. About two kilometers beyond the village, on the grass between the lane and a barn, there was a very French sight. A couple had parked their car and taken out a folding table and two folding chairs and were eating a light supper on the grass by the salt ponds and the barn. It is a way-to-live thing that one doesn't expect to see in America. I came back into the village and was once again impressed by the Frenchness of it. The solid white houses with red tile roofs, the kitchen garden often set beside the house, the irises or tulips blooming in pots against the walls. There is a style which is solid and pleasing.

The post office was closed and the postmaster and his wife were out. They live in the quarters behind and above the post office; this is traditional in French villages, I believe. So I remounted my bike and rode down the main street. There is a boulangerie – Mirielle says that is what makes a place a village. If there is no baker in the village it is more a collection of houses then a village. L'Eguille also has an épicerie and a church – and a café in the tabac store. I haven't been in the tabac store but I heard the voices within as I passed. There, in front of the church, there is the monument that every village and city of France has – the monument to the dead of World War One. It is usually in the shape of an obelisk with a marble panel or two marble panels with the names engraved on them, usually by year – 1914 to 1918. And then there is another, smaller, plaque added on, with the dead of the Second World War. I counted, for L'Eguille, 33 dead of the first war, and 3 of the second. There is also one, in 1954, in Indochina. I think L'Eguille now has 700 inhabitants. 33 dead out of a small village like that is a horrifying thing.

So, I had a very interesting talk with Mirielle this morning during the class. (I am the only one in the class with Mirielle this week.) She is very open. She told me of the therapy group she had been in with Farrar when they were living in London before they got married – it was a gestalt group. It really turned her life around. She was in her early 30s then and through the group she came to her own age – not a child and not an old woman like her mother, as she expressed it – and she was able to marry and build a successful life. She seems to me now to be a fulfilled and content person. The group lasted nine months.

I wish I had had an experience like that to set me on the ground. I still seem to be floating – I have never quite landed, it seems to me. There are two things I want to do when I return home. One is to continue studying French – and for this I would like to do the Summer Language School at UC Santa Cruz. The other is to go into self-discovery – is that a good term? – work. I think of Esalen – doing some intensive work at Esalen. Picking up on some of the things I was doing in the 1970s, which I never finished to my satisfaction. Unfortunately, these two things that I want to do are both intensive and I don't think I can do both. So I will see when I return. Yesterday I sent in an enrollment form to the Summer Language School, but this is not an irrevocable act.

10:59 PM   And so to bed. Last night at the OK Corral.

~

La Ferme to Madrid

Shaking and rattling . . . essaying to keep my writing steady as all about me lurches and clangs. Outside, the bare beginnings of light and day over a yet unseen Spanish landscape.

La Petite Eguille   Thursday April 5 , 3:25 PM
Well, it's the last write-up at the OK Corral. I am sitting before the little white table and I look out at the red tile roof with the lonely white shoe there resting. Below, in the classroom, Mirielle is talking with Lucy and Michael, the two students who remain. Well, I should now go down with my bags to the living room and wait for Farrar to drive me to the train station at Saujon. Au revoir to La Ferme.

3:39 PM   Now in the living room. Dans cinq minutes, said Farrar – he wants to see whether his mother-in-law wants to go to town also. Out the window, I see dark clouds over the sky and yet there

4:06 PM   Saujon station.
I was going to say above: and yet there is pale sunlight on the building across the yard.   Here at the

station I sit outside and the sky is completely covered by gray-white clouds. The report this morning was that it is raining in Spain. Here is the train.

4:09 PM   So – here I am riding backward, sliding, slipping, gracefully, softly out of Saujon. We go past a garbage dump – all the blue and white plastic bags sprayed about the ground. And now the green fields. There is a road I bicycled down. A brown plowed field. Old familiarity, because I have gone slowly over this land. A maxim? You can't know anything unless you go past it slowly. Speed and understanding exclude each other. Is that true? I don't know – but it stands thinking about.

4:13 PM   The train is now clicking neatly and quickly down the rails. I was going to say nimbly because there is a sense of effortlessness. But – can something be nimble that is bound to two iron rails? Doesn't one have to be able to jump, sault, saunter to be nimble? Sault is, I think, not an English word at all, but rather is French for jump. And yet – there is the English word somersault – which incorporates the word.

Neat is a good word for France – certainly as compared to the American look, the French look of the land, of the town, is neat. But – some years ago – was it in the 50s? – I think so – call it 1957, I remarked the difference between France and Switzerland when I crossed the border near Geneva. On the French side, the houses looked neglected, worn, disheveled – not only the houses but the whole aspect. On the Swiss side, there was neatness, all in repair and fresh painted, the flowers and the fields flourishing. I don't think one would find as much difference today. Much disorder came to France through the two great wars. Now, after many years, France has recovered, I think, from the wars. It takes a long time. That has to be the great quest of our time – to develop a system of governance of all the world that decreases the possibility of war and the spending of the enormous amounts of energy and resources on preparing for war.

Anyway. The train is rolling fast through the green fields, past trees, under a small bridge – onward to Sainte. I feel sad in leaving. I have liked being in this green quiet countryside. I go now to a far different place. The jumbled city of Madrid – autos, fumes, people, problems. South, out of the fat land, the green land, the open and quiet land. South to new country, new language – into the land of the Arab conquest and the 700 year re-conquest.   Can this be Sainte already?

7:06 PM   Sainte

I have been walking about town since I arrived not long after 4:30. I put my bags in the locker at the station and right there, right then, my newly-won linguistics carried me through the difficulty my ignorance of language caused me. How? I couldn't turn the key of the locker, so I went to the station office and told a fellow there that I had put five francs in the slot but the key didn't turn to lock the little door. Wait, he said, and came back a few minutes later to tell me there was someone at the lockers now to help me. This fellow put *another* key in *another* lock.

Ah, here is my fish soup. I forgot to set the scene.

I am now the only diner – the splendid only diner – in the dining room of the Hotel de France, across the street from the rail station. Me, in my khaki pants and boots, amid acres of white linen – well, yards of white linen. There are two waitresses who watch over me. The older one speaks with an Italian accent. The younger one, when she brought the tray that goes with this soup said, in English, diffidently (after she had said it in French): The sauce is strong, taste before you put it in the soup. The tray had a little metal bowl of an orange sauce and a similar bowl of grated cheese and between the bowls a heap of toasted bread cubes. The older waitress came over and showed me that before putting the bread cubes in the soup, I could rasp them over a big clove of garlic also on the tray. She served me the soup – a rich dark brown soup – from a tureen and then set the tureen on a hot plate on the table.

So. That was soup. Now main dish, Brochettes de Agneau, which my years of study told me had something to do with lamb. And so it does. It is the dish called, in Charlie's American Diner – shish kebab. Skewer and all. Also an attractive setting of carrots, green beans and french fries. It is not gourmet fare – and I like it. I also have before me a *quart* – that is how it is spelled but it is not a quart – it is a quarter liter of wine in a little carafe. So I lift my glass and write: Blessed am I to be eating in Hotel de France this Spring evening. A stranger from a strange land who sits at the corner table and looks out, through the gauzy curtains, to the little patio garden of Hotel de France.

There are now four other diners in the room. A lone woman at one table and three men at another. There is music in the room – not at all loud and not the Bam Bam music. It is American swing music of the 1940s.

I will finish the story of the locker. The man with the other key said as he locked the locker: It requires two keys.   I didn't stop to read the instructions again but I suspect that they say that.

Anyway, after leaving the station I walked to Rue Gambetta, which is the main street – I know Sainte a little, since I spent almost the whole day here in 1986 waiting for the night train to Lyon. I walked up Rue Gambetta to the librerie (bookstore) that Mirielle had described to me, and there I bought the book by Anatole France I had been reading at La Ferme: *L'Orme du Mail* (I think that is right). And I also wanted to buy a French book recorded on cassette, so I looked through what they had and I bought the tapes of a book by Pierre Loti and I also bought the printed form of the book so that I can both read and listen to the book.

Who is Pierre Loti? Well. I first became acquainted with Pierre Loti while sitting on the toilet at La Ferme. That is Because. Because on the door of the toilet there is a large colorful poster – a picture of a fanciful room decorated in the style of Islam. And on the poster it says something about the house of Pierre Loti. So I asked Mirielle a few days ago who is Pierre Loti? And she gave me a long answer. Pierre Loti is the famous local writer of the Charante region. He lived in Rochfort. He was in the navy – or in the merchant marine? (This was all in French – so there are lacunae.) And Pierre Loti was an eccentric. Each room in his house was differently decorated. (Loti was a painter as well as a writer – and maybe a sculptor and a musician as well.) And Loti was very interested in Islam. If his mother had not still been alive, he would have become a Muslim, said Mirielle. So he had rooms decorated in the style of Islam. And he had a complete mosque, dismantled and then reconstructed, put inside his house. Loti wrote many novels. Were they of this region? I asked. No – most of them deal with the foreign lands he visited. His most famous is called *An Iceland Fisherman* (*Pêcheur d'Islande*, something like that). And that is the book they have the recording of in the librerie on Rue Gambetta – so I bought it.

As I was paying for my purchases, I asked, Where is a store where I can find music cassettes? The man said, there is a store, you go across the bridge and turn left along the river, go until you reach the walking street, it is there. Or, he said –   An elderly English couple sit down at a nearby table. Now they are helping themselves from the buffet table set in the center of the dining room.

     – Or, he said – You can go to the big store on the corner right after you cross the bridge. I did that. The bridge is across the river Charante – a beautiful big river – it is also the one that goes through Cognac.

Maybe I shouldn't have ordered an infusion (herb tea) because it is now 8:08 and my train leaves at 8:52. I will drink quickly.   So I went to the department store on the corner, went up to the third floor and bought two cassettes of songs by George Bassent, who Mirielle thinks was one of the best French chanteurs. Oh – I can't drink this tea fast, it is too hot. I am becoming too un-relaxed to write. I like the French word for relaxed: decontracté (uncontracted?). But I tell myself – You are just across the street from the station. Yes, I answer, but how do I know I can open the locker? There may be all kinds of difficulty. Once I get started on this kind of worry worry, it is hard to slow me down. Get me to the train on time, I demand. I asked the waitress for l'addition when she brought the tea, but she hasn't come back yet.

8:38 PM   So. Now I sit on a bench on Platform C, Voie 4, waiting in the evening light, the failing light, for the 8:52 train for Bordeaux. I didn't see the sign saying which tracks the trains were on, so I waited in line at the ticket window and I asked; "Le train a Bordeaux qui part a neuf heure moins huit – quelle voie?" And the young woman said "C" – in the French manner – and then seeing that I was not sure what she had said, she said, in English, "C, platform C". Merci, I said. The French now *do* speak English. It is the Millennium and the Golden Age – Peace and Good Will and Harmony. Now if only the English and the Americans will condescend to learn a couple of languages, we can all say Hello.

I shall stand and gather myself unto myself, for the train arrives in a few minutes.

9:05 PM   Through the night – the bluing into black night – clicking off the rail sections one by one, goes the sleeper train to Ventimiglia – or some such name. And some such name is in – Italy. I had one of those terror – kidnapped – lost and gone forever – moments, as I came into the compartment and the woman here told me all this. But, I said, it goes through Bordeaux, no? Oh yes, she said. I always have the feeling with trains that I have no idea which way is up and which one goes to Spain. But I've only gone way wrong one time and that was in 1977, when I went all the way to Osaka instead of getting off at some Imperial Palace.

What is happening now is that I am in the last compartment on this car and the conductor came in right out of Sainte and pulled down the couchettes for sleeping. So now I sit hunched over on one of the little beds with my writing folder on my knee. The other people in the compartment are a woman and a little boy – I think they are grandmother and grandson. She was very nice and decontracté when I came barging into the compartment at Sainte. I spoke a couple sentences, and she said, You speak English? (in English). Yes, I said (in French), and also a little French.

It is now 9:16 PM – the train arrives in Bordeaux at 10:09 and then I have exactly 17 minutes to find my train to Spain and the proper car. It will be a Little Liza Over The Ice Floes for a couple minutes.

The little boy is playing with a little computer game that goes buzz click ring etc. It is hard to sit back on this bed. If I scoot back so I can lean against the wall, I can't bend my knees. It reminds me of my sauna. I asked Michael to build the sauna benches wide so that they would be comfortable to lie on – but they are too wide to both rest your back against the wall and bend your knees. So goes the anatomy of it all. My – my thumb is weary of scribbling.

9:29 PM   This is a first-class car; it has but four little beds – two on each side. The sleeping compartment I will be on from Bordeaux to Madrid (not first class) will have six people in it. I rather feel as if I am now imposing on my compartment mates. I just walked up the length of the car and all the other compartment doors are closed and I suppose people are making ready for the night. And a flash of a thought: I should establish a contact with the woman and the little boy – I should be confident and able – that is kind of what I expect of me. But then I have the other thought of myself as not formed – still young and unformed and not confident – this is a view

I have of myself. But – I am a rather old fellow. So this way that I see myself is interesting. Although the whole thing is a whirl about. Something like – why do I ask that I be charming and confidant, able and at ease?   I am also just a bit fuzzy from the carafe of red wine I had for dinner at the Hotel de France, back there in a gone away place in a gone away town.

9:37 PM   A half hour to Bordeaux. Of course, there is the language problem. Now the women and the boy – he is about seven – are sitting across from each other by the window, with a little game placed on the little table between them and they are playing together. I like the way they are with each other. They like each other – they enjoy being with each other. Maybe they are going on vacation together. Maybe they are going back to the parent's home? If so, the parents live in Italy. They are both clearly French.

Outside the train windows, it is now dark night – nothing can be seen but, every so often, the lit façade of a small town station twinkling by, and occasional blue spots of streetlights. I think – it is interesting – here I am – going lickety-split away from La Ferme. Right now, the four people at La Ferme – Mirielle and Farrar, and Lucy and Michael, the couple from Portland, are probably just rising from the dinner table. I have left the community – as others have left before me – Diana, the woman from Rome, and before her Alan and Jennie, the English couple, and Carolyn, the woman who is an editor for the Wall Street Journal. They are gone and traveling separate roads. A coming together and then separating and traveling far and fast in separate directions.

It is 9:51 now. The train is slowing. I think it is too early for Bordeaux – but sometimes it seems the schedules give leaving times instead of arriving times. I had expected to arrive in Sainte later then we did arrive. I better begin to gather myself together. I'd hate to have some of my things go on to Italy.

Somewhere north of Madrid   Friday, April 6, 7:17 AM

Shaking and rocking and rattling – outside, the bare beginnings of light and day over a yet unseen Spanish landscape. I stand at the rear of the car leaning against the wall, carefully essaying to keep my writing steady as all about me lurches and re-lurches, chunks and clangs. One might think that the car was being pulled by a team of mules over a rough mountain track. The railroad beds of Spain are a long long time coming to the slick effortless lines of France. Spain is going to convert to the same rail width as the rest of Europe and perhaps they are not putting a lot of effort into maintaining the old lines for that reason. In any event, my feeling is that if we went 5 kilometers per hour faster, we would jump off the rails altogether and tumble down the mountainside, mules and all.

This car belongs to SNCF, the French railroad, so pride of place in all the printed notices goes to French. On the door at my right there is a notice in five languages about not leaving the train at Hendaye, at the French-Spanish border, when the car is not at a platform. The train stopped there for at least an hour – maybe more – because I think they put other carriages under the cars – or do something to the existing carriages so they can travel on the different Spanish rail gauge. The French announcement says at its finish DANGER DE MORT, then there is German LEBENS-GEFAHR, English

DANGER, Spanish PELEGRO DE MUERTE, and Portuguese PERIGO DE MORTE. It is an interesting touch that the English does not say danger of death but only danger. Is this because the English want understatement? Possibly – but more likely I think it is because if they had added "of death" they would have had to go to another line.

7:34 AM   The train has stopped – in the faint blue light of budding dawn. I can make out a few buildings and there are the blue street lights shining. And there are raindrops covering the window and the ground outside is wet. Now the train starts again, but it is going in the opposite direction. Two women are now standing next to me in the vestibule – I think they are speaking Danish. From their indignant tone I guess they are talking about the lack of water in the bathroom. Hey, I feel indignant myself. There will be no washing up, or brushing teeth or flushing toilets this morning in Car 669 of Train 303. I would guess that the other cars are in a similar state.

I will go see whether the other people of my compartment have risen so that it is possible to pull down the beds into seats once more – the daytime mode. 7:43 No such luck, they are all determined sleepers. Now I can see Spain passing by under the cold new light of morning. Whitish-tan fields, plant stumps in regular rows, an undulating manner of ground. Spain doesn't have much level land; there is always the up and the down of it. And there are green fields too. Not as in France, a vast greenness that covers the whole view, but corners and triangles of green among the brown. We . . .   A man just stopped and asked me a question in French. He repeated it three times and I could not understand. Maybe he had a southern accent, and he spoke fast. Alas, always the incomprehensible.

As I look out, the ground looks quite white. Could it be snow? Or is it just white soil? No, it is not snow, for there is a green field. Nine minutes before 8 AM and the light is still quite dim. The sky is overcast. The white soil is in the cut embankments along the track – it is a chalky soil. Now we are in a long, a dark, tunnel. We are two hours out of our scheduled arrival time at Madrid Chamartin station.

Now the corridors of the train are filled with people – mostly young people. I think next week is a school holiday. Ah, we pass an imposing stone or concrete bridge across a narrow valley. And we are again in a tunnel.

A stout bald man in a light brown button-up sweater, with a round jolly face, stops and says something to me in French about my writing. He is remarking on the difficulty of writing while the train shakes. Oui, I say, c'est difficile. You are English? he says. American, I say. He repeats his comment in English. Yes it is difficult, I say, but I like to write.

Ah – suddenly, the skies have opened up. There is pale blue morning sky fringed by black storm clouds; the edges of the clouds are bright reflections of the sun, which is yet to be seen from Train 303. And the countryside too, has become lively and lovely – new green rising in lines and patterns in the rolling brown fields. This is a richer countryside than the one we were passing through 20 minutes ago.   I'm going to check my compartment once again.

8:06 AM   No – they are still in the beds. I have, in my little shoulder bag, some fruit and rye crackers and Swiss cheese and a little can of orange juice. And my stomach is saying breakfast time. Also I have my little electric razor. My, this is a prettier Spain that passes than I have known. There is water on the land, a softening – Spain has relaxed, sighed, greened into La Primavera. But wait, here again is a dark scrub land.

I think the other people in my compartment are German and maybe some are children. This is my guess from the voices I heard in the night. When I came on the train last night at Bordeaux, they were all in bed asleep. Someone had occupied my reserved berth – the bottom forward one. I asked the conductor. He looked in and said, Ah, there were two reservations for the same berth. But the top berth on the other side was empty, so he took the valises off it and I went up there. During the night, when we stopped at Hendaye, it became very hot in the compartment. The woman on the other top berth asked if I could open the window and I did and I think it stayed open all night; it was not too cold – they seem to turn up the heat in the compartments.

Ah – coincidence, just as I wrote that, the woman came by and went into the washroom. She will find no water, unfortunately. When I came into the compartment she was helpful. She told me to ask the conductor for a sheet and pillowcase. She spoke to me in French and I noticed an accent, so since I didn't quite understand what she was saying I asked, Parlez-vous anglais?, and she then spoke to me in a German-accented English. Always the languages. It is an interesting yet a difficult problem for the new Europe. My, this is a train of late risers. 8:24 and I think most of the people are still in bed.

The sky is lightening – bright blue and the gray floating clouds. It is a fresh rain-swept morning. On the top of the bank of dark clouds on the southeast horizon there is a bright glowing halo – it looks as if God the Father is about to appear in Glory with a choir of bright angels singing Hallelujah, Hallelujah. Now we pass through rolling semi-savage looking land – rolling hills with scrubby trees, and – miracle of La Primavera, a soft light covering of green grass sprouting. Off to the right, a high hill rises and its top is covered by white mist. My idea is that this rail line is the one that runs south from Zaragosa – that I was on in 1988.

9:22 AM   If we are on schedule, we are a half hour from Chamartin station. A white haze has settled over the countryside. We are now all sitting in the compartment. The conductor has just come in to return passports. We are one American, one young English woman, one French man, and a German woman and her two daughters. We have had a pleasant talk as the train rolls south across the Spanish meseta. The German woman, who was the one on the opposite top berth, is going to Sevilla, where her husband has a meeting at the University; she has been on trains since 7 AM yesterday morning, coming from a town near Dortmund. The English woman is going to a wedding at Jaen, north of Granada. The French fellow doesn't speak English, so he has not participated in the conversation. The German woman is very pleasant – she speaks good English and also, I think, good French – she lived two or three years in Seattle, where her husband got his doctorate. Listening to her speaking German to her daughters, I am struck with the wish to learn German. I have quite a good ear for German – coming from my childhood listening to Yiddish and I think I could learn German fairly quickly. Looking out the window, I think Madrid will be in fog this morning.

9:43 AM   Buildings are appearing. No – now there is a green scrub forest again. And the sunlight is coming through. Madrid is a city that starts suddenly – there are not miles of suburban growth fingering out from the city. I like the Springtime look of the rolling Madrid hills – the green of the grass – not luxuriant growth as in the wet lands, but a sparse thin layer of green on the land. The train is slowing. Maybe this is it.   9:47   Chamartin is on the north edge of Madrid

9:50 AM   Maybe it is not Chamartin, the train creeps on through a wide rail yard. Now I see, off to the left, tall new white apartment buildings of Madrid. I just – for the first time – got a faint twinge of excitement. Madrid is not a new place for me – and I am not a lover of cities. And still, I have an old-time friendly feeling for Madrid – I know some of its nooks and crannies. Oh – there is a great red ziggurat of an apartment building on the right; Madrid builds on. Now, we shall see how easily I can make the transition from French to Spanish. And still not let go of the French – don't let it slip away from me. 9:55 AM, to the minute: Arrival at Chamartin.

~

Madrid and La Granja

I walk across half Madrid in cold rain flurries

10:57 AM   And, suddenly it is quieter. I am on the Madrid Metro, line 1 – going from one end of the line to the other – Plaza de Castilla to Portazgo. Now, at Atocha station, the car has suddenly emptied of people and the many shouted conversations have gone out of the car into the tunnels that lead away from the tracks. I am going all across Madrid – from northernmost to southernmost, from Chamartin to Vallecas. Then, at the end of the line, I take the bus for another 2 miles further south.   The woman in the gray coat sitting across from me lets out a deep long sigh. She has a problem she has thought of and it caught her in the heart. I look at her – her face is expressionless.

11:16 AM   At the Portazgo bus stop. Everyone seems to want to talk to me and I am doing 0 for 2. Two men asked me questions. I said ¿Como?; they repeated. And I had to say No comprendo. There is no one else waiting for a bus.   I wonder if there is a strike or something? I'll wait a while – and then get a cab if no bus appears.

1:42 PM   Here I am at one of the bad places of planet Earth. At Puente de Vallecas, underneath the M-30 expressway bridge, leaning against the iron railing of the Metro entrance. Pepin was to meet Marta here at, I think, 1 PM – and I walked with him from his apartment and we were late. He had to stop at the bank and he asked me to go ahead and meet Marta. So I continued walking down Avenida de la Albufera to the Puente. But – Marta is not here. I don't know whether she already left or whether I misunderstood and am at the wrong place. Anyway. It is a bad place. The great traffic of Avenida de la Albufera passes under the expressway bridge and another road intersects here and the noise and the concentration of auto fumes is incredible. I have been standing here 10 minutes and my throat is feeling sore. In 10 minutes I am getting a year's worth of Santa Cruz level auto exhaust. I will wait to see if Pepin shows up. I have my umbrella stuck into the railing, opened, to dry off. Because when we left the apartment it was raining.

Going back a couple hours, I think I know what those two men at the Portazgo bus stop were asking me. What I didn't know was that the Madrid buses have been out on strike for three weeks. So they were wondering why I was sitting there. The first asked me if a camioneta was coming by – this must be some kind of informal transportation system. The second asked if I were waiting for a "particular". He must have meant a private car. Anyway, after I had waited 15 minutes without seeing a bus, I tried to get a taxi – no luck, they were all engaged. Then I started to walk with my bags hanging on my shoulders. After I had walked half a mile, I happened on an empty taxi, which took me the rest of the way.

1:56 PM   Now I am wondering where Pepin is? Did

I get the place completely wrong? My Spanish is still a little rusty.

4:46 PM   On the Metro leaving the University station. What a day! I have walked across half Madrid in cold rain flurries. One always must remember that Madrid is a mountain city and has mountain weather – it is now a good deal colder than it was in gentle France. I had lunch with Pepin at La Encarnacion, an old traditional and cheap but good restaurant near Cuatro Caminos and then we walked over to the university, visited Celso's wife, Isabel, who is in the

5:25 PM   Isabel is in the university hospital – I was about to write that when the train reached Novidades, where I got off to walk to Plaza de España. Now I am in the office of a travel agency where I am delivering a check to pay for six tickets to Spain for the conference next week. I had a devil of a time finding this office. Pepin gave me directions to go to the tower building at Plaza de España, which I think is the tallest building in Madrid, go to the entrance between the Varig Airlines office and a travel agency, take the Group 2 elevator to the second floor. I did, and ended up on a floor of hotel rooms – no offices. I went down and began over – maybe I had taken the wrong elevator. Nope. Same place. So I began to look for hotel room 18, which was the number of the office. Yes, there, in the dim light, was a small plaque beside the door, Agencia Brillante. I certainly am getting tired.

5:59 PM   Back on Metro line 1 to Portazgo.   At Portazgo I will have to walk a couple miles, unless a taxi happens by.

At La Granja – gentle blue sky, pale-white-shadow moon
. . . bright green fields after the rain.

El Colmenar   Saturday, April 7, 8:23 PM
And it is still light. Late afternoon, gentle blue sky,
rising pale-white-shadow moon. I am sitting on one of the
couches in the recreation room at la finca, El Colmenar.
[A note on nouns: Granja means farm, finca means
property or real estate, and also farm, El Colmenar is the
name of this particular farm – it means The Beehives.]

It has been a very pretty day – the bright green fields
and the open plowed brown fields under Spring sunlight
after the rain. This morning the passing storm clouds
from yesterday's storm, but by mid-afternoon the sky
was plain and perfect blue. We left Madrid this morning
about 8 AM – which is early morning in Spain. We
stopped for coffee (manzanilla (camomille) tea – for me)
at one of the bar-café-restaurants along the highway –
they are particularly Spanish places. Luis drove and as
passengers: me and Pepin, Javi (Celso's son) and Marisa,
a young woman.

In Carrascosa del Campo, the village some 10 kilometers
from the farm, we met Celso and several young men
from the farm. They had come to town in an old Land
Rover, which I was glad to see, for the last time I was
here, they had only the little ancient Renault, decrepit
and dangerous, which I named El Coche Bravo (The
Valiant Auto). I rode back with Celso in the Land Rover.
When we reached kilometer post 6 on the road between
Carrascosa and Huete, we turned off on the dirt road to
the farm. The first part of this road, which goes to the
village of Langa, is not bad. But the last part, to la finca,
is almost impassable after the rain, so I was expecting a

roller coaster, slip and slide and pray, ride to the farm after the heavy rains of the last week.

The ancient Renault (El Coche Bravo)

I asked Celso about the road and he made a face – the road was still a terror. But when we came to the turn off place, he pointed out the car window. I looked up on the hill and there was a tall metal electric transmission tower – and a line of towers going off in the direction of the farm – the farm was connected to the electric power net!! And then the second surprise was the road – it had been beautifully worked over and had a smooth surface with no ruts and no mud. Ah, Celso said, we didn't tell you – we wanted it to be a surprise. And the re-worked road went right up the hill to the main building on the farm. It is now 8:50 PM – and I can still see blue sky when I turn my head and look up and out the window. Now there are many people in this room – and the TV is on. So I shall continue later.

El Colmenar   Sunday, April 8, 8:52 AM
Almost nine on the clock, but here it is still early
morning. Perhaps, I think, in Spain 9 AM is early
morning until the middle of June. After that, 9 AM
becomes mid-afternoon until October.

I am sitting in the classroom, I took one chair down,
and I sit at a corner of the big table. (When the chairs
are not used, they are set, seat down, on the table along
its perimeter.) Now there is loud flamenco music coming
from down the corridor. I ate the desayuno (breakfast)
a half hour ago: an extra-large cup of hot chocolate with
the little flat cookies the English call biscuits and the
Spanish call galletas. (I am sure of neither the English
nor the Spanish spellings of the respective words.)

In the classroom (one of the fellows studying)

To continue with my discourse of yesterday about what

I found at the farm: Before arrival at the farm itself, I saw the rebuilt and greatly improved dirt road and the new electricity towers. (The lines have not yet been strung on the towers, so electricity from the power grid will not arrive at the farm for another month.) As I sit here, right now, I can turn my head and look out the window at the gray, cloud-covered sky, and I see, beyond the bright yellow of a blossoming thorn bush and beyond the two small oak trees on the ridge 50 feet beyond the end of the building – beyond and very high above all else, is the silver metal of the last electric tower, crisscrossed steel way up against the gray sky and matching and complementing the sky – gray on gray.

For me, as a visitor, aesthetically, from the search for nature of 1990 America – for me, I don't like the sight of the crisscrossed steel against the sky. But for the farm, it means much to have electric power. There is now a diesel generator which operates the lights at night, the television, and some few other things. But in order to have the carpentry shop and print shop that they plan and other things, it is necessary to have more electricity. So the farm will now be linked to all Europe – to the dams and reservoirs in the Spanish mountains, to nuclear power plants along the valley of the Rhone, perhaps to gas-fired plants in Holland, to a whole world of movement and construction and energy.

Yesterday, when I arrived up the hill in the ancient Land Rover, I saw that the main building was now painted bright white and that a broad concrete and placed-stone terrace had been built in front of it, and in front of the terrace there is a long narrow area of grass with young oleander bushes planted – and later Pepin pointed out the little – one foot high – almond trees and peach

Two views of the main building (a former dairy barn) at La Granja

trees planted between the oleanders. When we got out of the car, Celso took my arm and turned me about to look out across the narrow valley where the irrigated crops are grown – on the far side, in a level area dug out of the hillside, there was a large, low building being constructed from concrete blocks and red brick. It is going to have a large conference room and a kitchen and another 18 residence rooms. And, above and to the side of that building, there is another area leveled on top of a hill – it will be a sports field.

We went over to look at the new building. The main structure – the outside walls, the roof and some of the interior walls are already up – put up in only three weeks by three masons from Tarancon with the help of the fellows living here at la granja. There is also a large cut into the hill on this side of the valley in which will be built a reservoir for the irrigation water, which will also be used as a swimming pool in the summer. This is very important here, for the summer heat is fierce and a swimming pool will be a wonderful

5:37 PM   At the last word above, Celso came in and asked if I wanted to go into Carascosa with him. So I went in the big white van of Manolo with Manolo and Celso. And outside there came a cold rain, so we walked about

6:12 PM   Well, it is difficult to write for any length of time here. I am sitting on the couch in the recreation room and someone sits down next to me and we talk, or someone is leaving. Believe me, leaving in Spain – at least in this place – is an involved process. The person leaving goes about the room kissing everyone twice – once on each cheek – one doesn't simply walk out the door saying: See you later.

Emilio and Celso before the fireplace

6:18 PM   It happened again. Also, I have appointed myself the official door closer. There is a roaring blaze in the fireplace in this room but there are two doors from it – one to the hall that leads to all the bedrooms, and the other to the dining room. The dining room has a door to the outside. It seems that every few minutes the door to the dining room and the door from the dining room to outside are both open and a very cold stream of air comes in, for it is a fiercely cold day outside.

I made the second mistake of my trip last week when I sent my long underwear back to California – my thought being that if it was warm 70 miles north of Bordeaux, it had to be warmer in Spain. Not so. One must always remember that Spain is mountains on mountains and all of central Spain is the Meseta, 2000 feet up and harsh in Summer, harsh in Winter, and, I find, harsh in April. April flowers, Spring showers – yes, there are. But the flowers and the showers live with the cold – they come with the cold, they are Spanish Meseta flowers and Spanish Meseta showers. Also, whoever wrote The Rain in Spain Falls Mainly on the Plain, didn't know Spain. Spain is not a country of plains and the rain – when there is rain – falls on mountain and gully and rough and rolling hill.

6:30 PM   I am still sitting at the same place and the far door – to the hall – is open – but I have reconciled myself to the entrance of the cold air. Now, two older women from Huete, the nearby town, have come in. And three small children – grandchildren of one of the women. Pepin told me that one of the women has been afflicted with depression and she comes to see him. Depression seems common here. Or maybe it is only that there is much depression in the environment of the people who are around Escuelas Para la Vida, which, after all, is dealing with disfunctional families. There has been a middle-aged man here this weekend, who is the father of one of the young men here. He has the look of a solid citizen, the pharmacist at the corner shop, the grocer, the man at the post office window. But he sits without talking, in one place, all evening or all morning. He is depressed. Last night one of the boys put a jacket over the man's head and the man sat, thus hooded, for five minutes before he reached up and took the jacket from his head. And meantime one foot of his crossed legs bobbed up and down in a regular rhythm, as it had almost all evening.

Now. Let's see. I was telling of the day. In the morning I

went to Carrascosa with Celso. When we alighted from the van in the patter of cold drops, I offered him my hat, but he wouldn't take it. There is a saying in Spain, he said, that the rain of May grows the hair – and here, he said, showing me the back of his head, I need it. So we walked up to the little store where they sell newspapers and Manolo bought the Sunday edition of El Pais which I stuffed under my goretex jacket to keep it from the cold cold rain. In Carrascosa, it

11:01 PM   Madrid

Now I am in bed in the apartment in Madrid. It is warmer in Madrid then at the farm – or perhaps there is a warming trend in the day's weather. Anyway, I am not uncomfortable right now in this unheated apartment on the eighth floor of this red brick building in the barrio of Vallecas, on the far southern side of Madrid. I have the apartment all to myself, as both Pepin and Emilio are staying at the farm all week. So. What can I say in the few minutes before I turn out the light?

The impressions, sights, sounds, feelings, of the weekend have been many. As we left the farm this evening, we reached the paved road just about 8 PM. I saw a huge black cloud off to the right and low in the sky – to me it appeared to be in the shape of Iberia – the Spanish peninsula, the last south and west extension of the European continent. I thought of pointing it out to the others in the big new white Nissan van of Manolo: Celso, and Javi and Manolo and the middle-aged blonde woman whose name I didn't remember. But I didn't – it would be complicated to explain and maybe they wouldn't see the shape of the cloud as I did. Then, a moment later, after we had turned onto the paved road, Manolo pointed out to the left – there was a broad rainbow rising up from the horizon – but it didn't go arc-ing up into the sky – it was like a rainbow column into the soft gray clouds. Arco iris (rainbow), said Manolo. So there we have symbolism, and to spare. As for what I was saying before about the morning in Carrascosa . . .

11:22 PM   Since 11:20 is still relatively mid-evening in Spain, there was just now a telephone call that I answered.   Anyway, this morning in Carrascosa was interesting: Spain with the Spanish, countryside with country people. To the newspaper store, to the bar where the men of the village were gathered for Sunday morning coffee. To the panederia, (bakery) where we went in back where the oven is because that's where it was warm and I watched the baker putting in and taking out the bread on wooden paddles [Picture, page 234]. I like the bread of this bakery – much superior to the weak, spongy bread of France, a mon avis. And we went to the grocery store, specially opened for Celso by a woman wearing a long warm Spanish bathrobe. Then we went back to the bar to buy a bottle of wine and the bar owner ran out into the rain with us and climbed in the van and we gave him a ride to a house several blocks away.

When we came back to the farm I took over mopping the bathroom floor from the young woman who is an architect and designed the new building – Celso wanted to talk to her about something. Just before that, I encountered a unique etiquette problem. I wanted to use a toilet and I went into the bathroom, which has some six or eight toilet stalls. And there were Marisa, the very nice young woman who came from Madrid with us yesterday morning, cleaning the toilet bowls, and the young woman architect mopping the floor. I went into one of the stalls (which have a lot more privacy than American stalls –

with doors and walls all the way to the floor). But I felt ill at ease and in fact not relaxed enough to defecate. So I left – flushing the toilet first, however, for some obscure reason that had something to do with that is what one does. Anyway, I nodded and said murrph, or something, to the young architect as I left the toilet stall. And then Celso called her and they started talking in the hall. I listened in for a few minutes and then stepped back into the bathroom and took over the mopping.

After, I stepped outside and Manolo called out to me from in front of the kitchen: Did I want a bocadillo? Bocadillo is the Spanish snack sandwich. I called out Si, and I went back in to rinse out the mop bucket. (I had come outside to empty the dirty water onto the oleander bushes.) When I came back into the hallway there was Manolo with a large bologna sandwich for me. I set my vegetarianism aside and I ate it with pleasure, standing alone in front of the building on the wet walkway looking across the little irrigated valley.

So I ate today in the Spanish manner: At breakfast this morning at 8:30 AM, I had hot chocolate and a few cookies. This bocadillo was at noon. At 3 PM there was dinner, which was a large bowl of beans and rice with a little piece of chorizo (Spanish sausage) and a salad of lettuce, tomato and black olive (a Spanish way of eating salad is to set a large plate of it before several people and all eat from the plate). And then there was a slice of cake for dinner also, because there was a birthday celebration for Celso, who is 68, and for Luis, one of the farm's graduates, who is, I think, 27.

The birthday celebration was truly joyous. There were some 40 people at dinner and after the plates were cleared away, two cakes were brought out. Celso and Luis blew out the candles (rather, tried to, because the candles were of the kind that refuse to be blown out). Then presents were given to them and then there was a riotous demand that each stand up and make a speech. And then that each dance with someone. Celso did a truly pretty peasant dance with Marisa, kicking up his heels with great style and agility. Then, for an unknown reason, there came a demand that I and Marisol, the elegant lady from one of the wealthy barrios of Madrid, who is very active in the Collectivo, dance together also. So we got up – me quite reluctantly, but there was no way of not doing it – and we did a wild freewheeling, wave your hands and bend your knees, new-age kind of dance. And Antonio played the guitar and everyone sang deafening renditions of Clavelitos and Rancho Grande and a few others – very raucous and burlesqued. It was a high old time for all.

In the afternoon there was a general meeting of the residents on how to handle next week's conference and I sat in. I'm going to break this off now because it is past midnight. Maybe I can continue tomorrow. The fact that I am still up at midnight I attribute to drinking a half cup of coffee at dinner this afternoon.

SUPERwinterundearwearMAN: able to exist in heatless apartments where the blood of ordinary people would turn to frozen jello

Madrid   Monday, April 9, 9:24 AM
I sit at the end of the dining table in el piso (the apartment). I see out the window the grey cloud cover over morning Madrid. I hear the air bubbling gently

into the fish tank, and also an unidentified low hum —
perhaps the lights, perhaps the refrigerator. Before me
on the table is my huge desayuno (breakfast): Five slices
of Melba toast, one little container of yogurt, sliced-up
apple, pear and banana, a cup of manzanilla (camomille
tea). I did not wake this morning until 8:37 — when the
phone rang. Without the phone call, I might still be
sleeping. I was quite shocked at waking up at almost 9
AM. I hurried to dress — heaven forfend that Celso come
up to the apartment and find me still in pajamas after
nine in the morning! — that was my thought.

I hurried to call Marta — I had planned to call at 8:30 —
so that we would be in contact to coordinate what had
to be done in Madrid for the conference (mainly meeting
people at the airport). Someone else answered the phone,
I think it was her father. Although I didn't understand
all he said, I gathered Marta was still asleep. Call later,
he said. Nine in the morning is still early in Spain.

12:12 PM   Sitting down! What a comfort! What a
victory!   Sitting down on the Metro car at Portazgo
station. Sitting down because this is where Line One of
the Metro begins. I walked here from the piso instead of
taking the #10 bus to Cibeles because I want to go to a
photo shop on Gran Via and the Metro stop is right there.
I walked through a cold sprinkle of rain — mountain
spring showers, that is what it is, cold, and just a patter
of raindrops — with a hat or an umbrella, it is no great
problem to walk through. And I have both hat and
umbrella, as well as wool mittens. My hat is a Scottish
tweed that I bought in Hartford, Connecticut in 1979; it
is the most un-Spanish hat imaginable.

I feel rather tired this morning; I am not accustomed to

physical work – the kind I did Saturday and yesterday on the farm: hoeing with a short hoe, collecting stones and wheeling them about in a wheelbarrow, mopping bathroom floors. The stones are for the floor of the new building. The floors are to be concrete about a foot thick. But instead of using all that concrete, stones are placed to fill in the space as much as possible and then the concrete fills in the gaps and is a layer over the top. It takes a very large number of stones for this. There were two tractors making trips to the stone heaps that lie at the edge of every field in the area, towing large trailers and we workers threw the stones into the trailer, then climbed on top for the ride back. Something like a stone hayride.

So. We are coming to the Metro stop at Puerta del Sol. Gran Via is next. After the photo shop I will go to the vegetarian restaurant on Calle Amor de Dios. Looking forward to that.

1:11 PM   Restaurante Biotika doesn't open until 1:30, so I am around the corner at a bar drinking a cup of manzanilla tea.

1:36 PM   Aha – the prize for first customer of the day at Biotika is mine. And I am hungry. Since I was last here, the Biotika has changed its tables and chairs. They used to have strange chairs with backs on two sides, so you could sort of sit in a corner and lean against both backs.

My – the restaurant is filling fast – now three other tables are occupied – that is out of a total of only eight tables.

After the stone hayride (top); The stone gatherers (bottom)

1:41 PM   Ai – there was a POW and a puff of air from
the kitchen – it was a small gas explosion that startled us
all, waiters and diners. I just ordered the menu – that is
the meal of the day – el menu del dia. The menu is now
700 pesetas – in late 1988 it was 600. Spain has a fairly
high inflation rate, I think. The price of a Metro ticket
is now 90 pesetas – in late 1988 it was 60. (Although
you can still buy 10 tickets for, if I remember right, 410
pesetas.) Ah, the soup is good. This is my first vegetarian
meal since Paris. There are two English fellows at the
next table. I was on the point of saying several times:
If you need translation, I can help. But they seem to
be doing okay, so I refrained. I feel like staying within
myself today. I feel tired and subdued. I think of Celso.
At 68, he has such great energy – he is a remarkable
guy. I now have the main plate: garbanzos, cauliflower,
rice and a pickled salad. It is good, but not as good as the
Biotika of yore. A little too much salt, for one thing.

4:04 PM   At a bar-cafeteria near Calle Horteleza. A
Spanish "cafeteria" is a place that serves cafe (coffee),
so, is very like a French cafe, and a bar is practically the
same thing. I have two things I want to do before I return
to the piso. One is to buy a paperback Spanish/English
dictionary, and the other is to finish with the photo
developing. There were five pictures they are re-doing
because they came out with a dark line on one margin.
I walked some five blocks looking for a quiet place to
sit down again. All the bars, cervecerias and cafeterias
seemed to also be restaurants and they were crowded
with diners. I finally came on this place on a quiet side
street of this old part of Madrid. I am the only customer; I
sit at a little table sipping my manzanilla. This is a place
that I imagine is very busy from 11 AM to 2 PM and from
6 PM on. On the counter of the bar rest glass cases with

a variety of tapas, meats, and lobster. And a half dozen cured hams hang on the wall behind the counter.

6:33 PM   On the #10 bus at Cibeles. The sky is now clear and, outside, a sharp cold wind blows in the streets of central Madrid.

Madrid   Tuesday, April 10, 1:19 PM
On the Metro at Portazgo. I have been in the apartment all morning. An hour ago I came down – there is a bitter fierce cold wind on the streets and the sunshine comes and goes as great white clouds sail across the sky. I went to the bank and now I am on my way to the vegetarian restaurant near Lavapies – I think the street is Calle Argoso – something like that. I shall leave the Metro at Atoche station and walk over. I wrote two letters before I left the apartment. One is to Jonathon B., who is dying of cancer, and the other to Carol M., who also, I fear, may have a re-occurrence of cancer. Very hard letters to write. It is bare and simple when one can't say I wish, I hope, I expect.   I think Atoche is next.

10:04 PM   I may look like an ordinary guy, dressed casually in a Madras-looking shirt and a spring sweater – just like all the ordinary-looking Spaniards I saw today walking with their jackets casually opened to the icy wind. But though I may look ordinary, if I step into a telephone booth and tear off my shirt, it will become apparent that I am SUPERwinterunderwearMAN – able to exist in heatless apartments where the blood of ordinary people would turn to frozen jello. I went out this evening and bought thermal long underwear.

11:49 PM   I can only write for a few minutes, because I don't have my survival gear (long underwear) on anymore, and I must soon bury myself in my three blankets – it's a three dog night. Just at 11 PM when I was turning out the last light, the phone rang. Someone in Chile – they haven't gotten the tickets for the flight here (for the conference). So, I called Celso and Marta, and Marta will call back to Chile to check that I got the story straight. (Hey, long distance crisis calls in an imperfectly understood language are Aaaaarrrgg kinds of things.) Marta will also give them the airline – so they can check.

Madrid   Wednesday, April 11, 12:44 PM

Just a few words to open up the day. I am on the big red #10 bus heading to Cibeles. The street is incredibly bumpy. This is one of the reconstruction areas of Vallecas we are going through. Also I am sitting in the seat back of the rear wheel; I think the bounces are bigger and badder back here. I feel deeply tired. I want to watch my diet and pace my physical exertions a little better. Right now I am on my way to Calle Amor de Dios to Restaurante Biotika.   I also have some letters I want to mail from the main post office at Cibeles. I was all morning in the apartment awaiting a call from the fellow driving down from Holland, but he didn't call; perhaps he is not coming. This evening I will go out to Barajas airport to meet the fellow from Denmark. There are only five people on the bus now – this is not the time of day when people go to the center of the city. Today the weather is much warmer.

4:56 PM   There has been a great change in the weather. After the immense cold of yesterday, now I am sweating. I took off my sweater up above – in the Plaza Colon. Now I am sitting on a metal bench in the small underground waiting room. Waiting for what? The airport bus to Barajas airport where I am to meet the Dane and conduct him into town.

5:01 PM   On the bus – a very comfortable bus. Spain is on a trajectory out of poor Europe into rich Europe. In front of the main post office, a new sidewalk is being placed and there is installed one of the public toilets you now see in Paris and other French cities. And the Plaza Colon has been reconstructed – all the style approaches French style.

5:08 PM   The bus goes along Calle de Valasquez, past well-kept shops, restaurants, banks. This is the Salamanca district – one of the wealthy barrios. Interestingly, los suberbios (the suburbs) here are the poor neighborhoods; the rich neighborhoods are central.

5:33 PM   Before Gate 2 on an orange plastic chair – orange plastic is standard for the airport. The cleaning people at this airport have been on strike for a week and that is what it looks like all about me. Nobody has been sweeping and emptying and mopping.

Myth, tradition and the sweep of culture . . .
Good Friday at La Granja

El Colmenar   Friday, April 13, 9:30 AM
Friday. The 13th. Good Friday. A conglomeration, from out of the past, of myth, tradition and the sweep of culture. I am sitting on my bed in a room of the residence at the farm. The cold air comes in the half open window, along with sounds – voices, clucking of chickens, footsteps. The farm is a-stir – there are some 50 people here, taking part in the seminar. I came here

yesterday morning, in the bus from Madrid, along with Antonio and Torben, the fellow from Denmark. At dinner

Introduction...walking slow

yesterday (at 3 PM) we sat – all 50 of us – at a long table set out on the terrace before the residence and the sunlight on the white wall and the white paper covering the table was near-blinding. We ate macaroni with tomato sauce and bits of meat – great heaping portions, and there were plates of salad set before every four persons – to be eaten in common, in the Spanish home style – and a large orange at each place. In the afternoon, about 5 or 6, we met in a wide circle of folding chairs on the new football field– which is not yet a football field but only a leveled space of the chalky white earth. And first we did introduction games – walking fast, walking slow, embracing, holding hands, making faces.

Then we separated into three groups. I was doubtful; they were such mixed groups. There were the 13 and 14 year old girls from Orcacitas, a poor neighborhood of Madrid, the young men of the farm, from 13 to 30 years, and visitors from Madrid, some highly educated – a doctor, a veterinarian – university students, and the people from abroad – the social worker from Chile, a teacher from Denmark, me. Our subject had to do with *animation*.

This is not a word, or perhaps even a concept, that means much in English. We think of Walt Disney when we think of animation. But in Spanish (*animación*) it means something different – it means animation in a social and cultural sense. It means the motivation and the motivator, the inspiration and the inspirer – to do something in the society or in the culture. But still in Spanish – language and society – it is a rather vague term.

So our group started by talking about what we would talk about. Josele, who had been here at the farm for a year and now is continuing in Madrid, said he did not know, and others did not know, what exactly *animación* was. Then, the doctor said: Well, it has to do with leisure time – how people are led or taught or encouraged to use their leisure time. No, said Marisa, the kind and energetic young woman from Madrid (maybe a university student?) – no, it goes far beyond that; it has to do with the way we live.

This was yesterday afternoon, the first session of our group.

1:58 PM   The second session of our group was this morning and ended about 1 PM. Again we were sitting outside, on folding chairs in a circle. This morning we talked of our ideas of the society that now exists. The

people from Argentina talked of what was happening
there, the man from Denmark said something about
Danish society – I translated from English what he
said. Two young men who have lived at the farm spoke
of their experiences. Javi said he felt the rich did not
much care for others – only for becoming richer. Nor did
workers care much, he said; they are interested in their
earnings. He is pessimistic of the future, he said. Josele
talked about feeling himself outside society and about not
wanting to be in a society he felt was unjust. Later they
also talked about the difficulty they have in talking about
their past. They don't tell people they meet about their
past as drug addicts (and for Josele, his stay in prison).
Josele says he feels that those who know his past have a
conditioned relationship with him.

Our group...sitting outside, on folding chairs in a circle

The man from Columbia talked about the difficulty of

changing his society, about the rich and powerful – the 10% who control the country – and the rest who live in misery. He said the drug chiefs come from those who live in misery. He also talked of the schools for killers – of the death squads – of the alliance between the Mafia and the military. Of how dangerous it is to work for social justice. How it is necessary for social justice to work from the bottom up and to organize. He said some things about where authority comes from that I did not understand.

So. Now it is 2:12 PM. I am sitting on my bed scribbling and waiting for dinner. The morning was cool and warm, by turns, as the sunlight came and went. Now, the drifting storm clouds have mostly covered the sky. But I have taken off my pajama bottoms, which I have been wearing as improvised long underwear. I left my newly-bought long underwear in Madrid, in the mistaken belief that Spring had at last sprung.

2:17 PM   I sit here and keep my ears tuned to the talk outside. As long as there is talk, I assume that the meal has not yet begun – in the dining room at the other end of the building. And twice now I have put my head out the window to see if the people are still outside on the terrace. When 2 PM arrives and one has only eaten thus far one large cup of chocolate . . .

2:28 PM   Pepin looked in at the window. He was with the "retarded" man, who follows him about. This is the man who was abandoned on the streets of Cuenca and who now lives here. He takes care of the plants in the invernadero (the greenhouse).

As I was saying – when one has eaten only a large cup of chocolate, half-dozen cookies and a little wedge of cheese until now, one anticipates the dinner which is soon to begin. What will it be this afternoon? Probably garbanzos. It is always something filling and cheap like that. Although last night it was meat – which was quite tasty. I believe it was the last remains of an unfortunate kid (a young goat, that is). There are some 20 goats roaming about the farm hills now. Well, I shall go out and enter into the life of the house and the group on the terrace.

Jose Luis (the "retarded" man) on the terrace (left); Jose Luis with Pepin and Celso (right)

El Colmenar   Saturday, April 14, 8:47 AM

A brilliant morning, brilliant land, brilliant sky. From inside, a warm-looking day, but outside the air is quite cold. Now I sit on my bed, the middle bed of three, wearing my blue turtle-neck shirt, my blue wool sweater, my scarf, and my jacket, zipped up all the way, as well as assorted underwear and shirts, pants etc. Outside, from the hall, comes jumpy rhythmic music.

Last night I went to bed early – which here means 11 PM. To my regret, for after I went to bed there was an explosion of music, foot stamping, shouting, and hand clapping. This morning I learned that there were Sevillianas (dances of Seville) and singing and all sorts of unplanned spontaneous entertainment. There is a group of teenage girls from Madrid, and the boys living here, and they have tremendous good-will energy. Yesterday evening – in late sunlight into the darkness at dusk (at close to 9 PM – for dusk arrives late here) they were playing singing games – or traditional village singing – I am not sure what. In one we were in two lines and one person danced up between the lines and then back and picked a partner

A line dance

and both danced up and back and then the partner repeated and so on. In another, we were in a circle and we sang: Juan (as an example) robo el pan de la casa de San Juan – or something like that (Juan stole the bread from the house of St. Juan). And Juan, standing in the middle of the circle, says ¿Quien? ¿Yo? (Who? Me?). And everyone in the circle points at him and says Si! Tu! (Yes! You!) and Juan says Yo no fui (I wasn't there) and the circle says ¿Entonces, quien? (Well then, who?) and Juan points.

1:09 PM   Ah. I see that I didn't finish what I was writing this morning. That was because, at that moment, Pepin opened the door and said: Do you want to go to Huete with Celso? Actually I would have liked to be here at the beginning of my group meeting at 10 AM, but Manolo asked me yesterday to go to town because Torben, the fellow from Denmark was going and he doesn't speak Spanish. So I went and, as always, I enjoyed the visit to the town and going about to the stores with Celso.

It was clear and sunny and sharply cold in Huete. We went to the general store, which sells everything from flashlight batteries to clothes to kitchen stoves, and Torben bought some film. And then to the grocery store and then to the little open plaza, up the hill a little way, where on Saturdays there is an open air market of vegetables and fruit and spices and dried fruits and nuts and clothes and dishes and kitchenware. I bought a small towel, for I have been doing without a towel the past few days, since I haven't wanted to bother the people to ask for one and I wash only my face in the cold mornings and a sleeve serves just as well to dry my face. Maybe I shall take a shower with my new towel – which is closer the size of a washcloth than a grand towel. And maybe not – I don't need to be perfectly clean and neat – this is the countryside of the far country and I wear my gray boots and my blue Santa Cruz jeans.

When we returned from Huete about 11 AM, I went to

my group, which had the good sense to meet in the
great plastic-covered greenhouse. So we sat in summer
warmth, safe from the April chill of the air outside. And
by the time we emerged at almost 1 PM, the outside air
had taken on a gentleness and a softness that welcomed
us.

Inside the greenhouse – Celso gardening

So now, the people of the farm, the people of the
conference, the Madrillenos and other Spaniards, and
the South Americans are all standing outside, on the
sun splashed, sun drenched, sun washed terrace in front
of this long bright white building, and they are talking
quietly, in a sunny way, an April afternoon way. I am
sitting inside, on the edge of my bed – which I have found
to be the best place to write – for if I were in one of the
common rooms, someone would stop to talk and I don't
think I would write very long.

So. I should finish my story of this morning. I was talking about the singing game. We had Juan, who denies stealing the bread. And the group sings – Well who, then? And Juan points at someone – say someone named Marisa, and says, Marisa. So the groups starts again: Marisa robo el pan de la casa de San Juan, and the round begins again. The group last evening did not stay in one place, but saw someone at a distance and everyone ran to accuse *that* person of stealing the bread. So it was very active and everyone had great fun. Once we all went into the kitchen to accuse the cook.

Then the young people went into more active games, like a kind of line dance and a kind of leap frog, and I dropped out and began talking to the woman from Ecuador about her work. She works with a group called Fé Libertad – I am sure the first word is Fé (faith), but I am not sure of the second. I shall have to talk to her again. The group teaches and does other work to help poor people living in the villages of Columbia, Ecuador, Peru, Bolivia, Salvador and other countries. They are related to the Catholic Church, but there are also lay people and the work is not to teach religion but to teach living and to help. She works in a rural center, where she lives – they work a lot with los indigenes, the native people.   It is now 1:38 – I shall go out into the sun and be a person of the Sun.

El Colmenar   Sunday, April 15, 5:41 PM
So. The conference is over. The girls from Orcacitas left after lunch a few hours ago. The South Americans have gone off on a visit to Cuenca. The young men of the farm have been playing football on the land a half mile back up the valley. And I lay in the sparse Spring grass and listened to the talk of women and slept a little. And now

everyone has walked back to the main building and I sit in the classroom on a new corner couch, and I write. Down the hall comes the singing from out the radio or a cassette player. Jose Luis (I think that is his name), who is the "retarded" man, has just come into the room and we talked a little. He says: Now everyone is going and it will be more tranquil. Yes, I say, it is more tranquil now. I was told he was retarded, but I don't know it – because I, too, am retarded. That is, our use of the language is about equal. No – really not – he has more use of the language than do I. So, I have little ability to test his mental agility. I was surprised this morning when he read something to us in the concluding meeting as we sat in the sunlight and the sharp cold wind at the end of the building. He also had a drawing next to the writing and it passed about the circle. It was, he said, a picture of an old man sitting in a chair and looking at the stars. And it was – in about the same way I would draw that.

Right now, as I sit here, I feel rather sun-fried and tired.   Sun-fried, because while we ate, I loaned my ever-present canvas hat to Torben, the Danish fellow, because he could not endure the dazzle of the sunlight on the white building and the white table. (We ate outside this afternoon.) As we ate, the clouds passed lazily over the sun and the hot sunlight alternated with cool fresh shadow.   And tired – I am feeling tired because I went to bed about 1:30 last night (actually the last number I remember on my watch is 1:11 AM). And I woke about 8:30 (8:33 – these numbers somehow stick in my mind). I went to bed so late because, after the supper, there was an evening of entertainment.

The supper itself was a great event, for people began to arrive from Huete and Carrascosa del Campo and nearby villages. So there were some 100 people at the supper and temporary tables were set up – of folding sawhorses

Lunch on the sunlit terrace

and wood/formica tabletops – in the recreation room next to the dining room. In the dining room, every possible inch of space was taken up by tables (including those brought in from the classroom) and chairs. There was no room to walk between tables, so the dishes were passed down the length of the tables. The plates were re-used (higgedly-piggedly and mixed up) for the second course, and some of the people – Marta and Marisa and Antonio – never sat down and ate, for they were forever passing the dishes from the kitchen. And Lara, the boy who started to sit across from me, finished only a few bites of the first course of cheese and luncheon meat and olives before he got up and for the rest of the supper joined the noble unselfish plate-passers. Everyone was in good spirits and enjoyed the make-do quality of the meal. I did.

After the meal, at about 10:30, we all walked across the field to the new building. To go across the field in the darkness of country night, there were four autos parked at strategic places with their headlights on – another example of the way of we-can-do-it. In the new building – miracle on miracle – there were electric lights – for a cord had been strung that afternoon the 100 to150 yards from the main building and the diesel generator roared in its little building. The lights were concentrated at one corner of the large room where bed sheets on cords marked off . . .

9:29 PM   Madrid
That was the end of that writing, for as I reached for another sheet of paper, Emilio came by carrying things and I said, I will help, and then Pepin said, We are leaving. And so it was. In the van of Manolo, behind the solid line of cars on the road from Valencia to Madrid – the return from Semana Santa (Holy Week) of the Madrillenos. So now I sit in the piso on the bench by the dining room table – or rather main-room table, the television is on, quietly, the fish tank bubbles, and supper is almost on the table. The fish tank is a story. Apparently I turned off the wall switch that controls the air and heat for the tank. One little bright fish survived. I hope that two black ones will also.

Madrid   Monday, April 16, 11:42 AM
On the Metro, Line 6. I am on my way to a video services company in the rich neighborhood of Salamanca to see about transferring a video of the Spanish (European) system into one for Chile. I think Chile may have the same system as the U.S.. So I sit here – warmly. Warmly, because I am wearing the top of my winter underwear plus a sweater. And down here, in the bowels of the

earth, it is not at all cold this day.

12:45 PM   In a cafeteria off Calle Alcala, in the Salamanca district. Still warmly. A cafeteria here is not what it is in the U.S.; it takes its name from café (coffee) and it is a coffeehouse. There is actually little difference here between bars, cervecerias (beer houses) and cafeterias – they all serve all kinds of drinks, as well as sandwiches and light snacks, and many also serve meals. I shall now go back to page 12 or 17 or wherever I stopped reading over this letter and pick up once again, so I can mail some more of it.

4:44 PM   In the shade, because that's the kind of day it is. One who has walked a way chooses a table in the shade. The shade is furnished by a flowering chestnut tree in El Retiro, the grand park of Madrid. The table is furnished by the little food and drink kiosk at the corner of the great square pond of the park.

5:49 PM   I am sitting still (yet) and still (quietly) in the same green metal chair in front of the same green metal table by the same kiosk in El Retiro park. There are around me the same flowering chestnut trees. I look up and around. I have not been looking up and around for the past hour. I have been reading up to page 26 of the letter and when I walk back to Plaza Colon and the Telefonica building to make a call to the U.S., I shall make some copies of these pages. When the waiter came over I asked if he had ice cream (helados), for at that time I was warm. No, he said, but there is something with lemon and something with horchata. They are like ice cream? I asked. He said something about ice. So I ordered the horchata and a manzanita tea. Horchata, I found, was a drink – almond and sugar.

There is a jumble of pleasing bright green in front of me. It is the chairs and tables, fresh painted for the fresh new season. Over in the sun some 40 feet away, many people sit at the tables, people in pink and yellow, gray, maroon, white – singing colors under the afternoon sun. Here, on the shady side, there is only me and the two girls sitting two tables away. They look engaged in paperwork – one is leafing through a notebook, the other is writing. Beyond the green tables and beyond the flowering chestnut trees, there is a green hedge and beyond the hedge there is a wide gravel walkway. Many people walk along the walkway, I see their heads dark against the sunlight reflected by the white stones of the great monument on the far side of the square pond. Off in the distance I hear the sound of drums – earlier there was far-off jazz music. Nearby, from above and around, I hear the birds tweaking and twitting, little explosions of high-pitched sound.

A pretty woman in a bright red sweater has just sat down at the table in front of me. I noticed her as she stood and stared at something beyond me. Now she stands and turns and looks again. I look back and see the trees and the grass. She is taking out a camera. I think it must be the chestnut blossoms. But I was going to write that the – She is kneeling to take a picture. Then she goes further away and sits in a chair and holds the camera up to her eye – it is all very elaborate. She now has set a green chair out on the lawn to be part of the picture. She comes back to her table, but I don't think she has yet taken the picture. It is a ballet, a pantomime: "The Photo". She sets the chair further out on the lawn. She kneels down and takes a picture; I heard the very click of it. But I believe she has been taking pictures all along.

There is a very pretty effect of the afternoon sunlight lighting the leaves of a chestnut tree: bright, illuminated, sun-lit leaves against dark leaves. The pattern of sunlight and shadow; it is a life motif. The sunlight coming through the leaves; that is it, the beginning of Life and Spring.

As I started to say: But I was going to write that the birds, the trees, the sunlight – there is something not whole about it. Far away, I hear the rumble and roar of the traffic – I look up – for I wanted to look up into the sky and say: And there is a polluted cast to the sky. But when I looked up, I was surprised, because instead of the pollution, I saw a small bright white cloud past the trees, a little rectangular cloud. It is the only cloud in the sky. Now it is twisting away from its solid square shape. Now I see other clouds in the sky. They are not coming from anywhere, they are simply springing forth like mushrooms after the rain.

Now the pretty woman in the red sweater has changed her place at the next table and is facing me. The thought crosses my mind, Does she want to photograph me? I may be a picturesque subject: blue sweater and blue-check shirt, sitting in the bright green chair, my legs crossed and my green writing folder on my leg – on the table my gray fedora hat, which Emilio says looks like a gangster hat, and the two empty glasses and a saucer, and under the hat the pages that I read earlier. I now feel self-conscious, I don't want to look in the direction of the woman at the next table. Which is difficult, because if I lift my head from this paper, I am looking directly at her.

Well, I should be going, for it is now 6:32 PM – and I want to call California about 9:30 or 10 and depending on whether California has entered on daylight saving time yet, it is now either about 8:30 or 9:30 in the morning there.

I live like a Madrileño:
dinner at 10:30 PM, bed at 1:45 AM

Madrid   Tuesday, April 17, 5:39 PM
The slot machine plays a tune with lots of whistles and bells. The slot machine and me are in a cerveceria about three blocks off of Gran Via. It is a place I came on last week. Before 5 PM, there are no clients in here. Just me, sitting at a little formica-topped table in back. But just now, half a dozen other people have come in. This place is on the lower end of the socio-economic scale, as we socio-intellectuals would have it. In other words, it sets different sets of nerves twanging in me than the nerves twanged by the Cafeteria Nebraska on Gran Via.

This morning, at 11 AM, I was at the parochial church in the Ventas barrio and was at a meeting of drug addicts and parents of the Collectivo. Marta and Emilio conducted the meeting. Susanna, the woman from Ecuador who came for last week's conference at the farm, was also there. There was one fellow in his late 20s, well groomed and well spoken, who was on drugs; another fellow, small and wasted, wrecked by an auto accident, walking lamely.

A third fellow came with his mother. (The mother looked so young I thought she was his girlfriend.) He was quite aggressive and clearly not ready to give up drugs. He has some money – about $300-400 – and his mother has the passbook. He wanted the money; he has recently gotten out of Carabanchel, the main prison. He and the other two fellows left after about an hour and the parents talked.

There is blood all over the bathroom, says the mother, he is shooting heroin in the house. (I didn't understand all she said.) Marta advised the mother that she should set the rules for the house: If he wanted the money – for drugs, it was understood by all – she should give it to him and tell him he could not live in the house. If he lives in the house, he must leave the money alone, not shoot up in the house and not have a key to the house – he could not be in the house alone. All this was not for argument; he either observed these rules or he could go. She could not save him from the two ends to which the addict goes: to prison or to the cemetery. That was his choice and she could not help him unless he chose to help himself. She must care for herself; not allow him to drive her mad. The other parents agreed with this advice.

Then, the father of Paco, who is a man (about 32) out at the farm, said that Paco's wife, who had been living with another man, had left that man and disappeared, along with Paco's two boys, aged 6 and 10. He wanted to find the kids but for that it would be necessary to tell Paco the whole story and have him sign papers.

Other notes from the meeting: the small, wasted young man who limped, told of his auto accident and I think he said that, at one hospital, when they saw the tracks (needle marks) in his arm, they refused to treat him, because of fear of AIDS. I am not sure of this story – I am never sure I get the story straight when I listen to Spanish spoken fast and furious.

So. After the groups, at about 2 PM, the four of us –
Marta, Emilio, Susanna (the woman from Ecuador)
and I, got into Marta's Suzuki jeep and went to Cuatro
Caminos, where we met Pepin and a man from Chile who
was also at the conference. We went to La Encarnacion,
the working-class restaurant. There we met another
woman, who was already eating. I don't know if she was
there by chance or was part of our group (for we arrived
half hour late). She moved to a larger table for the
seven of us. I left about 3:35 because I had arranged to
call Chuck in Santa Barbara at 4. I took the Metro to
the Telefonica building at Gran Via. And after that call I
came here – to this people's cerveceria (I don't know what
its name is – I shall check on the way out).

I begin to know the little streets of Madrid, for I have
walked a lot in Madrid. In 1988 or 1987 or 1986, I had
breakfast one morning at a cafeteria around the corner
– quite a different place from this, a businessman's
kind of place. There is, at the corner, a low, square
modern building, which looks as if it might be a public
market. But it sticks in my mind from a few years back
that I looked at the signs and it has something to do
with meat. Slaughtering? No, I don't think they would
place anything like that within two blocks of the main
street of Madrid. Anyway, I shall shortly be on my way.
I am to meet Pepin and all the others at 7:15 at Plaza
Castillana, where we will take the bus to Colmenar Viejo.
It is now 6:15 and I figure it is about a half hour to Plaza
Castillana by Metro. But I want to leave plenty of time.

Did I mention Earth Day? Sunday is Earth Day and
I forgot all about it until Chuck mentioned it in our
telephone conversation. I want to talk to Pepin about it
and observe it in some way at the farm. After the phone

call, I bought a Herald Tribune and a TIME magazine to read about Earth Day in the U.S. TIME has it as its cover story. So. 6:19. All the people who were here an hour ago are gone. Now a group of four or five workingmen has come in and sits at the bar. It is becoming the hour for tapas, the evening snack.

6:39 PM   On the Metro. Corrections and additions: It is *Plaza de Castilla*. The cerveceria I just left is named Cerveceria-Bar Freiduria Gerbel, or something like that. Oh, and the low, square, modern building, by all signs and appearances, is a parking garage. I don't know how I happened on the subconscious idea that it was a slaughterhouse, unless it is the association of automobiles with slaughter. So. I am on an old Metro car – one of the roaring, rattling cars – of Line One, and stopped next to us here at Alvarado station, is one of the new cars. The new cars have the little handle on the door that you must lift before the door will open. That is like the cars on the Paris Metro, and it may be that the new cars are made in France. France is big in subway cars, I think. The Mexico City subway has French cars – and maybe Montréal also. San Francisco would have done well to go French also. Maybe the reason the new cars are so much quieter – one reason – is that they run on rubber tires, as do the new cars on the Paris Metro.

I find I have affection for French style: the rubber-tired subway cars with the handles on the doors, the pots of red geraniums on the windowsills, the intellectual conversation on television, the willingness of politicians – including and, particularly, President Mitterand – to talk like academics. I am somewhat misplaced now, in Madrid, just as I was beginning to appreciate the French.

Oops – another mistake I made. I see by a passing subway station billboard that the Madrid citizen is called Madrileño, not Madrilleno, as I think I wrote some pages back.   Here is Plaza de Castilla

7 PM   I stand on the sidewalk, leaning against the brick wall surrounding an empty lot. The lot is high in green grass. Near the wall I see some mounds of trash.

7:24 PM   On the bus for the long ride to Colmenar Viejo. The motor starts, and we move out into the traffic of the boulevard, go 40 yards and stop at a traffic light. The young leaves of the tree on the sidewalk bob about in the afternoon breeze. For afternoon it is, not evening – there is yet a strong sun up in the sky.

7:36 PM   We are outside Madrid; there are green fields on either side of the highway. There is full sun to the left and ahead and on the horizon the dark blue mountain distances of the Sierra Guaderrama. 7:44 There is a modern building, not yet completed, at the roadside; the sign says Nixdorf Computers, and beyond, in the green fields, sprout dozens of red brick apartment buildings.   7:47   Emilio points out the buildings of Colmenar Viejo, still far off, to the left in the green hills. Green the hills and now the nearer mountains come greenly out from blue shadow into the sunlight. Trees at the roadside glow green – the low sun lighting through the new leaves. We turn off the highway, at right is a field hazed yellow by sparse mustard flowers.

1:45 AM   Now I am living like a Madrileño: going to bed at 1:45 AM after a dinner beginning at 10:30 PM. The dinner, at Manolo and Nati's in Colmenar Viejo, was with twenty people, and it was mostly to honor the five

South Americans. Manolo drove us all the way to the front door in Vallecas from Colmenar Viejo – a 25 mile trip at one in the morning. And now he is driving back alone.

Madrid   Wednesday, April 18, 11:01 AM
Here I am. At last. The Prado Museum. Waiting in the long line before the entrance. It is because Marisa, one of the people of the Collective, is a student of art history and she is taking all the Latin American visitors through the Prado. Me too. Despite all the time I have spent in Madrid I have only been to the Prado twice before. I am looking forward to being a tourist among tourists. So here we are, in sunlight and street noise, among the visitors from all places.

1:45 PM   Ai – the work of the tourist it is very hard. I am tired after almost three hours in the Prado and now in the other building which has Picasso's Guernica. So I sit on this green-pillowed bench in the little shop while the others look at reproductions and postcards. Marisa knows a lot about art; we went through much of the work of Goya and some of Valesquez and then came over here to see Guernica. The late hours of last night begin to overcome me. At 2 PM we are to meet Pepin and Emilio at Cibeles. And then to lunch.

5:04 PM   At the Telefonica building at Plaza Colon. Waiting to call the U.S. I was shocked yesterday on finding that a half hour call to California at 4 PM Madrid time cost about $175. I have made many half hour calls to Madrid from California at 10 PM California time, direct dial, for $15 to $20. The partial solution, I learn, is not to use the Spanish telephone company, but to use the one telephone booth here in the telephone building where you directly contact an American operator and you use your AT&T credit card. But. One must wait. When I set down here, there were five ahead of me waiting to use the one booth.

So. After I make the call I want to go to a photo store to leave several rolls of film to develop. Then, I would either go to a café – maybe at the Plaza Mayor – or go back to the apartment for a siesta, since I didn't sleep until almost 2 AM last night. At 8:15 PM, I am to meet the group at the Manuel Becerra Metro stop in the Salamanca district. Tonight there is another dinner for the Collective and the visitors from Latin America. This will be at the apartment of Antonio and the three "graduates" from the farm: Luis and Josele and Sito.

6:06 PM   In a taxi on my way to Calle Montera, where I will look for the photo store.

7 PM   On Metro line 2, on my way to Manuel Becerra.

7:15 PM   So. On a chair before a cream-colored formica tabletop, with spotlights overhead bouncing light off the table into my eyes. Confusing sentence, but I am tired – of body, mind and kishkas. This is a cerveceria/cafeteria at Plaza Manuel Becerra. The sound of the women talking is like the light of the little spotlights – sharp and battering. This is not a place to rest the spirit among still waters. Not at all. This is a city place, and the grief of the city, the gnawing grief of the city, which comes in bites and pics and tics and tension, is bouncing about the formica tabletops and the beige-sparkle walls. I hate this place. I have been here only seven minutes and I hate it. I like the manzanilla tea – it is warm and kind as it goes down my throat, and warm in my stomach. It is the time of day to welcome warmness.

When I first came out of the subway, walking the weary steps, I saw the wood benches set by the little hedge in front of the roadway. On one, a man sat, reading a book. I sat on the other end of that bench. But then the chill of the shadowed air hit me, and I saw, in front, the sign "Cerveceria". So I walked in here. This is nothing like my cerveceria two blocks off Gran Via. This is in the solid middle-class, middle muddle, of the Salamanca district – it is all flash and sparkle and mirror and spotlight and the middle-class tension rolls from the women's voices in waves, spring-loaded, and it bounces off the mirrors and bounces off the formica and caroms inside my head. These women are not talking of Michelangelo.

7:30 PM   Still 45 minutes until the appointed meeting time. Way out there in the street under the sky. It is hard to believe in sky, sitting here. Or trees. Or sun. Formica and mirrors and sharp light, sharp voices. Where I am sitting is the back room, rather like a large corridor. There are only five of the formica-top tables. Each has four chairs – tan enamel over bent metal with gray-green plastic covered seats and backs. The floor is terrazzo, tan and black – I don't like it either. Three of the tables are set lengthwise against one wall – the wall that is set with mirrors from the height of one meter all the way to the low ceiling. I sit at the middle of these three tables.

At either side of me are a couple women. All talking fast and sharp. The two women at my right are both dressed in bright red – they are blonde. The two women at my left are older and dressed more somberly – one in black, the other in a dark greenish gray. Right now there is no one sitting at the two tables set against the opposite wall. These two tables are set with their short side against the wall. Until a few minutes ago a man and a woman, middle-aged, were sitting at one of the tables. They both sat on the same side of the table and they hugged each other before they left.

Now the two older women – the dark women – are putting on their coats. One wears a white coat, the other a rust colored coat. The waiter toted up their bill a moment ago – they had calamares (squid) and a couple of other things. This is the time of day for tapas – the snacks. The waiter comes up to straighten the chairs of the evacuated table. He wears black trousers, a white dress shirt and a little white bowtie – he is led about by his stomach, which stands out in front of the rest of him.

The room is a good deal quieter now – now that the somber women have left and the red women seem to have sputtered spattered away much of their tension. Maybe it is that they are no longer competing for the voice space of this little room. Now two young women, both wearing tight faded-blue jeans and white shirts, sit down at one of the tables across – the one occupied before by the couple. They both have long hair – one with dark blonde straight hair and the other with curly black hair tied back with what looks like a length of red knitting wool.

My, the time has passed. In 10 or 15 minutes I shall go outside, to stand by the Metro entrance or to sit on one of the wood benches. But, baby, it's cold outside. Well, coolish, anyway. This afternoon, when I was waiting in the telephone office, I was sitting next to an American girl who is spending a semester abroad in Madrid – she goes to USC and attends a school right up Paseo de la

Castellana from the telephone building. She said she likes Madrid – the weather is like California, she said. I looked askance and aslant – so she added, Well, last week was a little cold. But, she said, in February we had really warm weather, it was like Spring then.

The women in red talk; I don't understand what they say, I only catch words. One of the women said Hombre, etc. etc. – addressing the other woman. The Spanish use this expression to refer to women as well as men.

1:04 AM   And so to bed. Emilio says: There is not much time to sleep, so sleep fast.

Madrid   Thursday, April 19, 12:07 PM
The man next to me is whistling. Across the street there is the strong stutter of a jackhammer. A breeze with a chill edge on it rumples the new

12:11 PM   That was then: when I was sitting on the bench waiting for the bus, and deciding what to call the young green color of the new leaves on the trees across the street.

Now – the now-ness of the #10 bus bumping over the dug-up surface of Avenida de Palomares. I am all decked out in my weekend outfit – my granja (farm) outfit: boots and ChiPants blue jeans and wide cotton hat, plus assorted other clothing – I remind myself of that image of Walt Whitman that Bookshop Santa Cruz uses on its bags, bookmarks and T-shirts. No enterprise without a T-shirt – it is the norm of our time.

So – the day is bright and cool, the leaves are out and they cry **Life** in every street. The earth is aware that its day is coming. I am screwing up my courage to call Manolo and ask him to buy a little pine seedling that we can plant on the farm Sunday to commemorate Earth Day 1990. Pepin said Manolo could buy the tree and bring it out in his van. It is hard for me to converse on the phone and hard for me to ask someone I don't know very well to go to some trouble and spend money. (I will tell him I will pay for the tree – but I am afraid he won't take reimbursement.)

The #10 bus

Right now I am going all the way on #10 to Cibeles and then I will walk to Plaza Colon to the Telefonica building to try once again to reach AT&T. I gave up yesterday – the wait was just too long. But I hope that at 12:30 PM, which is 3:30 AM in California and 6:30 AM in New York, there will be no other people waiting to use telephone booth #1 at Telefonica. That is the only booth you can use to get the AT&T operator.

At 2 PM I am going up to Cuatro Caminos to meet the whole group for lunch. Then, at 4 something, Emilio and I will take the bus to the farm. My, there is so much nuance and personality and atmospherics that I have not been writing about. Maybe during the weekend I will do some of that.

Emilio looked quite tired yesterday. There have been the late night dinners – both last night and Tuesday night we didn't return to the piso (apartment) until after 1 AM. Pepin and Emilio have been sleeping on foam mattresses set out on the living room floor, since Emilio gave up his room to me and Pepin gave up his to Manuel, the fellow from Chile. Also, yesterday Emilio took Manuel and the two Argentinians on an enormous walk through Madrid – from Plaza de España to the Palacio Real to the Plaza Mayor to El Retiro – that must be some 10 kilometers through the rough and tumble and noise of the central city streets. He said to me last night: Ah, at the farm one can really sleep – there is no noise and the work is different, there it is physical, here it is anxiety and running about. Emilio really likes to be out at the farm. I don't know if he has ever lived out in the country before; he was born in Madrid and has been poor all his life.

1:42 PM   On a bench. I spend lots of time on a bench. So it seems. But it is hard to write while walking, running, swimming, bicycling. It seems that sitting is the best position – and benches are for sitting. This bench is on the sidewalk of one of the boulevards that cross at Cuatro Caminos (Cuatro Caminos means Four Roads). What I like about this bench is that it is in the shade and it is a nice solid bench with solid steel legs and arm rests and solid, stolid, wood planks for the seat and the back rest. There is, here at Cuatro Caminos, the acid smell of auto exhaust and the noise of the passing cars. Aside from the solid, stolid, bench in the solid shadow, there is little to recommend Cuatro Caminos.

Right in front of me, beyond the sidewalk and half the motorway, are the concrete supports of a road overpass, for one of the roads of Four Roads goes above the other in an overpass. And yet there are ground-level motorways on either side of the overpass, so we must mark the builders of the overpass as "unclear on the concept". Vehicles pass every which way, many of them the red Madrid buses and many of them the white Madrid taxis. That is another thing that is done far better in rather poor Spain than in rich America – the taxis are all clean modern cars, and the drivers are neat looking.

I must cross the street so I can be in front of Simago department store (sort of a Spanish Woolworths) at 2 PM

4:25 PM   Sitting again. The loudspeaker is on top of my head. Hey, nothing. There is a loudspeaker on top of every seat in the bus. And a television in front. We are going to see a bad loud movie, I fear. It is the traveler's castigation. Otherwise the bus is A-OK. Not that we are yet moving. We are still in the station at Plaza Conde de Casal.

4:28 PM   The motor starts. No, not quite the glamour of the airplane; but a voyage is beginning. Going somewhere – from here to there. *There*, today, is a place off a dirt road, somewhere in the countryside near Huete. Ballantines Scotch Whiskey, the voice says, with a Spanish pronunciation – that is the kind of radio station the loudspeaker is pouring over me. All-American

garbage music – in English even *I* can't understand –
and commercials for Scotch whiskey. When I went out
to the farm last Thursday morning, it was the beginning
of Semana Santa weekend and I think they put on extra
buses and, blessedly, ours – probably being an older bus
– had no television and the ride was quiet.

Emilio has already put back his seat and he is probably
sleeping through the garbage music. We left La
Encarnacion restaurant before 4 PM and took the
Line 6 Metro to Plaza Conde de Casal. The meal at La
Encarnacion, with 11 of us around three tables set
together, was the last with the Latin Americans. Marco,
from Chile, leaves on Saturday, the two Argentinians on
Saturday or Sunday and Manuel, from Chile, on Monday.
Only Susanna, from Ecuador, will stay a longer time.

El Colmenar   8:54 PM   And not yet dark. The gray
clouds floating have the white light of day yet on the
lower edges. I sit on one of the much-used couches in
the recreation room. The television set is on. All for me,
as I am now the only one in the room. Jose Luis, the
"retarded" man (he speaks, and, I think, reads better
than I – so what does that say of me?) turned on the TV
and then left the room. Ah, now he is back. There is a
football (soccer) game on. Spanish television shows lots
and lots of sports.

It has been a pleasant few hours in the evening on the
farm.   In The Evening On The Farm – why, the very
words are to conjure with.   Celso is planting little
tomato seedlings in the greenhouse and I hung around
and helped a little – pouring water into the holes, picking
little stones off the ground. That is a definite sign of
progress on the farm: the size of the stones in the fields is

much smaller than it was a couple years ago. There has been a lot of rock picking going on over the last few years. Emilio is setting the tables for supper. I shall go help him. Yes, 9 PM and the supper hour is just approaching. So it goes.

9:10 PM   The table is set – 12 places. After I wrote that I realized that there were not enough places – for we are 13 tonight. My goodness, 13   Easter   Last Supper   Passover passed over. Yes. There are 10 residents here tonight – one having gone to Madrid to take the university entrance examination on Saturday. And Celso – and Emilio and me. Thirteen, and I think Celso just started cooking supper a short time ago – so it will be closer to 10 than to 9 when we eat. The fellow who went to Madrid is Paco, the oldest fellow here – in his young 30s. We saw him at the bus station at Tarancon. The bus from Madrid to Cuenca and the bus from Cuenca to Madrid both seem to arrive at Tarancon at the same time. The buses stop there for five or ten minutes, enough time to go into the bar and get a bocadillo (sandwich) and coffee or whatever. This time, we didn't go inside, but stood in Spring sunlight, leaning against the wall near the bus, talking to Paco.

9:19 PM   So, I am feeling an edge of hunger. I had a meal I liked at La Encarnacion this afternoon. For a first course I ordered Ensalada Mixta, which is a good-sized plate of lettuce, tomato, onion slices, black olives and chunks of tuna. Then, instead of ordering a meat dish for the second course, I ordered two more first course dishes: Arroz a la Cubana, which is a mound of rice covered with tomato sauce with a fried egg at the side, and Judias Blancas which is white beans. In Spain beans are called judias, not frijoles as they are called in Mexico. But at the

La Encarnacion (Pepin in white jacket)

serving, the waiter said they were all out of judias, and he suggested lentejas (lentils). So I had that, and I liked my whole dinner – I do now have an antipathy to meat. For dessert I had an orange, as I almost always do, for the oranges here and now are the best I have ever eaten. No comparison to the poor product, including organic, that I have eaten in California. These oranges have no trace of acid – they are mild, sweet and juicy, easy to peel and easy to split into slices. It has a lot to do with the time of year, because they are dead ripe.

10:19 PM   After supper. Which was a plate of fish and bread and an apple. Now I am back in the same place on the same couch.

El Colmenar   Friday, April 20, 8:02 AM
Out the window, the opposing hillside gleams and beams tones of yellow and green, reflecting the morning

sunlight. The sky is still the milky soft blue of morning. A cock crows, from far off there is the remote roar of the diesel generator. Everyone has been up for an hour. The masons from Tarancon arrived at 8 AM to begin the day's work on the new building and all the residents must be ready to pitch into that work. I was the last to breakfast – at 7:20 AM. Then I looked for some work to do. I got a broom; I swept the recreation room and then the dining room – it was more show than substance. I want to be busy – but I don't know what to do. So now I have retired

Masons at work on the new building

to my bedroom and I sit on the edge of the bed writing. At about nine I will go with Celso into Huete to do the shopping. And he calls Pepin every morning from Huete. I'll go look for him now.   [A 2016 note on driving at the farm in 1990: Pepin, Celso and Emilio never owned a car and never learned to drive, so they relied on some of the resident fellows, if they had a license and were settled enough, or on visitors – like me.]

9:56 AM   Sitting. Again. In another place. On a stool at the bar of the inn by the road in Huete. I just drove Celso here in the ancient Land Rover. We had some trouble starting it – had to call Carlos over from his work on the new building. He put some gas in the tank and fiddled with the carburetor a bit. For me, the Land Rover ride is a bit scary. The brakes go almost to the floor before they begin to slow the car, the steering wheel goes round loosely for a ways before it seems to send a message to the wheels, and the wheels drift to the left. I'd hate to have to respond quickly in this car; I don't know where it would go in response to quick movements of brakes or steering. I want to suggest to Pepin that they get these things fixed and I will pay for the work. The Land Rover *looks* much better than El Coche Bravo (the Renault) but it, too, has the failings of age and neglect.

So. I am sitting here writing and I just drank off my manzanilla tea. Celso is telephoning to Pepin and his café con leche is growing cold on the polished wood counter. The television set is on. The Spanish like to have bouncy noise-music in public places – and that is what is coming from the television at this morning hour. Before we started on this trip

11:24 AM   In the bank. We have been to the grocer's, the fruit store, the butcher, the dry goods store, the post office and a couple other places. Celso knows, it seems, all the people in town. Many of the merchants were at the fiesta-night at the end of the seminar last Saturday.

What I didn't finish above, because Celso returned from his telephone call, was that before we started on this little trip to town, I was hoeing weeds from in front of the carpentry building. I must do something, for sitting about idly is against the ethic of the farm. The other choice would have been to work on the construction of the building, which I don't feel up to – and anyway I was going into town in a half hour. So I hoed. And the weeds were very cold. (They don't have warm blood circulating, you know.) They were, I was mildly shocked to discover, as cold as the rocks and the air. So my hands became very chilled as I pulled them out of the earth.

11:42 AM   Last stop, after the stop for gasoline for the Land Rover. Actually, I think it took "gas/oil" (diesel?). Now Celso has gone to get the wheel of El Coche Bravo, the Renault, which has been left somewhere here. Or at least that is my understanding and I

2:06 PM   So.   After we got back from Huete, Emilio reminded me that a young woman, Irena, was arriving from Madrid on the bus at noon. I didn't get to Carrascosa until 12:40 and she was gone. I asked in the bar and they said she had left walking.   Ah – the call for lunch rings down the hall.

3:05 PM   After lunch. To continue: My trip to Carrascosa this morning was something of a comedy of errors. As I said above, Irena had left and by the time I caught up with her she was walking, some 4 kilometers from the farm, on the dirt road. And, I found out at lunch that Celso had wanted to go to Carascosa with me and as I rolled down from the main building in the Land Rover, he was running after me. But I didn't look in the rearview mirror – I was all forward at that time, concerned about arriving so late in Carrascosa.

3:30 PM   I am going to sit in on the English class at about 4 PM.

8:15 PM   So. I have been riding high this afternoon. Irena, who is a recent graduate in philosophy from the University and who comes here every Friday, gave two classes in English. I sat in on both of them. She divided the young men here into two groups. The first, of seven, is a little more advanced in English then the second, which had four fellows. But the first thing you recognize with these fellows is that they are un-schooled. They never had, I don't think, a good experience with learning and they have thought of themselves as people who can't learn. They seem bright outside the classroom, but when they are in a classroom situation – in the past they have turned to stone. So this is what they and people teaching them must deal with. There is one kid, Israel, who seems quite sharp and bright outside the class – he is a wise-acre, quick, street kid. He was in the second group and he kept saying there was no way he was able to do the simplest classroom thing – like repeating an English word. In the classroom, he just thinks of himself as beat before he starts.

Irena had to leave about 6:45, so I took over the second group and I taught them the American Indian song: *The earth is our mother/ We must take care of her/ Hey yunga, Ho yunga, Hey yung yung/ This sacred ground we walk on/ With every step we take/ Hey yunga, Ho yunga, Hey yung yung.*   And then we spent the rest of the time talking about the Indians of the United States.

Now I am sitting on one of the couches in the recreation room – I think I shall call this the living room rather than the recreation room. I am on the edge of being uncomfortably warm because I am wearing full muda interior del invierno (winter long underwear) – it is like being inside a mobile igloo; the storms may rage, icicles form, thermometers freeze – but what care I? All I have to fear is normal warmth – for with normal warmth I would asphyxiate. The other people in the room are sitting about the fire – I am at the other end of the room. So it goes – we all learn our survival skills.

So – now it is 8:38 – perhaps an hour and 20 minutes to dinner. Last night everyone went to bed right after supper. The chavales (young fellows) are pretty tired after working most of the day with the masons building the new building. And, at any event, the diesel generator is turned off at 11 PM. I was surprised this morning to be the last one at breakfast at 7:20 – that is very early for Spain.

9:41 PM   Supper was much earlier this evening. It is over and I am back sitting on the couch inside my mobile igloo. It was a big meal for me, because I had two bowls of chicken soup with rice. After that, a fried egg and an apple and   Just now, everyone but me and Pitu and Emilio rushes out of the room. ¿Que pasa? I ask. It is raining, says Emilio. Oh, I say, and I go out to see. But no, I don't feel or see rain. So maybe it is only raining in Spanish, or on the plain.   What was I saying? Oh – I also had a couple big chunks of bread.

El Colmenar   Saturday, April 21, 8:17 AM
New morning, bright morning. I am sitting. On the edge of my bed, having breakfasted on a big tin cup of hot chocolate and seven or eight little square cookies – 'tis the custom of the land. At 10:30 or 11 there will be meat and cheese sandwiches, bocadillos. Now, somewhere in

the land toots an auto horn. This is unusual. Ah – it is a truck with sacks of cement for the construction. It will make the boys dirty, says Emilio. And Pitu comes into the room to get a pair of gloves.

Delivering bocadillos

Today starts later because it is Saturday. I should go sweep now – everyone is working and I am feeling a sense of obligation. Work, for the sun is waxing; work, for the day is building; work, for the time is growing. Work, Work, Work. The salvation and the savior. Work. A paean to Work.

9:05 AM   Oh, my poor hands are *so* cold. For, though the sun shines brightly, it is yet a very cold morning. And I picked up from the cold concrete the orange peels and other vegetables scraps the dogs have spilled from a pail, and my hands cold-en-ed in the process. Much cold-en-ed. Before that I swept the dining room and living room and took the ashes from out the fireplace. I looked for things to clean the sinks in the bathroom, but couldn't find them. But now there is a bustle in the house, for the unloading of the cement and the bricks has finished and the music is going, and voices, and much to and fro. We will make the trip to town a bit later, for Pepin is coming in on the bus at 10 AM, so we will pick him up on the trip.

So – now I am sitting on the couch in the corner of the classroom and, my, the couch is cold. The cold comes in to me through all my layers of clothing – even the formidable muda interior del invierno. Earlier, I was sitting on the bed in the room I am sharing with Celso and Emilio, but Celso came in and I felt uncomfortable merely sitting there and scribbling. Celso is a natural worker. It is not often you see him just sitting about – he is always doing something. Emilio and Pepin are pretty much the same. Now me – I am a sitter-about. My typical occupation is reading or writing. Interesting – my mother was always doing something also. My father also – though he *could* sit, I remember him just sitting. Though, of course, he worked six days a week for 10 or 12 hours – at least when I was younger. Maybe it is that I am of another time and another place, as well as of another temperament. My work has always been sitting, sedentary work rather than hustle and bustle and sweat. (Question: Do sitting and sedentary mean the same thing – thus giving the last sentence a measure of redundancy? Don't know – there is no English dictionary hereabout.)

So. I had a long dream last night. Do I have time and warmth enough to write it down? I shall commence. Although it begins to fade from unstable memory. I am in a foreign city – maybe English, maybe French. I cross to another part of the city – not far away, but on the other side – of, maybe, a river. There is a pleasant inn there, run by a pleasant couple – particularly the woman is pleasant. (Right now, while writing, I think of Mirielle and Farrar at La Ferme, although I didn't associate them in the dream.) There was a lot in the first part of the dream about being at this place and it was pleasant. There may have been something of a Donut [2016 clarification; Donut means Threshold Foundation members] quality in what was going on. Now, in what seems to me to have been a later dream, I am at the same inn. And I am sitting with several people at a table. Richard B. is either there or he arrives with the priest. The priest is the priest of Tarancon, who Celso and I met on the dirt road yesterday morning as we were returning, in the Land Rover, from making the purchases in Huete. Yesterday, the Tarancon priest was in a car parked at the side of the dirt road not far from the entrance to the farm. He was with the two nuns. I had met all of them one day during my visit in 1988, when they came out to the farm. They are all rather frigid, rigid religious figures – more in the church by way of retreat then by way of compassion. Pepin avoided them when they visited in 1988; he doesn't mix well with the kinds of people it is necessary to have a

10:32 AM   So. We have made the trip to Carrascosa to pick up the passengers from Madrid: Pepin and Luis and Manuel (the fellow from Chile) and Carmen. (We have 5 Carmens, Emilio said to me the other day.)   It was a Safari in the Grand Manner – over the far country tracks in the Land Rover, me at the wheel with my white cotton hat, bumpety, pow, pow over the ruts and ridges. Soon we will go to Huete for the purchases of the day.

Meanwhile, back to the dream. I was saying that Pepin doesn't like to chatter with people it is necessary to have a bit of a front with, so he leaves it to Celso to talk to the priest of Tarancon. The priest and the nuns came by in their car to leave packages of Red Cross donated food.

So, anyway, in my dream the priest arrives and I find out – I am quite shocked and astonished to find out – that the priest has gone to my auto, which I had left parked on the other side of the river in a parking lot when

10:50 AM   So.   I have been going about putting the empty butane and diesel cans in the Land Rover.

 So.   The priest went to my auto and opened the trunk and took out my papers – particularly this long letter I have been writing. And, apparently, this had been made possible by Richard B.

2:03 PM   Almost lunchtime.   Since the last writing I drove Celso to Huete to make the purchases: grocery store, fruit store, general store for butane, to the fellow who is with the company building the electric line, then, to buy the newspaper, to the gasoline station for a container of diesel oil for the tractor, to the feed store for three great sacks of feed for the rabbits. Then, after we got back, I spent the last hour putting rocks in wheelbarrows and carrying them into the new building to form the base under the concrete for the floor. Mucho trabajo, poco dinero – as my father used to say. Now – on with the dream. So Richard B. had made a copy of my car keys and given them to the priest – that's how he got into my car. Afterwards, in the night, I kept on dreaming about this. Trying to figure it out. Why had Richard done this? Why had the priest done this? What harm could come to me from this? How did the priest know where the car was?   It was a puzzling thing. I didn't feel greatly threatened but I was puzzled and rather disappointed.   So, I shall go see how lunch is progressing.

Earth Day: pale blue sky of morning . . .
yellow patch of first sunlight

El Colmenar   Sunday, April 22, 8:33 AM
Earth Day. And the earth is here – under, around,
here, there and everywhere. There is the pale blue sky
of morning and, faintly through the thick walls, I hear
the tsquaks of the birds. As I look out the end window of
the building (for I am sitting in the classroom, the end
room) I see the hill across the valley. It is a flat dark color
against the sky, with a ragged fringe of little silhouetted
trees at the ridge. But now, right below the trees, on a
flat place at the top, I see a yellow patch of first sunlight.
Earth Day begins at El Colmenar.

I have just come from breakfast (el desayuno – which
has the same etymology as "breakfast", since "ayunar"
is "to fast"). Breakfast at El Colmenar is a big metal
cup of steaming hot chocolate and as many flat square
cookies as you want. Israel, who serves today as the
breakfast cook, said Colacao, (which is the brand name
of the chocolate), es el desayuno de los deportistas – the
breakfast of the athletes. Spain eats advertising with its
breakfast, as does the USA.

There is a rustling and scratching on the roof over my
head. I think it is the pigeons. In the early morning
before the chickens and ducks and turkeys are released
from the little buildings where they have been shut up
for the night, the pigeons come down in droves and
coveys, fleets and flocks to eat the leftovers in the chicken
yard down the hill from the house.

8:52 AM   I shall walk a way down the road – though
I wonder if there will be a shopping trip this morning

to Huete?   Celso is not here. He went to Madrid yesterday afternoon. Isabel, his wife, will probably go to the hospital this week for an operation on varicose veins and Javi, his son, had x-rays last week and the doctor says he has a mild case of pneumonia, so Celso is quite worried.

Javi (center) at the 1990 conference

9 AM   Yes, I walk along the terrace in front of the building and the pigeons stand on the eaves like sentries – one posted every couple feet. As I approach, they retreat out of sight, further back on the roof. The birds down in the chicken yard now are small gray birds that fly back and forth from an oak tree at the edge of the yard.

2:03 PM   It is before dinner, and I sit around the corner from the dining room – in the next room – which I call the living room. I have a pain running down my left leg which comes, I believe, from something in my back. And the something in my back comes from something in the way I have carried water and stooped and bent over the past few hours, watering the new tomato plants in the big greenhouse. We helped Celso plant these plants shortly after we arrived on Thursday. Some of them look woebegone wilted now and I thought water would help. Before watering the tomatoes, I picked some green peas and after I picked a bean called something like ave or abe in Spanish, which is either lima beans or a close relative. Before the greenhouse work, I took, with the help of Benito, the weeds I had pulled up the other day and put them in the feed trough for the goats. And so it goes. When I came back from my little morning walk after breakfast, I saw Manolo, the man from Colmenar Viejo, whose son is a resident here, sitting in his van with the motor running. He was going to Carrascosa for the Sunday purchases (the stores in Huete are closed on Sunday). So I got in and went along. We also picked up four people who arrived in Carrascosa just before 10 AM on the bus from Madrid.

I rub my hands together now and I notice how rough and dry they are. This comes, in large part, from putting the stones on the wheelbarrows. The stone dust is very hard on hands. Nani, one of the boys, who rode to Carrascosa with us this morning, has breaks and spots over the back of his hands from handling the stones for two days without gloves.

2:17 PM   It looks like lunch will be rather late this afternoon. It is being prepared by Nati, Manolo's wife, and her mother. They all arrived yesterday. In fact, Manolo and Nati come to the farm every weekend.

I don't think my Earth Day commemoration is going to happen today. We never did all get together so I could teach the Indian song. But, of course, I have celebrated the day myself in the best way – watering the young tomato plants.

4:19 PM   In the living room after the dinner. Through the one window comes full sunlight, but it is very cold. In the corner fireplace, there is a high fire, a hot fire, burning. Someone is practicing the guitar, several are playing cards, some are reading parts of the Sunday El Pais, and I, in the far corner, write. There is content, contentedness, in the room. At the end of the dinner, a cake was brought out to celebrate the birthday of Josele, who came in on the morning bus from Madrid. Josele is one of the three who "graduated" from the farm several months ago and are now living in an apartment in Madrid. He and Paco took the university entrance exam yesterday. This is an exam for people over 25 who do not have a secondary certificate. It is a difficult examination of general cultural knowledge. I would guess that 90% of American high school graduates could not pass it. Josele brought a part of the examination with him this morning and I looked at it. The English comprehension part of it was a passage from Truman Capote's *In Cold Blood*, with questions that tested whether you understood it.

The birthday celebration was the singing of the Spanish versions of Happy Birthday and For He's a Jolly Good Fellow, the opening of some small gifts, a few words from Josele (demanded by the others with a chant of ¡Que hablé!, ¡Que hablé!, ¡Que hablé! – That he speak!, That he speak!). Then a chant of ¡Que bailé! – That he dance! – at which Josele rolled up one pants leg, at which there was a chant of la otra – the other. Then there were demands for singing and they got the guitar from the next room.

Ah – there is a roll of thunder from outside – this is a *very* changeable day – there have been a couple short spells of rain, verging on snow in the coldness of the day.

So – after the guitar appeared, Manuel, the fellow from Chile, sang several songs and several people told funny stories – jokes – very few of which I understood. It was a high humored, high tempered time. And the good fellowship has carried forward into this other room, this later time.

4:39 PM   I moved to sit by the window. There is now a flash of lightning and then, the following thunder. And yet, at the same time, I see blue sky in narrow intervals between the clouds.

4:45 PM   There is a hard hail coming down outside – the brown fields are being covered in white.

10 PM   Madrid
I just took a hot shower. There are showers and hot water out at the farm, but in the cold mornings, I get dressed quickly and then wash the only parts of me not dressed: my hands and face. Manuel, the Chilean fellow, and I have showered and now Pepin is taking a shower. When he finishes, we will have dinner. The afternoon at the farm and the ride back were alegre (happy) and raucous. There were games with teams in the living room – like passing a little onion in a tablespoon held, handle first, between your teeth, to a tablespoon similarly held by someone else on your team. And then on the ride back to Madrid, there was a raucous game of tapping people on the head, and then singing all the rest of the way. I mostly listened, because I didn't know the Spanish songs,

but I did solos of When the Saints Go Marching In, Oh Susanna, and Oh What a Beautiful Morning.

Madrid   Monday, April 23, 8:09 AM
Morning. I have some millet cooking. I am the only person in Spain, I feel pretty sure, who eats millet for breakfast.

11:57 AM   At a bank on Calle de Atocha. Manuel is changing money and I am waiting. I am doing errands before meeting with the group for lunch at 2 PM at Cuatro Caminos. First I picked up photos from the shop near Gran Via and now we are walking to a computer store to pick up the keyboard for the computer that Pepin has gotten (with a grant from Tides Foundation). Also the manual for the Olivetti computer is missing. And I want to ask something about the modem and about the software. I am not sure that

Madrid   Tuesday, April 24, 12:29 PM
My. I have not a moment. I am coursing about Madrid getting estimates for the furnishing of a school for 30 kids in the barrio of Pan Bendito. Typewriters, a ceramics oven and clay, soccer balls and basketball hoops, television equipment and chairs and desks and on and on. And I can barely speak the language – I don't understand 30% of what is said to me in the shops. It is all in the Don Quijote-ish spirit of the whole enterprise. The impossible dream. Now I am in the Metro on the way to a furniture and carpentry shop in the Rastro –

1:33 PM   Again in the Metro, lunch-ward bound toward Cuatro Caminos.   Hungry and tired.   The Rastro is interesting – there are all the street vendors selling clothes and whatnot. I went to the furniture and cabinet stores on Calle Ribera de Cultidores, which is the street of the Rastro. The shops I went to are at the beginning of the street – the high end, for the street goes steeply downhill. After I went to four stores and got estimates I walked a bit along the street stalls. But I am foot sore and stomach hungry now. It has been a weary walking day. I walked all the way to Puente de Vallecas and then uphill a long way – I forget the name of the street that runs into Avenida de la Albufera. And then I took the Metro to Tirso de Molina and walked some more.

1:55 PM   Standing on the corner, leaning 'gainst the wall. The wall being that of Simago – the five and dime store here at Cuatro Caminos. None of the others – my compañeros of lunch – have arrived yet. I came here a few minutes ago and I went into Simago and bought a pair of socks for 225 pesetas. The body needs refreshment. I didn't go to bed last night until sometime around 1 AM – for we had all gone to the airport to see off Manuel on his flight to Chile. He

2:29 PM   Still standing on the corner – with Pepin. Marta and Celso have not yet arrived. I am a-weary, heavy in the head, heavy in the foot. Ears dinned by autos and trucks, wheezes and rolls and thumps and squawks and blares. Nose damned by fumes, gases and all manner of noxiousness. What a bane are the automobiles. What to do about them?

4:41 PM   So.   At a cafeteria just off of Gran Via. I came in here because the photo shop wasn't open – it re-opens at 4:30. I want to pick up the photos I left for developing yesterday. My other errands for this afternoon are to mail a letter at Cibeles, the main post office, and to check the bus times for Saturday to Aranda del Duero. Aranda is halfway between Madrid and Bilbao and I and Pepin, Celso, and Emilio are going there to meet José Manuel and his family, who are driving down from Bilbao. The bus station is at Palos de la Frontera, way down beyond Atocha station – so I have a little more walking to do, even with taking the Metro. Then, at 7:45, I will meet Pepin at Plaza de Castilla to take the bus to Colmenar Viejo where he has a group tonight. After the group we will go to the home of Manolo and Nati for supper – so it looks like another late night – getting back after midnight. If I work things right, maybe I can go sit in the Retiro park for an hour and a half before 7 PM. We shall see.

5:03 PM   Lucky me. I got a seat on the Metro car. I am on my way from Gran Via to Atoche. Atoche is – maybe *was* is the better word – the main rail station of Madrid. Chamartin is a new station that receives all the trains to and from the north, I think. But Atoche is where I first arrived – it was on a night train, arriving in early morning – from Granada, I think, in 1983. At that time there was a highway overpass uglifying the traffic roundabout in front of the station. It has since been replaced by an underpass. Old Atoche station is now being completely reconstructed.

5:43 PM   So. I am leaving Palos de la Frontera. By Metro. Line 3, on my map is yellow and I didn't see it – it melted into the background. Now I am going to Sol and transferring to the line to Cibeles. To the post office and then walk one very long block to El Retiro. And rest. Today is the first really warm day since I have been in Madrid. I think. I can't remember back all those days to April 6. It is a long time back – April 6.

6:41 PM   Retiro Park. Blessed oasis – trees and water, birds and Chestnut blossoms, a cold lemonade, and a hot tea – for that is the kind of day it is. Now that I have stopped moving and sit in deep shade, I feel a bit of chill in the air. I have been sitting here reading the Economist magazine I bought after I left the Metro, at a news kiosk in the underground passage. I also bought two books from a vendor selling from a long table in front of the Post Office: *Novelas Ejemplares*, by Cervantes – which he wrote before he wrote Don Quixote and that's all I know about it and that may be wrong – and an anthology of poems by Ruben Dario, a Nicaraguan poet who died in 1916.

7:14 PM   Once again in the Metro world, which is its own world. Once you go underground, you are not at Sol or Retiro, or Puente de Vallecas; you are at Metro. Airports are like this too. They are

7:24 PM   Lucky again – a seat on Line 1 – on the other line, from Retiro to Sol, there was hardly breathing space – on this one, the car is almost empty. Why? Don't know.

I don't know if all this scribbling is of any interest – it is a day in the life. But I have left out the most dramatic part. At lunch – which as usual was at La Encarnacion, Marta and Celso arrived from the group in Ventas with one of the young men – Manolo. He was also in the Ventas group last week when I attended. This is a guy who looks like he hasn't a problem in the world. About 27 years old, black hair, rimless glasses, square jaw and unlined face, very neatly dressed, he looks like the Spanish version of a Harvard law student. But he has a serious problem – the talk at lunch seemed to center around alcohol –

so maybe that is his addiction rather than heroin. He is quite at the end of the rope apparently and wants to change his life, to come out to the farm. I think he will be out at the farm this weekend, but there was also talk of his arranging things, and unemployment, and May 15. So I am not exactly sure of the situation. That is the way I capture lunch table conversations when the Spanish are talking, but not to me.

When we left the restaurant, Marta left in her car and Pepin walked on to his university class. Celso and I and Manolo went down into the Metro, then Celso took Line 2 and Manolo and I took Line 1 together. He asked me if I was a "monitore", which is one of the helper/teachers. I said no, I was a friend of the Collective for many years; I was an American. When we were on the car, he said, I don't understand, so I said I was visiting for a month, that Celso and Pepin were very good people. I didn't know what else to say and we stood silently until I got off at Gran Via and he kissed me on both cheeks in the manner of Spanish friends. I said Hasta luego. I will ask Pepin to tell me more of Manolo's story as we ride the bus to Colmenar Viejo.

As we were eating lunch and Manolo was telling his story to Pepin, I had a strong sense of what was happening and I was moved – this was one person helping another person – being a friend to a stranger. There was no money involved, no career involved – that is the power of the way Pepin and Celso work.

Valdeacederas – That's the name of the Metro stop we are now at. I am not watching the stops because Plaza de Castilla is the end of the line. I am already late – it's 7:47 PM

7:56 PM   I started hurrying out of the car and there was Pepin sitting on a bench on the Metro platform. We were to meet at the bus stop above, but he was to meet Celso here below and Celso has not yet arrived. So now Pepin has run on to see if he can get the 8 PM bus and I wait for Celso.

Madrid   Wednesday, April 25, 9:54 AM
So. I make notes for errands this morning. Pick up estimates on kitchen appliances, audio-visual equipment, typewriters and desks. Go to a sporting goods store for an estimate. To a bank. To a store to buy some gifts. For Carmen and Gonzalo, who I am to have supper with tonight. For the children of José Manuel and Lola, who I will see on Saturday.

11:16 AM   At the Puente de Vallecas Metro platform. I went to the kitchen appliance store – he doesn't have the estimate ready yet, I must return. I went to the Olivetti store and got the estimates for the typewriters and tables, then I went a couple doors away to the sports shop I had been in yesterday. The manager, who looks like an ex-football (soccer) player, said yesterday, in effect: What, how can I give estimates on sports equipment of 30 kids in a school; you must tell me exactly what you want and then I can give you estimates. So, today I told him I wanted prices for four soccer balls and four basketballs, two basketball hoops and 24 uniforms for football and 24 uniforms for basketball. (Uniforms, I think, are important here – and are simple – shorts and T-shirt.) Now I am on my way to the electronics store for the estimates on all the television and audio-visual material.   I am only getting about six hours sleep these days. Last night we didn't get back from Colmenar Viejo until almost 1 AM.

1:15 PM   So. In a bar in the Ventas barrio, near the bull ring. The waiter just came over, as I was thinking of leaving. For I only came in for a few minutes, as we are meeting at 1:30 in front of the parochial church, a block away. And I have been sitting here 7 or 8 minutes already. But I ordered a manzanilla tea. This is not the pace of this place: dash in and sit down for 15 minutes. This is a little place on a side street.   I think we are going to have lunch at Marta's house. Pepin has a wonderful way of orchestrating all the people to meetings and lunches and work without seeming to be too busy. But he has so much happening – the groups and classes in the neighborhoods, the farm, the preparation for the new school in Pan Bendito, his own university courses.

4:29 PM   On bus #143 – across the city – from the Plaza Manuel Becerra in Salamanca barrio all the way to Vallecas.   Here is a good photo – the space age television tower of Madrid rising futuristically behind an old red brick building, which looks like an 18th-century convent. The one more thing – no – two more things I have yet to do this afternoon is buy something for Carmen and Gonzalo, perhaps a plant, and pick up the estimate for the kitchen appliances. Ah – here we are passing a place I recognize: Hotel Colon, where there was a conference in 1988 on the European Community and I went there to get information on exchanges of youth groups between countries. Madrid is becoming a familiar city.

Madrid   Thursday, April 26, 11 AM
On the #10 bus through the narrow streets of Vallecas, on a cold and drizzly morning. I am again bound on

errands, the main one being to file the estimates of equipment needed for the school and a request for a grant with the city agency. Before that I must (naturally) make two copies of everything. The agency is next to

Through the narrow streets of Vallecas on a cold and drizzly morning

the Cortes Ingles department store and I will go there for little gifts for José Manuel's kids. We will meet José Manuel and Lola and the kids at Aranda del Duero on Saturday. The kids are the three boys, 10, 8 and 3, and the two girls (who must be about 17 and 19 now) from the poor family in Madrid, who José Manuel and Lola have adopted. José Manuel and Lola are committed Catholics and their charity comes in large part, I think, from their faith. They are very good people. I shall give up writing – it is a great effort to keep a steady hand, for I am sitting over the rear wheel of the bus and it is very bouncy.

11:10 AM   I have moved to the front of the bus, I

shall see if the ride is smoother up here. So. My time in Madrid now looks very short and I have much to do. I think I shall leave Madrid along about May 10 to go with Pepin to a conference in Denmark. From Denmark I shall go on to England. I have several tasks I want to do before I leave Madrid. One is to send in a Threshold grant application for the work here. Another is to prepare reports on the previous grants from Threshold and Tides. Another is to get Pepin's new computer operating and get word-processing software and get him connected to Greennet in England, and through that, to Peacenet in the US.

11:20 AM   The bus is now passing in front of the Prado and in a minute we will be at the end of line in Cibeles. I hope I am not getting a cold – this going to bed at 1 AM and rising at 7 AM is a wearing thing on the body.

1:27 PM   On the Metro – and suffering. The eternal question of the long underwear. You can't doff long underwear when the day turns warmer or you enter a heated building. That is one suffering. The other suffering is with the slings and arrows of outrageous officialdom. Not knowing the territory (or the language well), I erred when I went into the city offices. I showed the papers to the fellow who is the receptionist and he conducted me to the woman in charge of the matter. She leafed through the estimates and said: No, this won't do, and No, this won't do – and so on. She threw out all the carpentry estimates and furniture estimates because they were written on the back of large business cards instead of on printed letterheads. So I said, Well, can more estimates be submitted this afternoon? She: "We don't work in the afternoon, come back tomorrow." And I said, Well, can I get a stamp of receipt of what you will accept? She said something to the effect –

6:25 PM   Once again into the fray. I am now on
a bench waiting for the #10 bus. I will pick up the
estimates for the ceramics and the sports at the school.
–   What happened in my last entry was that I looked
up from my scribbling and saw that my Metro train was
stopped at Pacifica station (where I was going). So I
dashed out, paper and pen in hand. To continue my story:
She said that the stamping was done somewhere near the
elevators. I went back and the receptionist directed me
to an office of registration where they receive documents
and stamp your duplicate document to the effect that
they have received the original. That was all I had to do
in the first place – and if I had, I would not have been
bureaucracy-mangled. So it goes. It is very difficult to be
effective when you only have a six year old's command of
the language.

*Restaurante Biotika: filled at 1:40 PM with mad
foreigners who eat before 3 PM.*

Madrid   Friday, April 27, 11:06 AM
In the warmth of the middle-ing of the day – April day,
city-of-the-mountain day – I sit on the bench across from
the bushy park, waiting for the #10 bus. All about me are
cigarette

11:09 AM   On the bus.   What I started to write about
was cigarette smell. This is a highly addicted country.

11:12 The last few minutes I have been struggling with
my sweater. I guessed wrong on the day and I wear the
upper of my long underwear. So, off the sweater, off

the hat. Jump and jumble the bus – very hard to write, except when the bus is stopped. The little girl in the seat in front of me turns around and stares at me. Hola, she says. Hola, say I. ¿Que es? she says, pointing at the orange toothpick in my mouth. Nada, I say. She smiles, she thinks this is a funny answer.

Wow, warmer and warmer. I think I shall see if I can take off my long underwear in a bathroom at Atocha station. I am going to Atocha to check the train schedules back to Madrid from Aranda tomorrow. The buses leave at 4 PM and 8 PM. One too early and the next rather late. Maybe there is a train at 6 PM. Now the bus stops at Puente de Vallecas and we go up a grade. Before Puente de Vallecas, the road continually slopes down. So it is a place – the Puente – where I can imagine a valley and water flowing after the rains and an ancient bridge (puente). No more. The Puente now is a wracked jumble of autos and old buildings and highway, smoke and noise – gray-brown smoke and roaring, bombing, bellowing noise.

11:26 AM Now the bus climbs up another slope – up to the traffic roundabout near the end of Retiro Park – the roundabout circle is now planted in bright orange flowers, in the middle of the circle there is a fountain with three sculpted birds atop it. The wings of the birds move slowly up and down as if they are flying. It catches your eye the first time you see it.

12:16 PM On the Metro. After buying the bus tickets for tomorrow's trip to Aranda at the bus station at Palos de la Frontera. At Sol, I will walk up toward Gran Via to pick up the developed photos. I will look for a Caja de Madrid (bank) to get more money, and I will eat at

Biotika at 1:30.

12:27 PM   Waiting. In line at the main office of Caja de Madrid. Two women at the window are unwinding a life's time of finances and, so, us behind them are fidgeting and fussing. Here in Madrid I know a lot of little things as a result of being here so much and running about the way I do. For example, I know that behind an unmarked door in the lobby of this building, there are restrooms. So I shall go there and pee after getting money. Where to get money and where to pee – two important things to know.

1:44 PM   At the Biotika. The Biotika now has an erratic opening hour. They just opened a minute ago. Last time it was 1:30. And before that, I sat down at 1 PM, as I recall. So now, at 1:44, the place is instantly filled with mad foreigners who eat before 3 PM. The Spaniards have had their bocadillo at noon and will not eat for yet another hour perhaps.

I had thought of eating at another vegetarian restaurant – the one at the Plaza Marques de Santa Ana, but my errands took me to Puerta del Sol and so I walked here. Anxiously, quickly, so as to be here when they open at 1:30, for by 2 PM there is no place left in the restaurant. That habit of anxiously quickly has grown in me and I don't like it – I would like better the more tranquil way – being in each step, resting at each step, sensing the things about me. But. The things of the city are themselves so rapid, so anxious; there are not bright flowers and open green.

Ah, my salad.   A Japanese woman with a cello sits opposite me. She doesn't ask permission or acknowledge me. I think because in Japan sharing a table with a

Restaurante La Biotika

stranger is quite common in restaurants. The American sense of "my space" is much more expansive than the Japanese. I love this food. There is a small salad of lettuce and fine sticks of carrot. And a very good dark brown, rich soup – very tasty and I cannot further identify it. They certainly serve fast once you sit down. Zip Zap Zoup. Zip Zap Zalad.

I start meandering in my mind about the projects I would like to do here before I leave. Connect the farm with people here who know about organic farming. Help them start with beehives and honey. Get the computer working with a good word-processing program. Talk about having American students come here under a regular program and also help some American Hispanics attend the next seminar in the Fall. Zip Zap Zoooey. Though I don't feel too Zippy Zappy right now.

The fellow at the next table leaned over and asked: At what hour do the breads close? Or so I heard it. I said: The bread? The banks? He held up his hand, palm toward me, in the silent gesture of Stop, Go no further. His companion leaned over and asked at the further table. They received a short reply and were satisfied.

2:22 PM   I have finished my main plate of rice and chard and sort of a tofu pizza and pickled cabbage. I love this kind of food. Now a dessert. The waiter told me the four choices – the only one I recognized was manzana

2:47 PM   I didn't finish the last sentence – the finish is: manzana asada (baked apple). So. Now I am at one of my favorite Madrid places – the Cerveceria Alemana on the Plaza Santa Ana – an old-fashioned, very Spanish kind of place. I don't much associate with this kind of place in Madrid – it is a gracious-living kind of place – comfort and middle-class complacency. Not that it is very expensive – I just ordered a manzanilla (chamomile tea) and it cost maybe 300 pesetas – say $2.50. Although maybe that is expensive. But you are not buying the tea – you are buying the Cerveceria Alemana.

People are eating now at the tables, although many tables are occupied by people with only a glass or a cup of something before them. On the next table – all the tables are small and marble-topped – on the next table there are two platters of Arroz a la Cubana and two platters of something else. But no people are at that table. Now the waiter moves them to another empty table, and adds a couple more dishes and two bottles of beer. Well, well

– for whom it is all this colorful food? Ah, the mystery may be solved. *The waiter.* The waiter sits down at the table covered with food. And he digs into the Arroz a la Cubana. And next to him now sits another white-jacketed waiter. This is a great place – may it live and prosper forevermore.

I came here partly to consider my next move, so I pull from out my trousers pocket my little list of errands. I have gotten a railroad schedule from Aranda del Duero to Madrid. I have bought the bus tickets to Aranda, I have been to the bank, I have bought little books for the three boys of Jose Manuel and Lola. Now I want to buy little gifts for the two girls, pick up my developed film, mail a letter. The problem is that most places are closed until 4:30. The other thing I would like to do is to get estimates for the items (mostly furniture) for which the woman at the city agency found the previous estimates inadequate. Now, if I could write a sentence like the previous one *in Spanish,* I would be very proud of myself.

The idea that just occurred to me is that I could go over to Cortes Ingles, which is the biggest department store of Madrid, and ask them for estimates on the furniture. I wonder if they would do that? *They* are open now – they do not close during the midday – only mad dogs and stores named English and etc. I was thinking of going there anyway to get something for the girls – like handkerchiefs. Now – I am not being sexist, buying books for the boys and handkerchiefs for the girls. I really don't know the girls – I met them for the first time on my last visit. They are the two older girls from the family of the woman of Vallecas who threw herself in front of a train three years ago. Jose Manuel and Lola took them into their home and treat them as their own children. I don't

know if they like books. I can't think of anything else as
a very simple modest gift – more a recognition than a
material thing.

4:53 PM   In the photo shop – which is up a flight of
stairs on the street that runs from Gran Via to Puerta
del Sol. I paid for the developing of my photos (darned
expensive) and then I asked: Is there a store to make
photocopies nearby? Nosotros, he said – we do that. So
now I sit on the red velveteen bench in the reception
area and wait for my photocopies. This place is mostly, I
believe, a photographer's studio, run by the photographer
and his wife. This is about my fourth visit here – bringing
film in, picking photos up. There is a good photocopy shop
in the pedestrian walk under Plaza de Colon, but I am
beginning to feel weary and my plan is to walk to Cibeles
from here (or take a cab), mail a letter, and then take
the old red – the #10 bus – back to the piso (apartment).
A day in the city gets to be a weary-ing time.   I   am
beginning to get a little worried – this is taking rather
long – is he just xeroxing the pages I gave him or is he
doing some elaborate photo-copying? I am always on an
edge of uncertainty – that is a consequence of being in a
society and yet not knowing the ropes – the greenhorn
syndrome.

6:08 PM   On the #10. Homeward bound. Weary.
Standing here the last 20 minutes watching the traffic
go by was an astounding experience. There go three dark
blue cars flashing blue lights and sounding sirens – looks
like Mr. Mucketymuck is going to his important office.
Anyway. The cars going by with one person. One person
encased in metal, king of 100 cubic feet and miserable
captive of everything outside it. What a horror of a
system. The air, the noise, the aggravation of isolation.

Aranda del Duero picnic . . .
fat Spanish tortillas, green peppers fried in olive oil

Madrid   Saturday, April 28, 7:35 AM
On the #10. Early – 20 minutes ago, at the bus stop in
Vallecas, there were rose-colored clouds spread out on
the morning sky.

7:58 AM   In the bus station at Palos de la Frontera –
the Station of the South. But we are going North. So it
goes – life and bus stations have exceptions. The station
is littered, packed, infused and infested with people,
people, people. People standing, people sitting, people
talking: waves and murmurs and flows and ebbs of talk.
It is a puente (bridge) – that is what the Spanish call it
when there are midweek holidays and by taking a day
off you can create for yourself a bridge with the weekend.
Tuesday, May 1, is Labor Day and a national holiday.
Wednesday, May 2, is a holiday of Madrid only – to
celebrate the day the women of old Madrid threw boiling
oil on the soldiers of Napoleon. So. Take Monday off
and Voila! – un puente – 5 days in the pueblo, or at the
beach, or hiking. And all Madrid is up at 6 AM Saturday
morning and waiting for the 8:30 AM bus to Somewhere
Else. Me too.

It is the Consumer Society, says Pepin. Hey listen – there
would be no boiling oil in 1990 – las señoras are on the
beach at Torremolinos or visiting Aunt Juana in the
pueblo south of Sevilla. Napoleon is but a cake filled with
whipped cream – why, on the walk from Atocha to Palos
de la Frontera a few minutes ago, we passed no less than
a "croisanteria". There goes a young fellow equipped for
the Himalayas: backpack, sleeping bag, boots and etc.

8:27 AM   On the bus, seat #20 in the no fumar (no smoking) section. I have my fat little shoulder bag on the floor between my feet. It is too fat, I think, to fit into the overhead rack. No – no – never say die – the shoulder bag *does* fit and now it sits above in sur-real splendor and my feet are free. The motor is turned on, the bus backs up and backing, turns. We are deep in the bowels of the station. You go *down* from the lounge area to where the buses are. And now the bus goes up a tunnel-ramp. Daylight. But, oh, treacherous Madrid and its mountain weather! – in the 40 minutes we have been in the bus station, the sky has become clouded over.

Over a bridge – the river Manzanares, and down a ramp to M30, the belt highway around Madrid.   Away, away, past the red brick apartment buildings – solid, sedate, glum, under the pearl gray April morning sky. When I get down my shoulder bag in Aranda, I must look at my map of Madrid, for we just passed Puente de Vallecas on M30. That, I would think, puts us in a southward trajectory – but we are going North, on the road to Burgos. Now, we pass, on the right, the Plaza del Toros, which is in Ventas barrio. Emilio points out – something of the Arabs – a modern and expensive-looking white stone building being constructed on the left. What is it? I ask. Oh, a mesquita (mosque) or something, he says. So. Now there is more greenery alongside the road. We pass Piscina Club Stella, a curvilinear white building. We pass Pinar Chamartin (the names all come from Emilio) – and now we are on the highway to Burgos, he says.

The horizon to the north shows yellow-bright beneath the gray sky – so perhaps we shall outrun the gray clouds. Yes, I think so, for the yellow-bright band is broadening.

8:52 AM   The bus stops in Alcobenas. There are people waiting to board in front of Hostel El Fronton, which has a bright green awning over the entryway and ivy along the façade. It is exciting to be out on the road, going Somewhere Else in the morning, an April morning, under a pearl gray sky. Now there is no more city along the roadside – there are brown fields and new-grass-green fields, bare trees just now fuzzing out, greening out in April leaves. Along the right side, maybe 5 miles away, there is a line of blue gray hills, under the pearl gray sky. Now, overhead, the gray is broken into puffs and swirls – but beyond the puffs of darker gray, there is still gray – that is what gives the sky the pearly flavor – the translucent gray beyond gray. It is an expectant sky. Expecting sun or expecting rain.

9:01 AM – says a lighted display on a concrete column in front of a building beside the road. Now, the line of hills has come closer and turned greener. Although it still is behind a transparent blue haze. That is the mysterious quality of the morning – the light blue ground haze and the pearl gray sky – we swim through them to the North.

We pass a turreted building with a sign, Monte Viejo – I have a recollection, I think, of that building. From 1984, when we went weekends from Madrid to the summer encampment of children in the Sierra Guadarama. That was a different set of people. Every time I come to Madrid there is a different set of people. The volunteer work with Pepin is difficult and people do it for a few years and then drop away. Now, overhead, there is a flying wedge of blue sky striking into the gray. And beyond the blue, north of the blue, is a hazed, stippled, white sky. Now the Sierra looms gray black ahead of us. There is snow on the Sierra, says Emilio, and soon we will pass Cerezo de Abajo. That is the village we visited in the Winter of 1987, when the snow was on the ground, to see whether we could start a farm there. We talked with people of the village council.

Oh, a gray sun is coming out. If the sun does come out, it will be full on this side of the bus and it will be very warm. Myself – I prefer the pearl gray sky. But the sun grows stronger and whiter and now the hot light is on my right ear and on this page. But it is only the blue wedge – the sun has reached the blue wedge. When the white haze that is beyond the blue wedge reaches the sun, we will once again ride in shadowed splendor. But now, it is warm. I take off my blue sweater – my trusty blue sweater – once, a few long months ago, it was new. Since March 15, it has lived three or four sweater lives, and now, it is a weary and a hearty veteran of a sweater. I ask Emilio for my gray felt hat, which is up in the rack. And I perch it over my right ear, against the hot sunlight.

I suddenly feel uncomfortable, hot, tired and I smell the cigarette smoke that comes from the back of the bus. My eyes begin to water – from bright light and acid smoke. Now there are rocky sharp ridges along the road. The road is climbing into the Sierra.   Two rows ahead, I see a reddened bald head, gray yellow hairs straggling, struggling over it. It is a weary head, a juiceless head. And the acid cigarette smoke burns my throat. These transient things – do they create the weariness?   Or does my weariness create them? I mean – create them in the sense of giving them importance, noticing them? It goes both ways, I suppose. But I give first place to the transient things. But – there are all sorts of transient things. There is the fresh delicate green of the new leaves on trees along the road, that very appealing delicate yellow green of Spring. There is the blue black apparition of the Sierra. There is a sprinkling of yellow mustard flowers. There is the great sun itself, which is not a malignant thing but the very source of life.

The bus slows. We are in a village. Here is a roadside inn named Madrid-Paris.   So. Yes – the sun has two aspects. It is the life-giver. And it is the destroyer. The Indian idea. I would like to study that more. The same force as life-giving and destroying. Life and Death. Change. It is all change. Life itself is change – that is its essence. So, being change, it is also death, which is a more noticeable form of change. Although death is happening all the time – even in the body. It is important to be consonant with reality. Perhaps the biggest source of dis-consonance with reality is resistance to change. This resistance comes from fault of security, fear, ignorance. There has to be that feeling of being part of it all, being accepted, belonging, security, before one can enter into the dance.

The bus now climbs through a mountain village. The buildings right on the road are rather rag-tag. But, beyond, down a ridge, there is a pleasing presentation of red tile roofs and a church tower. Now we pass a shallow green valley with grazing white cows. The cigarette smoke, the smell of cigarette smoke, jars against the sight of the lively life-full green grass. We pass Somosierra – this is la puerta – the summit. The road now winds downward. It is 9:30 AM, the bus goes down slowly at first, behind a motorcyclist, then passes the motorcyclist and picks up speed.

Now – this sheet of paper, # 95, is the first of a pad of writing paper I bought the other day in a papeleria in Madrid. I have now used up all the paper I brought with me from California. I cough. The cigarette smoke is awful. Smoking in Spain is terribly rampant and the rights of non-smokers are but little acknowledged. Strange – how malleable humans are. People can be convinced that they are somehow glamorous smoking. Ah, Cerezo de Abajo – we just passed through it. I didn't see any of the places we were, in 1987. Or was it 1986? So. How would it be if we legalized heroin and made tobacco a crime?

11:14 AM   Aranda del Duero

Sitting on the wall that goes about the new bus station, a lively breeze catches this page and rustles the plastic bag in which lie the two round breads. Celso and Emilio just walked to a nearby panaderia and bought the bread. We are standing outside the station waiting for José Manuel to come by in his car. He and his family are coming by car from Bilbao. Traveling to Aranda is not too difficult, for it is but some two hours from both Madrid and Bilbao and one does not have to enter into the streets of a large city. On the other hand, driving from Madrid to Bilbao is a long journey – over four hours and not a excursion for one day. So – this meeting in Aranda makes much sense. We will all go to a park and have lunch together. My hands are becoming cold – I shall dig my gloves from my bag.

11:37 AM   Still waiting, on the wall. The wall is not what you might imagine: high and formed of ancient stone. No. This is a brand-new bus station, built on empty ground toward the outskirts of town. The wall is concrete to about one meter high and then it rises in steel bars another 2 meters. The unfortunate aspect of this new wall is that the concrete is some 18 inches wide, which would make for a comfortable seat, but the iron bars are set so that only 6 to 8 inches are available to sit on. So I am perched rather than seated on this wall. And now, as the breeze dies away and the sun comes stronger, I begin to feel warm. Just 10 minutes ago I stood here on this rather deserted stretch of street and took off windbreaker, muffler, sweater and shirt and put on the upper of my long underwear.

7:12 PM   Aranda del Duero

Sitting in the bus station, waiting for the 8 PM bus to Madrid. It has been a pleasant day. José Manuel and his family came by the bus station about 11:40. He also had in his auto two nuns from Bilbao who were going to hitchhike the rest of the way to Madrid. They are unusual nuns – they live in a small group in an ordinary apartment in a poor section of Bilbao and they hold menial jobs – doing housecleaning or such things. And they work with the people of the neighborhood – being of help, babysitting or whatever. José Manuel drove his family and the nuns to a roadside restaurant outside of town and then came back for us. At the restaurant, the nuns left to stand on the highway asking for a ride, and the rest of us walked to a grassy area behind the restaurant and sat on the ground and talked for a couple hours.

Then we went back to the car and got out the big canvas bag of food we brought from Madrid – that Celso had spent all afternoon yesterday cooking: cold meat cutlets and big fat Spanish tortillas (tortillas in Spain are thick omelettes and a Spanish tortilla has lots of thin sliced potatoes and onion inside) and green peppers fried in olive oil. And two big rounds of bread bought in Aranda plus the one half of a round loaf of pan integral (organic dark bread) that I bought yesterday. I went into the restaurant (which has a market attached) and bought three liter bottles of water. So we had a very good lunch. After lunch and the exchange of little gifts we all went into the restaurant and had coffee or tea.

Then we walked back of the restaurant and past a vineyard, across a strip of plowed and planted land, to an island of trees in the middle of the planted field. There we sat on the grass under the trees and talked some more, until about 5:30 when we saw a tractor at the far end of the field spraying something on the land. We walked back to the car, said goodbye to Lola and the three boys, and José Manuel drove us to the bus station.

We walked into town, looked at the ancient church, which has an interesting facade, walked about the center and then, it being past six and there being general agreement that we were hungry, we walked down to the river bank (of the River Duero, which is a wide muddy stream going through the city). There, under the trees and on the grass and watching the ducks paddling in the river, we opened up the canvas bag again and ate again of the tortilla and green peppers and cutlets – and fruit – I forgot to mention the bananas and apples and oranges. Then we walked back to the station – the bag a good deal lighter. Rested and refreshed – a good day, a good break from the tension and pollution of Madrid.

Now we will arrive back in Madrid about 10:15, then take the city bus and get to the apartment about 10:45. To bed and early tomorrow morning take a bus in another direction – east to the farm.

7:44 PM   We have transferred ourselves to a bench outside, where the buses are parked, from the bench inside. I see flatness. The tiled sidewalk is flat, the asphalt where the buses are is flat, the fence around the station has a horizontal bar at the top, the buses are square and flat on top, the countryside beyond the fence goes on without a rise or a ripple.

7:49 PM   Now we are standing near the bus, waiting for the door to open. Pepin and Celso are doing a crossword puzzle, they have been working on it all the time we have been waiting in the station. I think one purpose of this whole trip, on the part of Pepin, is to give Celso a rest and a break. Celso has been under a lot of stress, for his wife has been in and out of the hospital. She has a problem with varicose veins, I think, and cannot walk and there is some problem that seems to need clearing up before the doctors will operate. Also, his son, Javi, has been in the hospital for the last week with a diagnosis of pneumonia. Since Javi was a heroin addict until three years ago, one thinks about AIDS – but he has been tested and is negative for AIDS. I think. Anyway – it is all worrisome.

8:02 PM   The bus backs, turns and heads out.
  Ai Ai Ai – not so lucky this time – this bus has a TV set and it is on. It will be a noisy ride, I fear. Other un-luck: the sun, going lower in the sky, is going to be full against this side. But. It is an attenuated sun. It is, again, a pearly sky – half pale pearl, half pale blue. Green fields, brown fields. And sharp, irritating, selling voices from out the television set. Suddenly, the TV goes from loud to louder. A movie is starting – a bad, grade F, Spanish movie. Now, we pass the roadside restaurant and the grove of trees we sat under this afternoon. Oh, now the sun is coming forth, shining forth, blasting fiery rays horizontally across the earth and right through the

bus – little heat, but much light. I am sitting in seat #8, which is in the second row. I look out the window – the countryside, bright green grass and reddish soil in rolling hills, glows and reluces and refulges in the evening sunlight – a glorious vision for a passing moment. This is a new four lane highway here – cut slopes, sweeping curves, black black and white white. There is a flock of white sheep crowded together not far off the highway.

8:21 PM Now the sun has disappeared behind the pearl gray – I doubt that we will see it again on this trip. And, at almost the same time, the four lane, brand new, road ends and we are on the old two lane road to Madrid. I look up, every now and again, at the TV screen – I don't understand 80% of it. I shall glance at today's El Pais before the daylight disappears.

A day at El Colmenar . . . hoeing weeds
from rows of garlic plants.

Madrid Sunday, April 29, 7:22 AM
Out again in the dawning hour. In the #54 bus going down Avenida de la Albufera to the Puente or Pacifica – where I assume we will walk the rest of the way to Plaza Conde de Casal, to board the 8 AM bus to Cuenca for the 2 ½ hour trip to the farm. I woke reluctantly at 6 AM on hearing sounds of activity in the kitchen. For I went to bed along about 11 last night shortly after we arrived back from the trip to Aranda. I feel rather weary this morning – this dim, clouded over, half-night morning. Besides the lack of sleep, I have had a nagging cough for the past five or six days – something down in the respiratory passages is

7:46 AM   In the bus station – bus stations are crossroads in Spain – here again at this early Sunday hour, this station, like yesterday's station, is awash with early morning people going Somewhere Else.
What I was saying above, when Emilio nudged me

7:52 AM   On the bus – as I was saying – when he nudged me that we were about to arrive at Pacifica and I had to stop writing and rise. So: something down in the respiratory passages is awry. Sometimes I think it is post-nasal drip – other times I think it is lung cancer or throat cancer. The cancer hypothesis comes up at 11:30, just as I am falling asleep; in the morning, waking in morning air, it appears as a post-nasal drip. How do you like that phrase: post-nasal drip? A medical mish-mash term. Meaning "after your nose is gone, there is a drip"? Or "beyond the nosalities, deeper than the nosalities, back of the nose"?   Who knows?

Emilio has seen a girl who is boarding. I suppose it is someone going to the farm, but I don't recognize her – if it is the person I first saw when he first said something. He also said, a couple times, it is going to rain.   Ai Ai – there is an awful burst of noise – the torture begins. Why? Why? Why? Who wants it? Who needs it? What is wrong with silence? I hate and I shall hate until the furthest reaches of consciousness this infernal racket which is a near-inevitable part of a long distance bus ride in Spain. At least, here, the driver turned down the volume from its first lunatic level. Yes, as I was saying – Rain. I didn't bring my rain hat, my waterproof jacket. These are the little things that give me a sense of security. Like the long underwear – they are like money in the bank – against the rainy day, the cold day.

Just before, when I wrote about the loud music, I came into a reverie as I looked out the window at the great blocks of new red brick apartment buildings passing by and the mounds of earth – little constructed hills – at the side of the highway, planted to grass and trees. I thought: I may be too old to feel easy with the strange customs of a strange land. I thought of Agnes, the German woman who has lived here in Madrid for many years. How does she feel? Does she feel easy? How about my parents coming to America? But then, America is a different land – many people, many cultures. At least then – in the early 1900s. I am not sure if the impact is that much less. But I thought of something else in my reverie. Which I cannot now remember – it is like a disappeared dream.

Ah – Emilio taps me on the shoulder. He says, Las cigueñas. ¿Que? I said. For he was pointing in the direction of a field of tall radio antennae. There, he said, in the small tree, they come every year, they are young ones. So, I think it is a pair of nesting birds. Storks? Swans? I will look up "cigueñas" when I find a dictionary.

Oh, that reminds me. Many years ago – or maybe it was only two days ago, on Friday – I wrote about the Japanese girl who sat opposite me at the vegetarian restaurant Biotika. Oh – there is an odious odious loud mindless pow pow pow piece on the loudspeaker and the cigarette smoke drifts up from the back of the bus. I feel utterly intolerant of these two things right now.

Anyway, the Japanese girl was American; she said "my parents live in Los Angeles" when I asked where she was from, implying that she has left Los Angeles. And her instrument, which she carried in a red plaid fabric case, was, I believe, a guitar rather than a cello. She said she was leaving that night for Geneva and that the instrument kept her company. Her talk thus hinted at a minstrel's life, although she looked quite the middle-class child.

Well. I am long way from my reverie, just as the bus is now a long way from Madrid's red brick apartments. It is 8:29 AM and the insides of the windows are becoming fogged over with moisture. I rub the window beside me with the back of my hand to make a little clear porthole for me to look out of. I am feeling rather glum and gripe-y this morning. I would like to be home in bed in Santa Cruz with the heat on and reading a book. I yearn for creature comfort, ease and softness. This is a tough life, here in this corner, in this cultural corner, of Spain.

The bus moves slowly, cautiously, from one set of highway lanes to another. This whole road to Valencia is being re-constructed into a four lane divided road. Now (8:41 AM) the bus turns off the highway and goes down a small road and into Villarejo – a village with an ancient castle tower off the main plaza. Works are in progress in Villarejo – sidewalks and a new stone pavement for the plaza, and white concrete benches and a stone terrace before the castle tower. Spain is everywhere building and beautifying – entering Europe and rich country status in a concrete and stone kind of way. I cough again. I don't like the feel or the sound of this cough. It comes up through, chortles through, the phlegm.

9:26 AM   Tarancon

The bus stopped here, the driver said 10 minutes. Anyway – I met the three girls – who are with us on the bus. They are university students coming out for the day to the farm to help. They are lively and fresh. I feel good

watching them. So I feel better. Did I see sun? Yes —
now there is a bright spot behind the gray. The sun
is there — at least we know that. Before, the sky was
massed gray, dark and light, but the sun was excluded
and occluded. It seemed colder standing outside the bus
in Tarancon then it did in the streets of Madrid: this
countryside is colder than Madrid.

The day rises, the sun rises, the year proceeds, the
grass is green. A vast flotilla of dark gray across the sky
to the South. The sun is on the edge of the flotilla. The
flotilla has something of the shape of all Europe; the
sun is somewhere around Norway. The bus curves along
the highway and suddenly I am looking at the grayness
beyond Siberia. Another curve and again I face the
Atlantic coast, but the sun-bright spot has disappeared
into northern France. And so it goes: bus, road, cloud and
sun.

Here is a very neat grove of pine trees on a slope a little
away from the road. The bottom branches have been
trimmed away so that I see the dark trunks and then a
round umbrella-like canopy of green above. Now the
bright-sun spot is out over the light gray Atlantic. It may
not rain today.

The road rounds a curve. This is my favorite place on the
road – where there is a short tunnel cut into a rocky spur
and a little river valley alongside, with the railroad to
Madrid on the other side of the little valley. We are now
about 15 minutes, I think, from Carrascosa. The movie
on the TV monitor at the front of the bus is about the
Spanish in Peru in colonial times.

9:49 AM   The bus pulls off the highway into the

pueblo of Alcazar del Rey. This is the last stop before Carrascosa.

3:09 PM   El Colmenar

After dinner. Sitting in the living room. The name "living room" is not quite right for this square, brown tile floor room with old couches along two of the walls. I feel fairly tired since I have led a hard and peasant life all morning since arriving. I did a couple hours of hoeing weeds from the rows of garlic plants. And then I did about an hour and a half of planting potatoes. Hey, hard work. For both of these tasks I used a short-handled hoe – which you use while bent over. I think this hoe has been banned from commercial use in California because it is so hard on the worker. Planting the potatoes, we first set the little seed potatoes on top of the ridges that had been hoed up. Then we went along with the short hoes, pulled the ridge forward to leave a space in back, dropped in the little potatoes and then tamped down the earth on top.

10 PM   Madrid

And so to bed. The earliest I've gone to bed since being in Europe, I think. I have lots of sleep to catch up on. Emilio and I and Celso came back to Madrid in the car of the brother of one of the fellows at the farm. It was off to the races all the way. I worried a bit at the beginning but I decided there was nothing I could do, so I dozed off most of the way. Emilio, who was sitting in front, said the speed was up to 150 at times – that's 90 mph.

At the corner of Calle Amor de Dios and
Calle de Santa Maria

Madrid   Monday, April 30, 11:01 AM
So. Monday in the Metro. Line #1, departing from
Portazgo. Me seated – a rare privilege for the Metro
rider. Feeling rather tired even after nine hours of
sleep. That potato planting is hard work. Right now – on
Monday morning, the Monday morning of the puente,
when one half of Madrid is off on a mini-vacation – I am
going to a bee store, Moderna Apicultura, on Calle Doctor
Esquardo, 47.

11:08 AM   Now I am waiting for the other subway train
at Pacifico – this is Line 6, the newest and deepest line –
it goes underneath all the others.

11:10 AM   I got a seat again. How lucky I am –
probably it is because of the puente, only mad dogs and
foreigners are in Madrid today – a great exaggeration but
many Madrileños are gone. I only go three stations on
this line so I must not fall into inconscient scribbling. So.
After I go to the bee store, my next definite appointment
for the day is to meet Emilio at Restaurante Biotika at
1:45.

12:12 PM   So. I went to the bee store. There are no
hives right now. It will be 15 to 20 days before they have
hives. Now I sit in a small bar-café around the corner.
I have fixed up pages 27 to 40 to mail and off they will
go this afternoon. After lunch, I think I shall go to a
computer store and find out about software for writing.
The question is whether the stores will be open today –
and, if open, will they be open before 5 PM?

12:42 PM   The Metro. Going to Cibeles to mail letters and then I will walk to Calle Amor de Dios. I am feeling pressed now to do all that I want to do before I leave. I just stopped at a travel office and asked about flights to London. The regular flights are about $350 and the charters are about $170. There is now a fellow who has walked on the train playing a guitar and a harmonica at the same time and singing loudly. How does he do that? Don't know. Maybe not a harmonica. And then goes about with a cup jingling with coins.

1:39 PM   I find I don't say much in this snitch-snatch kind of writing – usually no more than where I am and where I am going. Right now I am standing on the corner. The corner of Calle Amor de Dios and Calle de Santa Maria. I am leaning against the corner of the Biotika restaurant building and I am waiting for Emilio. We are to meet here at 1:45. The day is warm. For Warmth has, at long last, come to Madrid. Not hot, just pleasant. When I sit down, I shall take off my sweater. The sidewalks here, in this ancient part of the city, are so narrow that I, leaning against the corner with my shoulder bag held between my feet, block half the sidewalk.

4:03 PM   A bar near Atoche station. This is a modern bar – all the style and all the furnishings right out of The Modern Bar Magazine, sold by a salesman from Modern Bar, Inc. It is sort of a McDonald's version of a Spanish bar, and Frank Sinatra sings over the loudspeaker. I am waiting for 4:30 to arrive and the computer store, on a nearby narrow dog-shit-spattered street, to open. The street and the computer store are a surprising pair, but this is a serious kind of computer store – not a splashy flashy kind of place. Rather more an industrial kind of place. I was in there last Monday to pick up the keyboard and operating manuals for Pepin's new computer. Now I want to inquire about the software for word-processing. I don't know why I don't say writing instead of word-processing. Maybe writing can't be done by computers. What is the difference between writing and word processing? Writing is an intellectual – Oops – process. Word-processing is a word processing process. What is a process? A process is a thing. What is a thing? A thing is what comes out of a process. Next question?

Emilio said it is going to rain. He said that when we came out of the restaurant. The weather had changed while we were eating – gotten colder and the sky had clouded over. Emilio was quite serious over lunch. He talked of Celso. Celso is having a difficult time now. Emilio said something about Celso's wife. I think it was something more than that she has trouble with her leg and must be operated. But I didn't understand exactly what he said. Celso's grandchild, a baby, died about six months ago – the poor baby choked on some food. Pepin was talking about it to José Manuel and Lola last Saturday and he said that Celso's wife had been very depressed. I think he said something about her having been present and giving the child the food, but I am not sure. It is difficult for me to pester people for clarification when they are talking about difficult things.

My, the sky looks awfully threatening – lead gray. Maybe it is due to the windows of The Modern Bar.

And, of course, Celso has the worry about Javi, who is still in the hospital and who ran a high fever yesterday. The doctors don't seem to know exactly what he has or how to deal with it. That's what I understand from what

Celso says. Yesterday, at the farm, Pepin said he felt
Celso was in much better spirits as a result of the restful
day on Saturday. But then the bad news of the high fever
has been depressing for him.

And then, Emilio also talked at lunch about himself and
the work. He said he was content, he didn't want money
– so long as he had food to eat and a minimum of other
needs met; he had the love of many people and he loved
them; he was helping the boys at the farm. Everyone has
problems, that is life, but things were going forward and
it was necessary to go forward. When someone left and
went back to drugs, he felt great pain, but it is necessary
to go forward. Like when someone dies, one must ir
adelante – go forward. Emilio is feeling hurt, I think,
because his children have not kept in contact with him,
especially his daughter Marisol. He is going to see his
sister this afternoon. I will probably be back late, he said,
I will probably have supper at the house of my sister;
don't wait for me for supper.

So. It is now 4:33. I will pay for my manzanilla and walk
up to the computer store.

10:32 PM   And so to bed. I came back to the apartment
about 6 PM, went out later to buy some photo albums,
had a little supper and spend a couple hours putting my
recent photos into the albums so I can show them at the
farm tomorrow.

Unlike English, which is like the air I breathe,
I must work to understand Spanish.

Madrid   Tuesday, May 1, 9:34 AM
The Ides of May – or the Oops of May – but May. And
what is May? May is a gray sky and a coolness of air. I
am in a bus station. Again. The bus to Cuenca and I will
get off at Carrascosa and so to the farm. This will be the
10 AM bus that Emilio and I will take. This morning I
have in mind to conserve my strength, for I had a sore
throat during the night and I may have a cold coming
on. The question is: Can I rest while in motion? Today,
the First of May, is a national holiday in Spain. The
lead headline in this morning El Pais is that 85% of the
gasoline stations in the country are going on a week's
strike, starting tonight at 10 PM. As we rode the bus
down Avenida de la Albufera in Vallecas a half hour ago,
we saw that there was a block-long line of cars waiting to
get gas at the station near Puente de Vallecas.

I look down at the floor here, which is made of large off-
white tiles, and in the tiles I see the reflection of the
images coming through the glass doors that lead out to
the bus yard. I see that the reflection of the door posts
is offset a bit from tile to tile – it jumps a bit to one side
as it comes to another tile, then with the following tile it
jumps back into line with the last tile but one. Now, why?
Maybe the plane of each tile is a little different.

There is the call for our bus – although there is yet 13
minutes to 10 AM. Emilio seems unperturbed. He is
sitting in the next seat reading El Pais. Of course, he is
something of a commuter between Madrid and the farm,
and has the commuter's savoir faire and grasp of the
nuances of the travel. So he is resting while in motion.

When walking up to this bus station – a distance of the some five or six blocks

9:55 AM   On the bus. We sit in the two seats immediately behind the rear entrance. I fear it is in the smoking section. But. I have a defense against the second bane of my bus-traveling life. I bought a packet of Kleenex tissues, which I will use to stuff my ears. One problem of these seats is that there is not as much leg room since there is a metal panel between the seat and the door area. The door is cleverly done; it is all below the window level – one descends steeply from the aisle, but it works and it is convenient to have a rear door. I think these buses are Mercedes. Oh Lord, will you give me a Mercedes bus, my friends all fly by air and I must make amends.

Anyway – what I was saying when Emilio said Let's go (Vamanos) was that when walking the five or six blocks from where we got off the city bus to this station, I was oppressed by Madrid. The stained sidewalks, the iron bind of concrete and brick, the mechanism of cars and buses. I was (we are starting, so it becomes harder to keep my writing steady) I was also thinking of something similar when we were on the city bus. Wall scribbling and subway and bus scribbling – a la New York – is becoming very apparent in Madrid. And I thought: Why? To see your name or emblem on a wall? – to say this is me, this is me different from all the others? What is the purpose of it all? Life, human life. Why to live? To go about with the sun and get something to eat.

Oh sheeeeeet – I am in the smoking section. The smell of cigarette smoke is a very ugly thing. These poor creatures who afflict themselves with this. It is so destructive. It is like the city with its dirty sidewalks, relentless buildings and gasoline air. It is walking away from Being. Where is the Pure Land? That is what I want. Don't other people also yearn for the Pure Land?

Ah, we pull up at the side of the road and the conductor gets out. Emilio nudges me and points out – the storks – I look, and yes, there are two storks in the big nest on the little tree right beside this busy highway. Golly, if I were a stork, I would settle in a more tranquil place. The nest is on the edge of an industrial area, where new factories are on both sides of the road. Emilio says, in answer to my question, that this place is called Gargantua. At least that's what it sounded like to me and will suffice until I see the name written. The television has now started, but so far the noise level is below the pain threshold.

I am conscious of my mild continuing sore throat. My sense is that I am on the edge of a week of illness, balancing precariously. I am actually looking forward to leaving in about two weeks – it is a very demanding life here, and I am – what? A sheltered plant? An ornamental flower? A hothouse vegetable? In other words, I have grown accustomed to a rather easy and sheltered life. I am also on the cusp of 60. But look at Celso – 68 years old and he works so hard and gives so much.

Well. We pass the strangely un–together looking restaurant off the road where the road begins a long descent. The places along the road are becoming familiar to me. And there, below the road, crowding into a tunnel underneath the road is a great flock of white sheep. So. Let's see. Can I pick up the thread of my previous thoughts? Something about the natural rhythm of life being so disturbed in our present-day industrial society. Where do we find meaning among the iron rhythms of the machines? There is an olive grove – the little trees have a beautiful gray-green sheen, reaching almost to white in the highest leaves that reach up to the sky.

11:14 AM Tarancon

No. The bus is not a Mercedes, but a Setra? – is that the name? These buses are far better than poor, tired, huddled, Greyhound. In <u>public</u> goods, the US of A is a <u>poor</u> country. My, my – I feel a delicate creature this morning – Ralph with a sore throat, heading for the potato planting mines. Lift that hoe, and dig that furrow, get no rest till the Judgment Day. I don't even have a note from the Doctor saying "please excuse Ralph from potato planting today". Maybe I can pretend to be totally taken up with intellectual labors. Furrow that brow and lift that pen, Jewish folk work while the Goyim play. I hesitated before writing the last sentence – which is something to contemplate.

As we pull out of the bus station, I notice the little improvements in Tarancon, like the stylish white concrete benches on the street. Earlier, when we were coming into town, I saw the modern statue of a family in bronze on a white stone pedestal, and the rebuilt little plaza with benches and neatly cared for ornamental trees. I like this kind of thing – it is community and a taking-care-of-things. Aaaarg, more cigarette smoke from somewhere behind. The sun now comes from behind the gray clouds and there are yellow-green sun-lit patches across the green fields. I see the sign Barajas del Melo – A village somewhere off the highway. I feel I pass a fixed way here – there is not time or space or mechanism to explore the by-ways. When I am in Spain, I am very much involved in the work.

11:33 AM   I like the pace of this bus, it proceeds steadily, stolidly, sturdily along the highway without derring-do swoops and swipes. I think it comes from the character of the driver. So many Spanish drivers drive as if they are competing in races. We had an extraordinary – and dangerous – ride to Madrid last Sunday evening.
The darkness over this page signified the bus was passing through the little tunnel through the rocky spur – a picturesque spot on the road.

5:32 PM   El Colmenar
I looked at the last sentence I wrote just above and I was a little surprised. I left myself way back there on the road. I think I mix this letter a bit with what passes in my mind. This morning on the bus seems a long way off. Not because so much has happened, because for me it has not seemed too active a day. I have been rather hiding out because I feel like being quiet and taking care of myself. There are 30 active people about and I feel awkwardly separate right now.

There was just a meeting here in the classroom – where I sit on the brown couch in the far corner and the four others who remain in the room are at the fireplace at the opposite corner. The meeting lasted an hour and a half. It started as a review of the conference of a couple weeks ago. Pepin and people in the Collective and people living here talked of what they felt about the conference. I felt very sleepy, tried to look alert but lost concentration every few minutes. In any event, I didn't understand much of it. When I am tired, it is very hard for me to follow Spanish. For, unlike English, which is like the air I breathe, I must work to understand Spanish. In fact, the person I most like to be about today – and I am just reminded of this because he just walked in the door – is José Luis, the "retarded" man. He always has a rather sweet, childish expression (although he complains a lot, but not in a whining way – just in a curmudgeonly way) and I feel I don't have to strain to make sense with him. Maybe I feel that he won't be judging me.

Madres on a walk near La Granja

So. There are some ten university students here today. One of them, during the afternoon meeting, said something about his religious feeling and Pepin said something about his (Pepin's) relation to religion. He said something about having his hopes for justice and a better way of living, and that what he does, he believes in and he lives. (I hesitate to write more in report of what he said, for I fear I am misreporting it – which goes to poor understanding in the first place and loss in remembrance in the second.) He said he had studied philosophy and had worried a lot about religion and philosophy, but now he doesn't. He respects the beliefs of each person.

So. So. I feel I am a very un-Spanish and isolated type now. The Spanish value <u>warmth</u> a great deal – at least the Castillanos. The Castillanos consider themselves quite a different people from the Catalans and from the Basques. Yesterday at lunch, Emilio was telling me that he felt that the atmosphere at the farm was much better now because all the young men here now are Castillanos. Before, there were several Basques, who had come through José Manuel and his group in Bilbao. They were a group, separate, he said. And that is a view I have heard a number of times – the Catalans, the Basques, are much more for themselves – they don't have the giving quality of the Castillanos. I haven't had the same contact with Catalans and Basques to learn what they say of Castillanos.

So. Before the meeting there was dinner and after dinner Pepin and Celso took me on a little walk to see the little almond tree seedlings.   Marta is leaving – her car is right beyond the far wall and several of the fellows have gone out in the continuing light rain –   Right here, Gabriel, one of the young fellows who has learned a number of English words, sits on the arm of the couch and looks at this page and points out the words he knows.   So – as I was saying – they went out into the rain to see her off and to sing Que se vaya, que se vaya, which means: I hope she leaves, I hope she leaves – this is often a derisive refrain to the parting song which says, Don't go, you can't go, etc. etc. I was just thinking that we don't get the flavor of the country from immigrants to the US. The old country flavor is diluted and depreciated –

but here it comes through with great charm. Same with France – though I don't know France as well.

Celso, Pepin and Emilio on the upper field of La Granja

Anyway, as I was saying, we went out to look at the 5000 almonds seedlings. The ground around them was beautifully neat – all the weeds have been taken out and rocks and pebbles picked away. Pepin always has these tasks to do and I imagine that the whole group worked at it yesterday.

Before dinner there was a major crisis which I know caused Pepin and Celso and Emilio considerable pain. Sito, who had lived here for over a year and is now 17 and living in Madrid in an apartment with two other fellows who "graduated" from the farm, and is going to a special school to get his high school certificate and is a bright young fellow, has been being a bit irresponsible: going back to his old neighborhood to hang out with his old buddies and dressing in a kind of punkish way. Pepin feels he is still too immature to be on his own this way and proposed that he live the next year at the farm and take the bus each morning to Tarancon to continue his studies. Sito refused and I think he is leaving the program.

That was just before lunch. Now I feel apprehensive about writing this lest Gabriel should come back to look over my shoulder – for he is Sito's brother, and he is able to recognize names from the page.

So. After that (the Sito event, which I was not at) we held a little meeting to talk about a Threshold grant application, but they were all too upset to really function well on that subject. And before that, I was rather hiding out (from myself mainly) – not wanting to go down and join the potato planters. For, after all, I do feel sick and I am trying to take care of myself. And going further backward in time, for this is the day's story backward told, when we arrived on the bus in Carrascosa, the Land Rover from the farm was not there. So first we went into the bar (the second bar, the people of the farm never go to the first bar, which is on the corner – I asked Emilio why today and he said: They are very serious there). In the bar, Emilio bought me a manzanilla tea. (Earlier, when the bus stopped in Tarancon, we went to the station bar and Emilio ordered a coffee for himself and a manzanilla for me, but the hot water machine or something didn't work and I never got my manzanilla and Emilio was embarrassed.)

Incidentally, it is an unwritten rule of the Collective people that no one ever pays for himself – someone always pays for the whole group – even if it is 10 people having lunch. The group pays – not the individual.

After I finished my manzanilla – Emilio had nothing, because he didn't want another coffee. (I told him at the bar in Tarancon: If I drink a coffee I will not sleep Friday (today being Tuesday). Yes, he said, I do not drink coffee at night– when I was young, yes.) After I finished my manzanilla, we began walking. We walked out of town, past the construction materials company and past the cemetery and out another kilometer along the road. I saw little purple flowers along the roadside that I had not noticed before; we passed a man walking in the opposite direction who nodded and said Buenas Dias. Then the Land Rover came over a little hill and we got in and drove back into Carrascosa and to the gasoline station on the further side of the pueblo. There, Celso and Paco filled four big plastic containers with diesel (which they call gasoil). They were afraid they might run out of fuel for the diesel electric generator and the tractor during the coming week of gasoline station strike (huelga). The young man at the station said that his station was not going to close, but I think he said they would close if there were pickets.

7:02 PM   Ai, I just broke training. One of the kids started to take plants inside – all the indoor potted plants were sitting outside soaking in the light rain. So I said ¿Necesita ayuda? and went out into the cold rain to carry in plants. I fear I shall be sick for a week. We shall see.

7:10 PM   I have moved over to the living room. The video of the conference is to be shown. What I want to see is the Saturday night show. I saw most of the other part of it and it wasn't that interesting.

9:09 PM   I saw the video of the Saturday night program of the conference. The last part, the play put on by the fellows living here, is very moving. At the end they sing two songs. One is a song that was sung against the dictatorship of Franco.

The refrain is:

Habra un dia en que todos	There will be a day in which we all
Al levantar la vista	On lifting up our eyes
Veremos una tierra	Will see a land
Que ponga Libertad!	That is put in Liberty!

The other song is from Beethoven's ninth symphony.

Cancion de la Alegria

Eschucha, hermano, la cancion de la alegria,
el canto alegre del que espera un nuevo dia.
Ven, canto, sueña cantando, vive soñando el nuevo sol
en que los hombres volverán a ser hermanos

Listen, brother, to the song of joy,
the joyous song of he who hopes for a new day,
Come, sing, dream singing, live dreaming the new sun
in which men will return to being brothers

El Colmenar   Wednesday, May 2, 1:47 PM
Just before dinner and I am hiding out. In my usual place, sitting on the tan couch in the corner of the classroom. Here, all is quiet, all is peace. I have done practically zip work today. Everyone was up and bustling at dawn at 7 AM. I stayed in bed another 20 minutes and

then washed up (face only – a dab and a dib of the cold water) and had breakfast (like the washing, minimal: a big cup of hot sweet chocolate, a little cupcake, five or six cookies – one drinks and eats with a spoon).

Then I got a broom (a little push broom, I haven't seen the straw-bristle broom in Spain) and began sweeping the living room floor (tile). I got a gratifying amount of dust and dirt in front of my broom. (It is no fun sweeping when no growing mound of dirt appears in front of the pushbroom.) Actually, these brooms are often used like the straw-bristle brooms: standing sideways and sweeping the broom past you – like a bullfighter making a pass with the cape, though with less grace and less danger.

After, I went down with Celso to the carpentry shop and looked at the beehives they already have. I am going down to the store tomorrow and order three hives and also some wax panels for the hives. Actually they have the beehive *boxes*; they don't yet have hives. The boxes are what I looked at.

Then, along about 9, I went in the Land Rover to Huete, with Celso, and Paco as driver, and also Benito. First, we went to the dry goods store and bought Benito a pair of shoes.

But. Before I go further – and the call for lunch may come at any moment – I want to say a few words on long underwear therapy. I have just discovered it. First, my sore throat and general malaise seems to be clearing up. I attribute this in part to wearing long underwear yesterday afternoon and so far today. Why? There is no scientific evidence. Simply let the record show the co-incidence and the belief. Second, I have discovered psychological security through long underwear. There is the feeling of being protected, quite secure. Your body is in a place – you are in-folded and ensconced – in a word you are secure. I do think there is a psychological security. Who is it that wraps the baby tightly for the first year? Was it an American Indian tribe? Or is it some contemporary culture? Anyway, that is, maybe, something of the same thing. The sense of being wrapped.   So, I am going to help serve the dinner.

3:31 PM   After dinner. Back on the couch, in the classroom. All the residents are out working: putting up the interior brick walls of the new building (working with two masons from Tarancon) or planting potatoes. The university students are milling about in this building; they are not as disciplined and think of rest after dinner. Also, I think they are leaving for Madrid soon, and I with them. Celso, Pepin and Emilio are doing one of their walking conferences. They talk as they walk together down the dirt road in the direction of Huete.

6:15 PM   Madrid
Ah – a life comfort. The students left early, just after 4 PM. And now I am by myself in the piso (apartment) – Emilio and Pepin stayed at the farm. And I am going to treat myself to a siesta. I think that on waking I will be in perfect health, rid of my cough, rid of my sore throat, rid of the specter of the week-long bout with a cold. Hurrah. Hurrah.

A week in Madrid
shopping for bee hives and furniture.

Madrid   Thursday, May 3, 12 noon
On the #10. Bumping down the street-in-repair. I must
say that I don't feel 100% this morning. I feel like I am
coming out of a week of flu – I have very little energy.
There is a lot of running about and doing I feel I should
do and I don't feel up to it. Right now I am going to
the bank and then I'm going up to Cuatro Caminos to
meet Antonio and Marta for lunch and talk about the
Threshold grant application.

1:16 PM   At the Metro station Cuenca

3:57 PM   On the Metro again. After lunch at Cuatro
Caminos, I am on my way to talk to the people at the big
department store, Corte Ingles, to see whether I can get
estimates for furniture and equipment for the school at
Pan Bendito. I am sniffling and snuffling a bit. After the
visit to the commercial office of the department store, I
think I shall go back to the piso and lie down.

5:01 PM   Just a comment – café-bar comment. I am
in the same place, near the O'Donnell Metro stop, where
I was the other day – near the Casa de Miel (the House of
Honey), where I have come to buy three bee colonies. The
comment is that high above the bar, near the door, there
is a little platform with a little TV set. The set is on, the
volume is up; it is deafening. Yet – not one person in the
bar is watching the TV. The tolerance for noise here is
very great. Oh, now a young man reaches up and turns
the volume down. The reason I am in the bar, drinking
a cup of manzanita, is that Casa de Miel opens for the
afternoon at 4:45 PM – and at 4:55 it was not yet open –

so I decided to relax to Latin imprecision. I shall stroll by at 5:30 – <u>then</u> it will be open.

10:24 PM   And so to bed. I just remembered a snatch of a dream I had last night – during the first part of the night – for I had several dreams last night. I went into a room, which may have been an ancient burial chamber, and there was a brown, mummified, woman. I wasn't frightened and in the dream it didn't seem to me to be extraordinary. I had a dream later in the night which I never did quite remember.

On the 8th floor of the building on the right is the "piso"

Madrid   Friday, May 4, 9:40 AM

Sitting in the apartment (piso), feeling zero energy. This cold I have isn't a lot of sneezing and so forth, but I feel completely wiped out.

3:59 PM   On the #10 Slash, which is different from the plain #10; it doesn't go all the way to Cibeles. But it does go to Puente de Vallecas, where I can get the Line 1 Metro.

6:29 PM   On the anden (platform) at Opera – Line 5. I am to meet Antonio and Celso and we are going to look at the site for the school in Pan Bendito. I want to ask for a Threshold grant to help start the school. I have my camera and I am going to take pictures of the place and the barrio. Pan Bendito, Pepin says, has a population of mostly Gypsies. I am still sniffling and snuffling along with this cold. But I am not going to the farm tomorrow. I am going to meet with Gonzalo, the computer whiz, tomorrow morning to put Pepin's computer into full operation.

6:33   I don't yet see the others – hope I am at the right place. This meeting at remote locations in the city seems to work most of the time. I wonder if this is the way Madrileños fix meeting places generally – or if it is just a thing of the Collectivo. Probably it is general.

So. I don't feel much energy and so I don't much feel like writing. But I scribble along, here in the dimness and the noise of the underground world. The red and white cars rumble up and the doors open with a popping air blast sound and the people spill out and along the platform and are gone. Now a little boy sits next to me. He is holding a paper maché model of a hot air balloon. The balloon is red and the little car hanging below it is silver color. My, they talk English – the little boy and his little sister and their father and the older man – who may be the grandfather. 6:41 PM I'd better make sure I am in the right place.

9:29 PM   Now I am really really tired, tired in
the bone and tired in the blood. I just got back to the
apartment a few minutes ago from the trip to Pan
Bendito. We walked a long way, from the Metro stop to
the site of the school.

11:32 PM   So to bed. Very late. Celso arrived very late
for dinner, so it has just finished. Celso and Pepin are
leaving at 7 AM for the farm. I am staying here, to work
on the computer with Gonzalo and because I feel in no
shape to go to the farm.

Madrid   Saturday, May 5, 8:47 AM
A quiet breakfast. I woke just before 8 and Celso and
Pepin were long gone – to catch the bus to the farm. So
I am cooking my big American breakfast of oatmeal, and
I will sit here quietly in a recuperative state of my cold
and read yesterday's El Pais and eat my oatmeal. At 10
AM Gonzalo comes over and we will put the computer in
march (as a direct translation would have it).

9:29 AM   Having finished breakfast, I sit here at the
table with my companions: Sniffle, Snuffle and Ache. I
almost never get colds at home. Here it is a combination
of unaccustomed food, unaccustomed physical work,
city noise and pollution, great variability and extremes
in temperature, stress. Put them all together and every
time I come to Madrid I seem to catch a bad cold. Take
yesterday. I was riding about in the subway for an hour
and more, and then walked over 5 miles, I think, in the
back and forth from the subway to the place where the
school is to be in Pan Bendito. Hey – at home with this
kind of cold I wouldn't go out of the house.

2:03 PM   Gonzalito was here until 12:40, putting programs in the computer. This afternoon, I am going to see whether I can operate on a computer using MS-DOS and Spanish. After he left, I went down into the street and bought a newspaper, lots of fruit, a bar of bread (The Madrileños call it a "pistola"), eggs, artichokes, a can of sardines and a bottle of cooked lentils. I think the stores close at 2 PM in the neighborhood and will be closed until Monday morning. I have had a big bowl of lentils. And I am cooking up the eight or nine small artichokes; some I will eat cold tonight or tomorrow. The news kiosk was sold out of El Pais, so I bought El Mundo – but I so much prefer El Pais that I am reading yesterday's in preference to today's El Mundo. There is an interesting article on the new and radical mayor of Moscow who has been in Madrid for a conference on perestroika.

9:55 PM   And so to bed. Still feeling quite energyless. I need a few more days of quiet and rest. Tomorrow, at least, will be such a one.

Madrid   Sunday, May 6, 11:34 AM
I am feeling quite sick. I got up to eat something and have gone back to bed.

Madrid   Monday, May 7, 3:33 PM
So. I have a dizzy doozy of a cold. I think it has now gone to my sinuses, something that hasn't happened for years and years. In fact, I rarely get colds. I think the last one I had was – yes – in Madrid in 1988. This is just an awfully stressful place for me. So. Now it is after dinner and Pepin and Celso have left – and also Josele, one of the fellows who was at the farm and is now living in Madrid. He was over for dinner.

10:22 PM   And so to bed — feeling a little better. I worked most of the afternoon on the new computer and I am finally able to get it to print things for me. I was working on the Threshold grant application.

Madrid   Tuesday, May 8, 12:26 PM
My father died 20 years ago today. How quickly 20 years seem to have passed me by. And I am in this then unforeseen place — the Boyle Heights of Madrid, with a terrible head cold. If I think back, I think I may have had a bad cold each of the last four times I have been in Madrid. I had a bad cold in 1988, a week after I arrived. I remember one other bad cold — either 1986 or 1984. Otherwise, other where, I rarely get colds. This is an extremely stressful place for me. That is something I have to take into account for the future. One idea is that I should limit my visits to a shorter time — maybe no more than two weeks.

9:04 PM   I must make a report of this — how nice a guy Celso is. He came by here on his way home and insisted on cooking a Spanish tortilla (an omelette of potatoes and onions) for my supper.

Madrid   Thursday, May 10, 7:40 PM
Strange how early in the day 7:40 PM seems. It seems like about 3:30 PM on a California day. And me? Sitting at the table in the main room of the apartment. Not feeling bad but not feeling good. This morning I went out for the first time since Friday — I mean out into the city. I went across half the city by bus and Metro to FAX the Threshold grant application to San Francisco. And when I got to the FAX place, their copy machine was broken so I walked eight blocks in futile search for another copy machine, feeling hot and then feeling chilled, and then

hot and then chilled. And my teeth hurt when my foot hit the ground and the jar went up into my head. I think that is sinus trouble. But I got through it all and even so, I feel definitely better this afternoon.

Tomorrow I start off on a mad round – it is hard for me to refuse to help when they need help. Pepin has planned a trip for all the fellows at the farm to El Escorial, which is the place to the north of Madrid where el rey Felipe (I think the Philip of the Spanish Armada) built his huge castle-monastery. So, that trip is for Saturday. And Josele, who is one of the "graduates" of the farm – who was supposed to drive one of the vehicles on the trip, had something of a falling out with Pepin this morning. That was because Josele says he is going to take a job in a bar. And Pepin is dead set against Josele working in a bar because Josele had an alcohol problem as well as a drug problem and Pepin doesn't want him in that environment.

So, Pepin asked me if I could drive. And I said Yes. That means that tomorrow I have to take the subway, and then a bus from the northern tip of Madrid at Plaza de Castilla to Colmenar Viejo – about a 2 hour trip altogether. In Colmenar Viejo I pick up Manolo's big van and then I must drive it to the farm, which is a trip of some 150 kilometers. That's on Friday. On Saturday, I load some 8 of the fellows in the van and I drive back to Madrid, through Madrid, and on north to El Escorial; it has to be a 3½ to 4 hour trip. And then in the evening, back again. So that is some 8 hours of very stressful driving in one day, after a week of a bad cold; a Don Quijote-ish thing to do.

I rather hate to admit it but I am looking forward to

the peace and quiet and non-commitment of being in England. I got my ticket this morning. I am leaving early next Saturday afternoon and by Saturday evening I hope to be at a vegetarian health spa, or something like that, in Sherborne in Dorset. And I shall be with John Clausen, which I am looking forward to – for John is demanding in the places he stays – he demands a certain level of creature comfort. Creature comfort is what I am much looking forward to. It will be a sharp break with the past month and a half in Spain. I hope I am in adequate shape for walking half a dozen or 10 miles a day, for that is what we have been talking of. I certainly don't feel in that kind of shape today.

11:07 PM   And so to bed. Feeling better. The worst of my cold is past.

Madrid   Friday, May 11, 11:20 AM
On the #10 bus again. Again going through Boyle Heights – the streets of the past, the people of once upon a time. For the streets of Vallecas, this poor neighborhood of south Madrid are for me the streets of Boyle Heights, the poor Jewish neighborhood of east Los Angeles, where I grew up 50 years ago. But not the streets. No, the streets are quite apart, quite different. But the essence. The essence. The people. The way the people are. Way down inside. The net of living, the way of being together, the worries, the hoping. Boyle Heights is gone – lost somewhere in the pastness of the dark universe. But, here is Vallecas with the essence. But, there are no Jews in Vallecas. The essence, though, is not Jewish – it is the struggling, the uncertainty, being poor, not being in control of it all.

So. The #10 goes up the narrow street, with shops on

both sides. And now turns downhill into Avenida de la Albufera. An old man across the aisle coughs in a sick man's way. I look up at him. Heck, he's not much older than I. He is wearing a dark suit and a white shirt, but no tie – and a working man's cap. And on his feet, the felt slippers that many people wear in their apartments here. I shall buy a pair to bring home with me. Vallecas is wearing, yes – but I have an affection for it. The living is hard here – it is the poor side. Things are so much easier – in the day to day kind of things – on the rich side. My American life seems much less real than life in Vallecas. But is it American life? Or is it my life? I live a rather disassociated life in the US. I have no responsibilities or strong family ties. Several people on the bus now cough in succession – in that wet, sickly kind of way. Is everyone feeling like me? Is there an epidemic of head colds in Madrid? Could be.

So. I have a busy day in front of me. Down to the sea in ships – or rather down to the center in bus. I will walk up the Castellana to Plaza Colon and the Telefonica building, where I will call France to talk to the young woman, Diane, who was in my French class in Santa Cruz. She is now working on a farm in southern France, and wants to come to work with the people here, in June. She wrote a letter to Pepin, in Spanish, which arrived a few days ago. Oh, my, now I am very warm. It is beginning – the hot and the cold of it. So I am going to call her to tell her there is a place for her here. And then there is monkey business with some money I have here that I must chase a bit on. And then lunch. Where? Biotika? Or another veggie restaurant?

Here we are now going past the Prado. I did go once in my present trip. It is so awfully crowded. One more long block to the end of the line at Cibeles. Madrid is now greening in the full of May.

1:58 PM   Ai Ai. At a restaurant. The story of my morning has an O. Henry turn. After I made my telephone call, I crossed the street to get a taxi – I was treating myself well, instead of schlepping about on Metro and bus. But. A rendezvous awaited me and it wasn't in a taxi. So, I couldn't get a taxi. So I walked to the nearest bus stop; I would take any bus going up the Paseo de Castellana. There were some 30 people waiting on the bus island. I took out my wallet to get my bus pass. It wasn't there – I had just put it in my other pocket. A bus stopped and I walked ahead to get on it. There seemed a crowd trying to get on – some 10 people. A well-dressed middle-aged man in a brown checked suit crowded up to the stair in front of me and others were pressing behind me. The man in the brown suit stopped before the cashbox on the bus. The fellow behind me, wearing a dark blue suit, called out to him – something, I suppose, like Are we going on this one or not? Brown suit turned, they both scurried out the bus, the doors slammed.

I looked up and saw that actually few people had gotten on, the bus rolled down the street, I reached for my wallet to put the bus pass in – and – suddenly – I became the star in an American Express commercial. Wait, I cried to the bus driver, they have my wallet. He opened the doors and I ran off. Brown suit and blue suit were nowhere to be seen. There I was in Plaza Colon: peseta-less, dollar-less, franc-less and VISA-less. Suddenly a bright angel in the form of Walter what's-his-name – the tough guy of the AmEx commercials Wait a minute – maybe <u>he</u> was the guy in the brown suit. Do you think

AmEx hires these guys? Anyway, the vision spoke to me and said, Yes, But. Yes, but you have been carrying 10 hundred dollar American Express checks in your other pocket for, lo, these two months, day in and day out. And this was day out.

So I went to the Barclay's bank on the corner. It was closed – a sign on the door said "Closed May 10, 11, 12". I walked up the street. Another bank. I went in what I thought was its entrance, but it was the entrance of the building. The porter was standing at his desk. I am looking for the bank, I said. Which bank? he said. Any bank, I said. The banks, he said, are on strike today. All the banks? Yes. Ai Ai Ai, I thought. I don't even have bus fare to Colmenar Viejo. But then he added: the Cajas de Ahorro (saving banks), they are open. Ah, I said, is there a Caja de Madrid nearby? Yes, he said, just keep going up the street. So, that is where and how I cashed my AmEx check and re-entered the world of the money-ed.

I attribute the whole incident to my clothes – the gray fedora and the gray wool pants – I had an American tourist look, I think. Usually I wear my nondescript Santa Cruz khaki and I look like a fellow not worth robbing. Today I was the little pig going to the banker. So it goes.

3:54 PM What a day! On my way to the Metro, I passed a police station to make a robbery report. So now I am running late. And running. I ran from the Metro exit to where this bus is because I was afraid I'd miss the 4 PM bus, which would make me hopelessly late. As it is, I may be only 15 minutes late. Smartly, I wrote the address in Colmenar Viejo on another slip of paper, which wasn't in my wallet. So I have that, though I don't have the phone number.

4:08 PM   So. I sit in the bus, the hot sunlight comes through the window. I sweat. Alongside the road, in the green which is now peaking and darkening, there are now many flowers: red, yellow, violet and white.   And I feel away from it, connecting more with my stuffed nose, the heat, the noise of the loudspeaker, the heavy lunch I ate, the bad of the city which we have just left, the sense of the robbery a couple hours ago.   I want away from this stress – I want peace and tranquility – the Pure Land, pure air, pure water. I don't know how Celso and Pepin go on year after year with so much more stress and struggle and yet keep on and keep on, in good will and good humor, no matter what. After a mere month and a half as a mere hanger-on, I am limping and lagging and lacking.

Tomorrow is going to be a toughy for me. I look out over the green gray land, I hear the chatter of the loudspeaker and the shake and the rattle of the motor and the metal. I have such a longing for the Pure Land, the fresh land, the nurturing natural land – the place beyond the mountains, by the clear waters where the flowers are not mixed with, not muddled with, the loudspeaker voices.

Fiesta in Huete: a military band . . . a lively drum march, and at regular intervals a brilliant flourish of trumpets.

El Colmenar   Saturday, May 12, 7:26 AM
Morning of the morning of the first day. A quiet sky, wakening blue, new blue, freshness of morning. Soft colors, soft sounds, pure air, fresh light. There are rows

and rolls and curls of soft gray and white clouds across the new blue of the sky. The trees are a light bright new green on the hill across the valley, the hillside is open white-tan soil and dark green bushes. Away, faintly throbbing, there is the diesel generator, and the birds are twiting highly softly and brightly. Four white doves fly past the window, past the hillside, then return, flutter past and return again.

I am hot and I take off my wool scarf. Wool? Hah! Cashmere, and a long time with me – since the year 1979. And I take off my windbreaker, bought in March 1990 in Saujon, France. And now I feel a little hot and a little cold. That is the way with colds – one doesn't know if it is too hot or too cold. I have had my big mug of hot chocolate and 14 cookies. Could have been 16 cookies or 8. And that was the break of the fast – the des of the ayuna. Now I am waiting for the gathering of the forces, for soon we head to El Escorial.

Ah. 7:38 AM   Pepin just came in. He said, We are calling a doctor in Madrid so he can go today. Pepin is talking about Jose Luis, the "retarded" man. Jose Luis has some trouble with his eyes. Apparently, for a long time he has not seen out of one eye – that was long before he came here. Now, he says he cannot see well out the other and he says he has pain in the eye. So Pepin and Marta are going to Huete to call Marta's mother in Madrid to find a doctor who can see him today, and we will take him there as we pass through Madrid. I started to worry about him last night as we rattled over the dirt road back to the farm from Huete. My, I thought, what if it is a detached retina like I had many years ago? He shouldn't be bouncing his head about rattling over a dirt road.

Last night, everyone on the farm went into Huete in the evening. We were invited by Mariano, the young man who is the government teacher who comes out here every afternoon to teach. We went to his home, where he lives with his parents, and in the narrow patio back of the house, on a big round stone table, they set out all the dishes – of meats and fish and Spanish tortillas and a big basket of bread and the lemonade and non-alcoholic beer and the inevitable, ubiquitous, everywhere indigenous, everywhere abhorrent Coca-Cola. And we snacked and snicked and stood about and talked. The singer, said Mariano's mother – the singer, who is so good, sings opera and everyone sits and stands and listens. The singer, he (or she, I never was sure which) cannot come, she said. So we did not hear the singer sing.

And after we ate, and after the dark came over Huete, we went out to the streets, to where the music was. For, you see, these are the fiesta days of Huete. Rather, of part of Huete – for Huete has a history – a fascinating history. About 2000 people live in Huete and maybe that many people have lived in Huete for hundreds, perhaps thousands of years – for Huete, I think, is an old old town. And yet the people of Huete form two communities – and have ever since the Middle Ages, as I understand the story. There are two barrios of Huete, of about 1000 people each and they are separate. They have their own, different, fiestas; they have their separate community lives. Until recently, there was not even inter-marriage between them. And the fiesta of last night and this week is of only one barrio – the other has its fiesta next week.

The story they tell is that, during the Middle Ages, one part of the town was Jewish and the other part was

Moorish – and so there was a separation. Now, and for many hundreds of years, they are all Christian, but still they are two separate communities. I think the barrio we were with yesterday was the formerly Jewish barrio; it was all of keen interest to me. The fiesta dance of this barrio of Huete is, they said, different from all other places and has continued, year after year, through the hundreds of years since the Middle Ages.

Indeed. There in the main street – which is not the main street of Huete, but, I guess, is the main street of this part of it, there were colored lights strung across and a loud band. First surprise: the band is a military band, consisting of drums and bugles, and played by soldiers.

Ah, 8:18 – I was going to go to the bathroom, but the hallway in the front of the building is being mopped – so I will wait a few minutes. Yes, the band is a military band – it places a lively drum march and at regular intervals there is a brilliant rising flourish of the trumpets. And the band marches slowly slowly down the street. In front of the band are the dancers – many circles of dancers that fill the street – they dance rhythmically, joyously, with the marching music and when the trumpets blare, they all raise their joined hands and sing out. The whole group of dancers – circles of children, circles of older people, younger people, pitch against each other in the crowd and move slowly, crowdedly, before the band. The dance is called something like the Gallope.

8:37 AM   So – everyone is standing in the hall, waiting for Pepin and Marta to return from Huete and then we will go.

Yes – and there are the pushers – this is in the

fiesta dance of Huete – there are the Pushers, the Empujadores, although I only saw one middle-aged man. To urge the people to move forward ahead of the marching band, the military band. I found the whole scene stirring, moving. Here was this vestige of the ages, this visible bridge to long ago times, long ago people. I saw in the dance a remote relation to the Israeli hora – this was a Jewish echo of Spain, a transmutation of the pain of centuries ago. For, as I have noted before in these pages, there are many purely Jewish faces among the long-time Christians of Huete. And Huete has an inglorious history of the sitting of the Inquisition. So a large part of the populace of Huete is, I think, the descendants of forcibly converted Jews. Unfortunate Spain, loser of great richness because its blind and stupid intolerance insisted that everyone come down, be pounded down, into the same gray, silent and abject state.

I joined the dance for 15 minutes – the music and the dance was very catching. I probably would have stayed on into the night but the couple I was with, Mariano's friends, suggested stopping in a bar, and I thought I should re-join the people from the farm – who were standing at the side of the dancers, along the sidewalk.

And we all returned to the farm about 10:30 PM. Nani, one of the fellows, sat next to me in the back of the Land Rover on the way back and he told me of the fiestas he had seen, especially the one at Sevilla on Holy Week, when there are the processions that go from 12 midnight to 12 noon, carrying the images of the Virgin – one is the Macarreno and the other is the one of the Gypsies. They do not cross, he said, they both stop and sing, but the one of the Gypsies is more spontaneous. I want to go, one

*Huete, seen from above, on the dirt walking road from La Granja (top);
Huete's main street (bottom)*

year, and see that.

I was thinking something like that yesterday as I was driving out here by myself, in Manolo's van. That was the first time ever that I had driven out to the farm by myself – and I saw the trip in a different way.

8:55 AM   I must look out and see whether we are ready to go. 8:59 Nope. Pepin and Marta have not yet returned so everyone is standing about waiting. I fear we shall be rather late and return rather late – rather later than late. Anyway.

So I was saying about my trip here yesterday: I saw everything in a different way. There was the countryside, green and tan Springtime patches, and the little white stone villages, and the rock forms of the cliffs and the drops into the river valleys. It was a strange and ancient land – all the overtones and undertones, the imagination, the history, the fantasy, came onto me. All this doesn't arrive for me most of the time in Spain, because I am so immersed in the grim daily struggle. It is poverty and problems and deadly struggle, very grim, very gripping, immediate, real people with real tough problems. It is a world that exists also, of course, in Santa Cruz – but in Santa Cruz I don't confront it. Here I do, and before it the fantasy of Spain, the imagination, the past and the unreality, or at least the imaginative, deconstructed reality, fades away like the white shadow moon under the noonday light.

Ah, here are Marta and Pepin. – We are off. At 9:08 AM

Rain slants down in silver streams, splashes over the rough terrazzo squares

2:46 PM   Somewhere near El Escorial

So. Here is the 2:46 PM update. I am not too near El Escorial, but that is the only reference point I know hereabouts.   Ping-pong and darts and rain over all. But not real rain, just the dark clouds overhead and sprinkles and splashes. The ping-pong table is at my left and the dart board at my right. All sheltered under a wide overhang of the second floor. The place is the mountain country home of Marta's family – a rather grand place – swimming pool   Ah, there is a roll of thunder overhead, and now a peripheral flash of light, the storm darkens, the storm approaches.   Yes, swimming pool Ah, now there is a hard rain falling, the skies have liquidized.   So – swimming pool and tennis court and dog kennel with Doberman, St. Bernard, two Pekinese and two non-descript.

My, what a heavy rain shower – the water slants down in silver streams, flies off the top of a parked car and splashes over the rough terrazzo squares. Loud thunder and it has become several degrees colder. For, yes, this is mountain country. Start at Madrid at 2000 feet and drive seven leagues sliding upward and there is highness and mountain rain, mountain cold. I say seven leagues because that is what the film at El Escorial said: Felipe II chose a site seven leagues from Madrid for his palace-monastery. Since we drove back from El Escorial a ways to arrive here, I will give us six leagues from Madrid. More sharp thunder overhead.

My, I am feeling some hunger. Since I have not eaten since the hot chocolate and 10 cookies at 7:30 AM. But if I were asked ¿Que tal? (How's it going?) right now, I would answer, Bien, bien, as I always do – and truly, because I do feel pretty well right now. A bit tired after the drive of some 3 1/2 hours – although we waited some 15 minutes at Plaza Conde de Casals, where two more cars joined our caravan, making for a total of six. Then we caravanned northward through the Saturday morning car crowd of Madrid and up through the green countryside, rumpled and bushed (the countryside – not us) to El Escorial.

El Escorial is an imposing brown granite edifice, classic and austere. Austere is a word applied to the Spanish Habsburgs. We parked the cars, waited for all, re-grouped and entered. One of the university students who helps the Collective works as a guide at El Escorial, and he met us and took us to the room where they show a film presenting the history of Philip II and his grand castle-monastery. We watched it – it was about 15 minutes and in Spanish, English or French. (You choose your language with a switch on the earphones. I listened mostly to the English, but I also listened to some of the Spanish and French. I found I understood the Spanish and French equally well.) And, after the 15 minutes, El Escorial was closed, because it was after 1 PM. So we left, back to the cars and drove here. One thing I do a lot of in my time in Spain is simply wait for instructions. There is a group organization which falls into place. I don't know
    Ah, the call for the meal.

6:39 PM   In the sunlight of this at times sunlit afternoon. Sitting on stone steps, looking across the tennis court to the distant line of far-blue mountains. In the near distance, the sun lights a green field and dark green trees – an all green, bright green dark green hillside. And, above all, gray and white clouds – just above the blue mountains a wide rolling row of mid-gray clouds; higher and closer flat sheets of white cloud against pale blue: a mountain landscape, a mountain skyscape. When the sunlight is on me, I feel warmish and I unzip my windbreaker a bit; when a cloud covers the sun and sunlight fails, I feel a chilly little breeze against the back of my neck and I zip up my windbreaker as far as possible.

At La Granja: quiet and order, progression of sun and clouds, night and day. One can be part of it all.

El Colmenar   Sunday, May 13, 9:25 AM
Sun-ly, warm-ly, chickens clucking, the day begins. Chickens chase chickens; it's a bird-brain life down there in the chicken yard.   We do better.   Don't we?

11:10 AM   I am hiding out. My philosophy of the farm is either to be seen working or to hide out. And, perhaps, writing can be seen to be working. I am being an example, an exemplar here. (Is "exemplar" an English word? Or does it come to me from an obscure store of French? – or Spanish?) Anyway, an example of Work. Work, for the day is waxing, work, for the day is waning, work, for the day is dying. Work, for in work is salvation. Work, for in work there is a place for you, a use for you. And so it is.

This morning I came out and Manolo was sweeping from the concrete terrace the stains and bits of mud from yesterday's storm. So I got another broom and swept into the sweep of it. And then there were three of us – three sweepers sweeping. (And – that finished, I went to look at the rabbits.) But really, there is a sense of the sweep of it all. You sweep the terrace, and after, you look down the length of the terrace and it is still damp from the rain and now it is all swept of the red mud and it shines spotless and damp under the morning sunlight. And you feel that the world is in its place and order and harmony reign in the world and there is contentment. That is the simple way of it all. Quiet and order and pattern and a place in the sun and the progression of sun and clouds and light and shadow and Spring and the springtime flowers, night and day. One can fall in with it all, be part of it all, sweep along with it all. Avoid the broken patterns, the jagged sharp edges of metal, and ragged noise.

An exemplar of work

11:17 AM   Ah, I heard the voice of Antonio outside and I went out to look for him because I wanted to talk to him about the woman who called Friday morning and offered – I think – computer equipment to the project. She said "equipo de informatica" which means something more than a computer – which is "ordenador". And she had to know in a few days, or else they were going to give the used equipment to someone else.   Pepin said, Talk to Antonio.   But I went outside – Antonio was there, but with 7 or 8 of the fellows, sitting on a rock bank beside the building, eating the bocadillos (the snack sandwiches) of mid-morning. I am not hungry, since I ate three little breadsticks given to me by the woman of the panederia (bakery) of Carrascosa del Campo.

That – Carrascosa del Campo – is what happened after the morning sweeping. I went there in Manolo's big white van (furgoneta) with Manolo and Pepin. In the little bar (the second one, not the one on the corner), we met Celso and Emilio, just arrived from Madrid on the bus. And there was also the man who owns the construction materials yard in Carrascosa; he seems to be a regular on Sunday mornings in the bar – and he knows me now so he put out his hand to me and said Buenas Dias.

Then we went to the bakery and Celso, Emilio and Manolo went into the grocery store.

You have to be a regular to know the stores of Carrascosa, for there are no signs – by all appearances they are houses midst the houses. But, push aside strings of long wooden beads in front of the bakery and enter a pleasant little world – of a big glass case full of cheeses and sausages and this and that, and long tables covered in orderly row with round flat cakes, and trays of cookies on top of the counter, and through the glass door into the back room, which is warm and smells of fresh baked bread, for it is the room of the oven and there stands the Baker with his long wood paddle, putting the lumps of dough inside and then turning the wheel so that the platform turns a little and there is new space for more lumps of dough. And the baker's wife counts out the bread by twos: dos, quatro, seis – and up to veinte, and puts them in a big empty paper bag of the flour. Manolo buys two round goat cheeses and then there is much computation – the baker's wife thrusts into my hands the half dozen thin breadsticks. Then we walked to the grocery store – where the woman always comes down on Sunday morning in her thick bathrobe and opens the door to the grocery store. And so it goes.

The baker of Carrascosa

Now, the day has darkened over – dark gray drifting clouds cover the sky and a chill is on the land. Earlier, when Pepin and I were getting into the furgoneta for the ride to Carrascosa, Pepin said, No es un dia catolica. Catolica? I asked. Yes, he said, that means it will not be a good day, a clear day. But, he said, you don't say *Catolica* to mean it <u>is</u> a good day. You only say *no catolica* to mean it will *not* be a good day.   Enter into the subtleties of 2000 years of church and people.

So – now it has started – the light rain, the patter of water. I get up and close the open door. Closing the door, I create the room – the classroom – into one space from the two spaces it has been for the last half hour. For I have been in one corner, sitting on the tan couch, and in the other corner, hidden from me by the open panel of the door, have been two of the college girls and Nani of the farm – sitting at the typewriter, tapping out something and talking. It is a background for me – the talking – for I don't understand the Spanish speaking among themselves. I don't even focus in on it – it is like the chickens clucking outside.

Now Carmen has come into the room with the four young children. There is the little boy, about five, and his sister, about seven – the children of Paco, one of the fellows living here. They have been staying here the last week. And there is a story about them and why they are here now. I won't tell it right now. I think I mentioned it before, a few weeks ago. And there is the little girl, about three, in the purple sweat suit. She is very cute, with straight blond hair; earlier this morning she was carrying about a purple flower she had picked, which just matched her sweat suit.

And there is the girl, about 12, who is the sister of Nani and who is a very nice girl; she wants to be helpful and she is always nicely smiling and friendly – now she is helping Carmen with the little children. She also knows a little English. She has a very silent father. When he is here at the farm, he sits in one chair, immobile and doing nothing, all the day long. Yet, when there was an evening at Manolo and Nati's in Colmenar Viejo after the seminar (for the Latin Americans), he (his name is Fernando) was the very soul of gaiety and conviviality – telling jokes one after the other. I think he is one of those people who is very afraid of a situation in which he is not in control, an unfamiliar situation. Here, on the farm, he is not in control and he sits silently.

My, my fingers become tired and stiff from the scribbling. If this were to be my method of hiding out all the way to dinner at 2 PM (it is now 11:59 AM), I shall have much stiffness of the writing fingers to deal with.   I lift my head and turn to look out the window – now there are patches of blue midst the clouds; perhaps the day is becoming less non-catholic.   I think I shall now go to reading my earlier pages so that I can mail them next week from Madrid – I am now reading around page 60, so I am far behind.

In Vallecas: a short stout woman, holding a shopping bag, waiting for the bus. Her life has not been easy; that at first glance. Where does one get the energy to go on?

Madrid   Monday, May 14, 11:38 AM
On the #10 bus. Feeling vulnerable in the pockets. Ever since being pock-picketed pick-pocketed on Friday, I have been feeling pocket-vulnerable in public places. Especially with these gray slacks, whose manufacturer never gave a thought to pickpockets. I look out the bus window at Vallecas this May morning, and it seems a far place. I wonder what I am doing here, whether I do any

good by being here.

Vallecas is a hard place to live, even on a May morning. There is a short stout woman, gray short hair, holding a shopping bag, waiting at the bus stop. Her life has not been easy; you can see that at first glance. Where does one get the energy to go on? With the shopping bag, carrying the shopping bag, waiting for the bus? The days go by. The people walk along through the sunlight. Wearing light sweaters – dressed for May, dressed for 1990. The people walk along, fashioned together, being of the same place, of the same time.

There is a screeching wailing siren behind the bus. Wailing through. Here are the little autos parked under an elevated roadway. And all about there are the little cars.   Now the sky is clouding over – this is still the mountain climate, always changing. The gray buildings – they never sparkle – they are always gray, whether they are red or yellow or white.

1:45 PM   Like the guy who went to the doctor sick and the doctor asked him, You've had this before? Yes. Well, said the doctor, you got it again. What I have is Monday Vegetarianism. And the cure is: Chinese restaurant.

It all happened before. I decided to try a different vegetarian restaurant, this one on Calle Marquez de Santa Ana. I arrived. Closed: "For rest, until the 20th", and the other one, Biotika, on Calle Amor de Dios, is closed every Monday. In 1988, I recall, the same thing happened. And I found a Chinese restaurant two blocks away. Many places are closed today in Madrid, because tomorrow is the Fiesta de San Isidro, the patron saint of the city. But Chinese restaurants never close. So here I am, the only client in the Chinese restaurant. And here arrives what I ordered. First, a big salad of just lettuce and tomato. The waitress understands me – we speak the same broken Spanish.

A brilliantly sunny May day,
patches of red poppies along the road

El Colmenar   Tuesday May 15, 5:19 PM
So. Sitting in the recreation room. Outside it is a brilliantly sunny day – a day in May. Driving here this morning we passed patches of red poppies (amapolas) along the roadside. Like the California poppies, the amapolas of Spain like cut slopes and disturbed earth.
Emilio and I left Madrid at 8:24 this morning and arrived at the farm at 10:01 – those are the figures and the facts. That was my fifth drive along that route since Friday evening. The sixth will start, I imagine, in an hour or hour and a half. This will be my last visit to the farm on this trip.

Today there were close to 50 people at lunch. There were a group of adult education teachers from Cuenca and from Guadalajara, as well as the alcalde (mayor) of Larnaca and his family. Larnaca – is that the right name? – is the village about 6 kilometers away on the road to Carrascosa. It was the best lunch thus far at the farm. They made a paella outdoors in the giant paella pan (must be 1 1/2 meters in diameter) over a wood fire. This was a seafood paella, with big shrimp and mussels and little lobsters and crabs. And there was a big common plate of salad – lettuce and tomato, lettuce from the green house – on each table. For dessert there were slices of watermelon.

Cooking paella

After lunch I talked a half hour (in French!) to a fellow here from Cuarto Mundo – which must be Quart Monde in French. This is a very interesting group, founded in 1957 by a French priest. Now there are about 300 volunteers who live with the poorest families, in projects in France and also now in many other countries. There are also some 15,000 "allies" who help part time and share their salaries with the volunteers, who each get the same amount of money, which is something equal to the minimum wage in France. They choose a project in a poor neighborhood and the volunteers live in the neighborhood – if single, maybe with a family; if a family, maybe in a separate apartment. They may work on a project five or 10 years – until they can get others, maybe a community group, maybe a government agency, to take it over. He told me of a project started in New York in a welfare hotel and one in Guatemala of a mobile library in the dump with the families who live in the dump. They work a lot like Pepin's Escuelas para la Vida, involving the poor and marginal people in the projects, working

Madres on the terrace – I am the shadow photographer (top); View from the terrace (bottom)

to give them a sense of self-esteem and psychological security. They try to set up a "maison du droits du homme" (so I understood it) as a place where classes of the "universite populaire" can meet and where people of the neighborhood can come to talk and for assistance. He gave me a pamphlet and a copy of their monthly newsletter – both in Spanish. The movement, though started by a priest, has no formal link to the church. The priest died two years ago. I am interested in this group and want to learn more about them. Their main office is near Paris and he told me to talk to the international director to get information about the project in New York.

The bus creeps along a narrow street –
wetness and umbrellas

Colmenar Viejo Wednesday, May 16, 11:11 AM
World War I is said to have ended at this minute. I am standing on a street corner, waiting for the bus – the bus to Madrid. Colmenar Viejo is a town some 25 miles north of Madrid (not to be confused with El Colmenar, which is the name of the farm (La Granja) near Huete). I drove up here this morning to return Manolo's van – which was loaned to me on Friday. The connection of the farm with this town is that the director of the Universidad Popular here was a friend of Pepin's and so Pepin started giving the Escuela para la Vida classes here and from that several fellows came to the farm from here and there is a network of families here involved in the work.

Manolo and Nati are very active – their son Carlos is out at the farm now. They are comfortably middle-class people – nice apartment, two cars. I think Manolo owns a hardware store.

So. I am feeling tired this morning. Matter of fact, I am looking to the green oasis of Dorset on Saturday for rest. I have a great deal of running about to do before I set sail on Saturday.   The day is May – warm but not hot. The sky was clear up to five minutes ago – now there are thin flat clouds spreading about above. The bus comes, I hope, to this street corner at 11:30. So I was told by the woman in the bakery across the street. Although there is no bus sign of any kind here. Ah – now, at 11:27, there are three women – who look dressed for Madrid – also on the corner. That is reassuring.

7:37 PM   Madrid
On the #10 bus. It is raining thunderbolts outside in this mountain city of Madrid. The bus creeps along a narrow street of Vallecas – wetness and umbrellas. The rains started about an hour ago. I was working on the computer in the apartment and I stopped with the thunder and lightning. Something about computers being wiped out by lightning strikes came up from my uncertain knowledge. So now it is coming-on-night darkness, as one might expect at close to 8 PM – but usually doesn't happen in Madrid these days until around 9:30.

7:49 PM   I shall see how long between subway trains – for one just left. I am at Puente de Vallecas station on Line 1. I shall go only one stop on Line 1 – then I change to another line – 6? – to go to Manuel Becerra. I forgot my Madrid map, so now I am going on city-memory. Two and 1/2 minutes – still no train. The woman sitting next to me on the platform   Ah – here we are – three and 1/2 minutes.

7:57 PM   At Pacifica station on the #6 Line. Here

comes the train.   7:58 On the train – four stops to
Manuel Becerra. Very few people are on this train –
everyone must be home already. Conde de Casal – it is
interesting to go underground between places you have
walked above ground. The walk from Pacifica to Conde
de Casal is the one I have made a couple times early on
Sunday morning to go from the bus stop of the 54 bus up
to the bus station from which depart the long distance
buses to Carrascosa del Campo (and the farm).   8:03
Next stop is Manuel Becerra, and I will be almost a half
hour early. Subway cars <u>do</u> get you places fast.

12:31 AM   Late to bed. Tonight was a good-bye supper
for me.   Such beautiful and open-hearted people. The
supper was over at the apartment of Antonio and Luis
and Josele – and there were Pepin, Celso, Manolo and
Nati, Marisol Marino, Marisa, Marta, Mane (who I didn't
know before), and Bertrand (the French fellow from
Quart Monde).

Madrid   Thursday, May 17, 9:26 AM
Almost at Cibeles on the #10 bus. It is a bright morning
and I am out early and feeling a bit of Spring, a little
lightness in my heart. I have felt terribly oppressed by
Madrid the last 10 days – and now there is a lightening.
I have money errands to do this morning: bankers and
brokers. Not a pleasant contemplation.

4:15 PM   Well, I tried. Here at the Cerveceria
Alemana. I have come in here before and asked for a
manzanilla (camomille tea) and the waiter has asked: "Of
herbs?" and I have said Yes, and wondered why he asked.
Then Emilio told me that there is also a fine Spanish
wine called Manzanilla.   So now, I came in here and I
said: I want a manzanilla, the wine. And the waiter said,

There isn't any. So I said, The other manzanilla. "Of herbs?" he asked. Yes, I said.

I just finished lunch at the Biotika on Calle Amor de Dios. I ate late because at 2:45 I was still in a bank office. My Spanish investments have been an unmitigated disaster thus far. And the dollar continues to drop like a spent rocket against the Spanish peseta. Spain has the third largest reserves of dollars in the world, I was told; that must be after Japan and Taiwan. Why? American companies are buying Spain, lock stock and toro. Spain is the financial fad of 1990. The peseta was once 180 to the dollar, now it is 102. Makes it easier to compute prices – just knock off the last two figures.

So – I have a choice seat in Cerveceria Alemana, right by the window. [2016 note: my computer tells me this was Hemingway's favorite seat.] And flights of gray pigeons flitter flutter above the Plaza Sanra Ana and puffy white clouds roll up across the sky. There may be thundershowers again this evening. I have two things – no, three things – I want to do before going back to Vallecas. One is to develop a roll of film and get my camera looked at; the roll of film now inside seems jammed, it won't advance. The second is to buy a book on WordStar, the word processing program on the computer. The third is to call Threshold from the Telefonica building. It now being 4:32, I think I can start off on this afternoon quest.

7:09 PM Wow. I think this is the first day in Madrid that I did all the things I wrote on the little list I make up in the mornings. And it took from 8:30 AM to 7 PM. Post office, two banks and three brokers, bookstore, camera store, two calls to the US, department store and bought several things.

And now I sit on the last row of the #10 bus, homeward bound, bouncing bumping through the sunlight and the smog. There is a gray-headed woman in a brown dress leaning on the windowsill of a second story window, looking out over the street and city. Another woman, another second-story window, black dress. It is that kind of day; there is a habitability outside. The temperature is habitable, the air is marginal. This is the last rush hour of the day – a May day, raged to rags by the autos. And yet, the hopeful people, the wistful people, sit out on the sidewalks in the white plastic chairs around the white plastic tables. They look so tired, here in Vallecas, drained drowned downed – a weary way – the city doesn't work. Doesn't work. Where is the joy? Morning joy? May joy? Is it me? Or is it the city? No, it's not just me. The faces in the street reflect my sense of it. Where is the Pure Land? Is there a Pure Land? What are we come to? Swimming in garbage noise and garbage air and garbage sight on a warm and sunlit May day.

By Air Madrid to England . . . Ah, Madrid. I knew you
when your trees were but bare branches,
when your streets were cold, when you and I and the
Spring were young . . . tomorrow at this time, I shall be
in England, an island of the Western Sea

Madrid   Friday, May 18, 12:24 PM
On the #10 bus, through the red brick streets of Vallecas. Off to Cibeles – to the post office, to send all the heavy unnecessaries home by ship. 24 hours more in Madrid and, much as this city tires me and discourages me, I feel sad, sad.   Echaré de menos, Madrid. I will

miss you, Madrid.   Ah Ah Ah, Madrid. I knew
you when your trees were but bare branches, when your
streets were cold, when you and I and the Spring were
young, Madrid.   But, yes, I am tired – I could go to a
tranquil land, a quiet land, clean air land. Is the Pure
Land in the County of Devon? One doesn't know, but
purity is a scarce quality, long time gone and but faintly
remembered in most places in a trampled world.

Not many people on this bus as we pass Puente de
Vallecas and begin the upward slope of Avenida de la
Ciudad de Barcelona

The red brick streets of Vallecas

3:30 PM   On a bench in El Retiro park. I am waiting
for the post office to open again at 4 PM. It is a long story.
Just before the bus landed at Cibeles, I looked in my
wallet to see how much money I had. I thought I had a

5000 peseta note, but no, all I had was one 1000 peseta note. Not enough to pay the postage on my book packet. I thought, well maybe they change traveler's checks in the post office.   Yes they do, but no, they just closed. I walked out and up the street to a Caja de Madrid branch. The guard at the door there said, "Closed" (in English). Usually the banks close at 2 PM, but this week, because it is the week of San Isidro, the patron saint of the city, they are closing at 1 PM. My watch said 12:59 – but it was closed.

Back to the post office and down to the package office. Here they wrap things for you and for 250 pesetas I got all the books and bangles put in a box and ready to ship. But the postage was over 3000 and I didn't have it. So I walked to Calle Amor de Dios to meet Pepin for lunch at 2 PM. On the way I passed the American Express office, and Sing Hallelujah, they were open and dealing. So I cashed a traveler's check there.   But. The package department (packages by sea department) closed at 1:30 and won't open until Monday. So now I am waiting to see how much more the air shipment is. If it is not outrageously more I shall send it that way. If it is, I will ask Pepin to send it for me by sea next week.

I walked over here (Retiro park) from Calle Amor de Dios with Pepin. He went on to the hospital where Javi is. Javi, Celso's son, has been in the hospital for a month now. It is heart-breaking to see Celso worry over him. When he went in, they said he had pneumonia – he was running a fever. But they can't seem to discover the cause or to cure it. He was given antibiotics and it didn't help. Of course, since he was a drug addict, everyone thinks of AIDS, but he has been tested twice and he doesn't have it. The doctors seem very uncertain. They have mentioned tuberculosis, and today they are doing a biopsy of lung tissue to see if he has a tumor. I have suggested that they have a second doctor see him, but Pepin says that the first doctor would then quit. Anyway, he seems to be deathly ill with an undiagnosed ailment, a situation that one would think is rare today.

So. I am now doing my last 24 hours in Spain. By tomorrow at this time, I expect to be in England, a far country, an island of the Western Sea.

3:52 PM   Well, I shall go over to Cibeles. If they open promptly, I shall arrive at about the opening.

11:18 PM   Last night in Madrid. A warm night. And I am mostly packed.

~

Madrid to England

*On the airplane . . . but Vallecas is not a place one can
leave by just driving to an airport and getting on an
airplane; it is necessary to leave plodding, step after step,
past the red brick buildings, along the gray sidewalks,
past the end of the city and into the mountains.*

Madrid airport   Saturday, May 19, 12:13 PM
Seated in front of Gate 15 – which has just now opened.

12:18 PM   What one finds on entering the door of Gate
15 is that the flight to London doesn't live there – it has
been changed to Gate 7, a long walk down the marble
corridors.   So. I have left. I spent the morning finishing
packing and wrapping up little gifts. Pepin and Celso
accompanied me to the airport in Marta's car. Everyone
had tears in their eyes as I said goodbye the last time
with the kiss on each cheek – they are very open-hearted
people and much affected by leave takings.

Right now, sitting in the departure lounge, the Japanese
women clustered about me, I feel rather glumly tired. I
have swum a dim sea – not understanding much of what
is said, being on the tough side of the city, of life, being in

the vast careless city (careless of air and quiet, order and color), doing a lot of hard city walking and hard country work, being sick a good part of the time, living in other people's spaces, going through strong emotions. It has been a tiring time. Actually – what was I thinking of, more specifically, when I wrote of the dim sea? Actually, what I started to think of is how well I know Pepin. I have the difficulties in language, my lack of experience in relating closely to people, my whole style of standing away from life. And I am well along – I have formed and followed my patterns for a long long time. I have a strong element of distrust, of suspicion, in my way in the world – the way I look out the window of myself at others.

And so I view Pepin. I have never talked closely with him – because of the language, because even with the language I have difficulty talking closely with people, and because I have so much admiration for Pepin and feel myself quite inadequate in being as good and responsible and sacrificing a person as is he. And his way in the world – and Celso's – are quite astonishing to me – being willing to open to the most apparently difficult people, and help them. Like these guys on drugs – robbers, thieves, murderers, people with terrible mental problems. People like Jose Luis, the "retarded" man who was an alcoholic living on the streets of Cuenca. Or like Roberto, who was a year at the farm and now, a few nights ago, put a knife to the throats

12:50 PM   Now I am back on the Madrid Metro – but no – there is light outside. It is not the Metro, it is the special bus that takes one out to the airplane. But it looks as if modeled on the Metro – although it bounces like the #10 bus going through the streets of Vallecas.

12:58 PM   So. Here I am in seat 15A, Iberia 727, flight 606 to London Heathrow. Just to finish the unfinished sentence: Roberto who lives in Pamplona in the house of priests of a teaching order – we visited there in 1988 – Roberto put a knife to the throats of the priests in the middle of the night and they fled the house, after which he destroyed much and tried to set fire to the house. He said the priests were ETA (that is, Basque terrorists) and he was the CIA. No – I think the other way round: They, the CIA, he the ETA. Anyway, Roberto is one of the persons, not terribly unrepresentative, to whom Pepin and Celso open their hearts and their homes. And they keep on – they seem not to become discouraged or tired – or at least they try not to show it. Celso, now, is not doing well because he is so worried about Javi, in the hospital now for a month with an undiagnosed lung disease and also about his wife Isabel, who has circulation problems in her legs and can hardly walk.

Roberto and me – probably from 1991

1:08 PM   Ah, just received a free Herald Tribune. Interesting that they give out an American, rather than an English, paper on this flight to London. They are also passing out copies of El Pais, which I bought in the airport, and ABC, the conservative newspaper.

1:10 PM   The airplane rolls – out along the runway. My my, I am on the airplane, but my sense of myself is still in Vallecas. Vallecas is not a place one can leave by just driving to the airport and getting on an airplane. Will I still be in Vallecas when the plane lands at Heathrow?

Here we go down the takeoff runway. Bouncing along – back to the #10 bounce. Ah, the bouncing ceases, we are up in the air and over the green and brown fields. The sky is clouded. This is the first time today that I have looked up to the sky. So now we do air bumps, which I little like. We are climbing very slowly and turning, still below the clouds. The stewardess didn't make a check of seatbelts and the fellow in Seat C had his briefcase on the seat of Seat B during takeoff. Ai Ai, the details slip. We are higher. Higher and higher – we avoided Madrid – I guess we skirted north of it. We are above the cumulus clouds, which stand in rows off a ways, but we are still below the flat solid gray of the higher clouds. Now we are over mountains. Must be the Sierra de Guadarama.

It is strange that I still don't feel I have left Vallecas and all that. I must have rooted my consciousness there – more so than on previous visits. Each time I go I seem to less and less be a visitor to Madrid where I do visitor kinds of things. Rather, I seem to be in the work right away.   I shall glance through the Herald Tribune.

1:54 PM   I have eaten my lunch – no, not the whipped chocolate dessert, nor the cheese or butter – but one of the fat and fatty slices of sausage and both the cold beef and the tuna salad. An airplane lunch.   We are now over blue water and drifting nets of white cloud.

2:04 PM   Over land again.   Could this be England already? The Spanish Armada never had it this easy. Oops – now the land is covered by clouds.

1:32 PM   (Switching to English time, which is an hour earlier.) We are descending, so that must be England somewhere under the puffy white clouds.

1:35 PM   Yes, it is a green and forested land below. I'm still in Vallecas. Maybe when we land and I hear English all about me, I shall leave Vallecas. I don't think one can fly out of Vallecas; it is necessary to leave plodding, step after step, past the red brick buildings, along the gray sidewalks, past the end of the city and into the mountains.   When one reaches the sea, I believe one needs to walk across the water to reach England.

The voice on the loudspeakers says, first in Spanish, then in English, that in a few minutes we will land and the temperature is 16° Centigrade – that is a good deal cooler than Madrid. And I left my long underwear and my sweater in Madrid. Closer and closer, downer and downer. England looks rather dry and hazy. There is a spidery highway intersection. No, not dry. There is a river. Thames? Oh, a gorgeous castle. Rich rich England. A big reservoir with sailboats. Lots of water.

1:50 PM   On the ground. At Vallecas International Airport.

2:09 PM   Waiting. The line is long – Britain doesn't waive the rules. Everyone must wait, be identified, stamped and certified. And I didn't even get a customs card on the plane. You had to ask for it, the people in front of me say. This is a second-class citizen line – the "other passports"; the first class is "European Community"

2:21 PM   Next step – at the baggage roundabout. Oh boy – I am anxious to get out of airport land.

3:03 PM   I must have left Vallecas, because I am spending £20 on a taxi ride. I am going to Woking – at least that is how it is pronounced – to catch the train to Dorset. I could have waited an hour and taken a bus but that would mean arrival near dark and I get there at 5:30 this way. But us Vallecanos don't spend $35 on cab rides, so I am entering a far country, a green country, a lush country, where the money grows on trees and the bobbinbill sings silver. And I talk English to the driver – me and him – me from middle Russia via Santa Cruz and Vallecas and him from South India via – where? God – I do feel relief – I have left the tough side and I am riding Easy Street in a brand-new taxicab through green pastures. And the air – by God – the air smells like – well – air. Rather than diesel exhaust.

Yes – it is spelled Woking. I thought it might be pronounced Woking, but spelled Woughinghamshireing. Say, these are nifty roads. We are in a rich country – the Queen's England. Only thing is that I look up every now and again and we are on the verge of death – going right against the oncoming traffic – but then I realize they are going the wrong way too. My – what pretty, green and fresh trees. Whole forests of them. What pleasant looking houses. Half-timbered and standing since the 12th century.　　　　B.C.　Or maybe even since 1920. Who knows? Anything is possible. It is a lovely day – greenly sunlit.

3:19 PM　　I hope this is Woking. The train is at 3:40. Yes it is – there is Woking Ford. And now Audi and Volkswagen. It's one world for automobiles.

3:26 PM　　It is all so very easy. Here I am standing on Platform #3, leaning against a brick wall and waiting for the 3:40 to Dorset. Me, a simple lad from Vallecas. No wonder Europe is uniting. It is easier to get from Vallecas to Woking than from Santa Cruz to Santa Monica.

3:36 PM　　Train stations make me nervous. Trains come and go and one might be the one you are to be on. But information is always in obscure places, and the trains don't wait long. One just went through on Platform #3.

3:39 PM　　My watch must be slow, because the 3:40 out of Woking is rolling, rolling. And I am on it. All I need is a boat voyage today to qualify for the Super Traveler, Hero of Land, Sea and Air Award. I am going through an amazing sequence – bip bip bip and it deposits me at a Vegetarian Health Spa in a village of Dorset – a reprocessed Marginado from the far south streets of Madrid – turned into a Gentleman Vegetarian in svelte green England. First thing you know, I'll be eating cucumber sandwiches with the beastly crust trimmed off and drinking herb tea from porcelain with an upturned pinky finger. So it goes on the roller coaster of life.

Although I have to say that Britrail does not have the silk gravy smoothness of SNIF – no not SNIF. SN?F? Anyway – the French rail company. But we are going fast, and the station announcements are in English. A barely understandable English – but, then, is the language in <u>any</u> railroad station understandable? I must not overdraw things. The rail station in Woking had diesel quality air. Not as bad as Vallecas – but not snow white and Pure Land. And in this rail car the diesel from the engine enters. Though I do appreciate the red sticker on the window, which has a cigarette with a bar across it and the words No Smoking – Penalty £50 Maximum. And fee fie fo fum, I smell smoke. Should I go on a hunt for the culprit and threatened a £50 fine? Maybe diesel smoke and cigarette smoke are indistinguishable.

3:58 PM   Basingstoke. This rail car has sets of four facing seats – two and two – on both sides of the aisle, with a fixed table between the facing seats. It seems an invitation to eat. A fat bottomed woman and a fat bottomed girl have sat down across the way. They have plastic bags bulging with – I think – food. I can see the girl. She first drank a soda from a can. Now she is eating a chocolate bar. They both love to eat; it is rather nice to watch – they are rosy and content. I am hungry and thirsty. I wonder if there are vendors selling food and drink, meat and mead, on this train?

I look out the wide window at the green countryside fleeting by. It is still unreal. Maybe part of that is that I went directly from Madrid to the English countryside without going through London. Pepin left on a 2:30 bus from Madrid to the farm. He just arrived about 4:30 –

which was about a half hour ago (it is now 4:08 English time, which is 5:08 in Spain). So – in about the same time I, instead of being in the Spanish countryside, am in the English countryside. Just now I started thinking about my sweater. I left it in Madrid for Pepin and I think I shall have to buy another here – for England, I think, even in late May, is sweater country. I then thought of the other gifts I left. I gave Celso a deerskin bracelet made on the Souix reservation at Pine Ridge in South Dakota. I gave it to him just before we left for the airport and I noticed in the car that he was wearing it. If I know Celso, he will probably be making something like it by the next time I visit – he is very clever. Though not with deerskin.

4:15   Andover. I looked at my AAA map of England. It doesn't have Woking but does have Wokingham. Same place?

4:41 PM   Leaving Salisbury. I have drooped off to sleep. I went to bed about midnight and was awake near 6 AM this morning. Well, we are <u>not</u> leaving Salisbury. Yet.

4:57 Rattling along. The countryside progresses. greener, hillier, Purer. The sky hangs grayly, lightly overhead, like the pearly canopy of a vast green bed. There is an old man in a red shirt bending over a garden beside the track. And a row of brightly whitely blooming trees. We stop. Tisbury. Tisbury? Yes 'tis. But Tisbury isn't on the AAA map. I am going to buy me a real map of Inglaterra. AAA maps are for autos, not people; I am a people, not an auto.

5:02 – Sherborne is at 5:26 – so in 15 minutes I will begin

to pull myself and my belongings together.

I started reading the book Pepin gave to me; <u>La Hoja Roja</u> by Miguel Delibes. Pepin says he is a very good writer. Pepin wrote, in the Spanish manner, a beautiful inscription in the book. The dust cover starts telling about the book this way: Retirement is for the functionary don Eloy, like the red leaf (hoja roja) that appears at the end of the little books (librillos) of smoking papers: an advice that now there are a few left, that it is at the point of finishing itself.

The train just stopped.   5:10   Gillingham – not on the AAA map.

To continue from the dust cover: That of "retirement is the anteroom of death" leaves off being a sentence to convert itself into a threatening reality. Etc.

5:12 PM   Fourteen minutes to Sherborne. People come and go on this car. Only one man – sitting across the aisle from me, has stayed through ever since I got on at Woking. Now – 5:14, the vendor comes by, "Cakes and coffee, cold drinks" he says. I hesitate but say, No, thanks – since I am soon leaving. The countryside is prettier and prettier and the sky more and more looks like rain is coming.   5:18 Templecombe,   Sherborne must be next.

~

England and Middle Piccadilly

. . . the stableman . . . the son
of the son of the son
of Lady Chatterly's lover?

6:12 PM   Sherborne

Seated. In the Three Wishes, the only place in town serving this early. Things are working like a dream. The train arrives at precisely 5:26, as scheduled. What? Mussolini in England? Or do democracies, too, run the trains on time?   Wine arrives. I thought I ordered beer – but heck – I can hardly speak the language.   So.   I come out of the train station; there is a cab at the curb. I show him the slip of paper: Middle Piccadilly Natural Healing Center – sounds right out of the Hobbits, no? Yes, he says, I know where that is. Another fellow walks up: Shall I put your bag in the boot? No, says I, I must call first. Ah, he says, you can use the car phone. He dials for me; he knows the telephone number. I sit in the car; the phone is answered. I ask, I have a reservation for tomorrow night – do you have a place for me tonight? No, I am afraid not, he says, your room is occupied. Can I speak with John Clausen? John comes to the phone. He is coming to Sherborne at 7 for a concert at the Abbey, he has an extra ticket. The cab driver takes me to a Bed and Breakfast. £12. I take the room, quickly put on my best clothes (shoes instead of boots, slacks instead of tan Levi's) and walk toward the Abbey, stop in three hotels to ask for dinner but they don't serve until seven. And so I come to the Three Wishes and Chicken and Mushroom Pie with potato in the jacket. And surrounded, I think, by Americans, dressed to the nines – I bet they are also for the Abbey this evening. I shall be the least dressed. Unto the least of them, if they wear not boots, shall, too, music be administered.

So, 6:34 and I finished eating. I was quite hungry. I wonder if there is an American group in town? In a town of 8000 (says the cab driver) in the pastoral country of Southwest England on a day in mid-May in a small café, why? Why should at least half the 20 patrons be Americans? Do Americans eat earlier? If they are hungry do they not eat? If pricked, bleed? etc. etc. The question is: Are Americans humans?

Anyway. I have this day made a great transition. From Poor to Rich, from there to here. And it was incredibly easy. Easier then driving over Highway 17 to San Jose from Santa Cruz. I am so glad I spent the £20 on the cab; I think that was the key. I knew not London and in that my spirit was not troubled. Anon Anon   It is 6:41 and I shall pay my just debt to the innkeeper and be off to the Abbey.

6:54 PM   I sit on a bench in front of the Abbey – a wood bench with a small metal plaque that says, "In memory of Barbara Helen Trower 1900 – 1975". In front of me is an elaborate stone monument with a bronze plaque dated MCM – oh, I can't remember the Roman of it – I took it as 1884 – High Victorian. The inscription is also Victorian – it is to somebody Digby of Sherborne Castle, who, born to a noble inhe . . .

10:02 PM   Well, it is a far different life I now lead. To finish the last sentence, which was interrupted when John Clausen appeared at the bench before me: Digby inherited and his first thought was to restore the Abbey and he thereafter led a blameless and praiseworthy life and died full of years, whereupon the citizens erected the monument etc.   Now I am in bed. At the Bridalways Bed and Breakfast, on the outskirts of Sherborne – no, I think it is <u>Bridleways</u> – for it is horses, not marriages. This is also a riding stable. Tomorrow afternoon I enter on my three day health cure at the Piccadilly. I would have said I need it much – this morning. But now – the stress and grind and grime of Madrid is four worlds away. Sherborne feels rather apart from life – the calm and quiet make me a bit uneasy – such is the perversity of the human experience or the gyroscope effect of life – I am still spinning in Madrid. Hmm – I seem to have come around in a circle in two sentences. Well I shall leave it there. So to bed.

Sherborne   Sunday, May 20, 7:49 AM
A cow is mooing. And all that. Sunshine, birds tweeking, green – green trees, green grass. And, yes yes yes – across the road is an old stone house with a thatched roof. Thatch, thatch, Mrs. Thatcher, there are yet thatched roofs in the land. All this I see from my second-story bedroom window at the Bridleways Biddy Boo Boo Bide a Wee Bed and Breakfast. No, actually, the Bridleways is not that cutesy. But, there below, is the stable man attending to the horses. Could he be the son of the son of the son of Lady Chatterley's Lover? Was

that Dorset? No, I don't think so.   John was talking last night of his Thomas Hardy walks. All the locales are about here. Castlebridge and et cetera. I think the only Thomas Hardy book I have read (rather, listened to) is Far From the Madding Crowd.   So, 7:56 – downstairs for the Breakfast part of the B and B.

8:07 AM   Breakfast. Being served by the wife of the son of the son of Lady Chatterley's Lover. Now I have gone and made myself nervous. Afraid of my shoulder being looked over. Can I scribble down to the end of the white space and turn the page before the fried breakfast part of the breakfast arrives?   I am   No   –   the fried breakfast has arrived. Fried egg, slice of bread fried in butter, bacon, sausage, and a fried tomato. Oh, and a fried mushroom. Not for a vegetarian – which once I was and will be tomorrow.

So, I look out the window as I chew my toast and mushroom. Across the road is an ancient stone barn with a thatched roof – it is probably the barn of Mrs. Thatcher's thatched cottage down the road a ways. And before the barn, in the foreground, on this side of the road is a little hillock of green plants growing and stirring about in the breezes of May morning. The green of the plants is fresh and new, the stones are stained and patina-ed – water and wind and time and toil, and all that. But. Which is older? Which has longer endured and will endure longer?   Obviously – the delicate grasses. So – God the Father (could it have been God the Mother?) found the answer: the circle, the cycle, renewal. Transformation, transmutation, transmogrification.

8:28 AM   I have left the scene of the breakfast. The Last Breakfast – the last breakfast of bangers and fried eggs and double strength tea and marmalade. Tomorrow. Tomorrow. Tomorrow I start a new life, an old-new life – I shall become a holy roller, bible thumping, more vegetarian then thou, Vegetarian. Give praise. Hallelujah. Today, however, I sit on the edge of my second-story bed and pick the bacon bits from between my teeth.

So. I have six hours before I meet John at 2:30 to take a walk. I get up and rearrange my things. I take a plastic bag from my satchel.   Ah, there are the horses below – all out in the yard, with much shuffling of hooves.

So – and into the plastic bag I put the various papers and whatnots from my blue shoulder bag. So now my blue shoulder bag has only my writing folder, the Spanish book La Hoja Roja, my written and yet unread pages of this letter, my windbreaker, bought in long-ago far-off Saujon, and my cashmere scarf of 1979 Connecticut, plus reading glasses and miscellaneous accessories and accoutrements. This is the countryside England May day packet.

And boots? Or shoes? That is the question. Why not boots? It is a country kind of place and a country kind of day. And a hat. My well-worn canvas hat that has withstood well being packed rolled up yesterday. No. I put on one boot and it doesn't feel right. I am a tired person this morning. I am not for striding through bush and bracken. I am for strolling and resting. Lolling about in verdant tranquility.

9:29 AM   Wandering about, following the sign to the castle, I come upon the country church – and I shall copy out the little history posted by the gate later. Right now I am at the side of the church, among the graves.

Here is what is on one gravestone – 6 feet by 2½ feet,
I would say – placed flat on the ground: "In memory of
William Boswell who died July 4, 1863, age 77. also
of Elizabeth Boswell, his daughter, who died June 2,
1860, also of Elizabeth Boswell, wife of the said William
Boswell and mother of Elizabeth Boswell, who died April
21, 1891 aged 92." The last four lines, starting "Elizabeth
Boswell", are hard to read, having been worn away,
especially the age at the end; I make out the 9, but the 2
could be a 0. The "said William Boswell" seems strange
on a gravestone. Maybe the text was written by the clerk
of the solicitor of the last of the Boswells.

Here is another inscription – this one on a stone placed
above one of the doorways of the church (I am now
walking back towards the gate): "Here lieth ye Body
of MARGARET BARNARD, an old faithful servant to
ye Earls of Bristol and their Successors above Seventy
years. She gave twenty pounds towards the building of
this Church (and departed this Life April the tenth) An:
Dom: 1716 aged 96"

Several questions: when it says "Here lieth" – is the body
actually placed above the door? Also note the parentheses
marks – it is as if to say her death was incidental – the
important facts are that she was a faithful servant and
that she gave 20 pounds to the building of the church.
Also, the stone looks almost new – so I would assume it
has been replaced.

Wow. There goes a train with a great woosh and high-
pitched sound of speed. The rail line runs right behind
the church (rather, in front of it) and down in a little

valley.

The church is not a large building; I say about 50 or 60 feet long by the same width; it is roughly square. Made of blocks of a pretty and mild yellow stone; the morning sunlight finds orange tinges to the yellow. The ground around it is covered by neatly mowed grass with the gravestones on the two sides. There are four large Gothic arch windows along the side, set with diamond-shaped pieces of plain glass. The roof is, I think, made of slate. There are two large cedar trees on either side of the walk leading from the gate to the church. I think they are cedar. Yes, make it cedar. The stones of this side, many of them, have flaked off the outer layer and so are a bit recessed. The stones of the front look much newer and are of a different color, without the yellow, but rather a gray-white. Here is the legend printed at the top of a card that tells of the services for May/June 1990 – the card is in a small glass-fronted case set on the wall beside the gate. At the top of the case it says "St. Mary Magdalene, Castleton." The legend is "The church is of St. Mary Magdalene founded in the 12th century by BISHOP ROGER of SALISBURY, in the ancient borough of CASTLETON, within the precincts of the Norman castle: moved to this site by SIR WALTER RALEIGH in 1601: and rebuilt by the 5th LORD DIGBY with the help of public subscription in 1715."

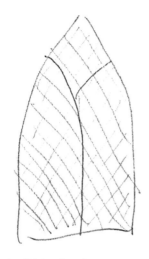

Scribble sketch - an ancient window

So. Margaret Barnard's 20 pounds aided in that.

Onward. Maybe to the castle, if it is not far. Or – maybe
to town.

10:04 AM   Ah, I find that the gate to the castle is just
across the road from the church. And here, just inside
the gate, is the sign "Sherborn Old Castle English
Heritage, Historic Buildings & Monuments Commission
for England (the last in small print) Opening Hours etc.
etc. 55 pence for adults. It opens at 10, so I am right on
time. There is only one car parked inside the gate. Up
the gravel driveway I go.

10:27 AM   I sit – rather half-sit half-lean – on a
remnant of ancient wall. Sherborne Old Castle is but
a tatter and a remnant. It was built in the early 12th
century by Roger dc Cain, Bishop of Salisbury and
second only to the king, Henry I, in power. Elizabeth
gave the castle to Sir Walter Raleigh in 1592. During
the Civil War it belonged to Lord Digby, one of the king's
principal advisers, and was held for the king in 1642 and
1645 – but fell, after a 16 day siege, on August 15, 1645.
Parliament ordered that it be dismantled, so now it is a
ruin.

And I am cold, for there is a sharp cold breeze. From
where I sit on the this remnant of the wall above the deep
ditch (oh, I'd say 40 feet down) I look out over the wall
on the far side of the great ditch and see a pretty lake
down below. The booklet on the castle (which I bought for
85 pence) says Sir Walter, by 1594, built and moved to
Sherborne Lodge – now forming part of Sherborne Castle
beyond the lake to the south. I wonder if I can walk there
from here?

11:50 AM   Here is a pleasant place: Oliver's, a tea

shop on the main street (is it called Cheap Street?) of Sherborne. I sit at a long plank table with chairs for 12 about it. I am the only one at the table now, the four people who were at the other end having just left. There is tranquil flute music, and the sound of a little fountain in the next room. I think I shall sit here until John shows up at 2:30. I may take a salad or a sandwich or I may just sit with the pot of peppermint tea I have before me now. I inherited, on the table, all but the front section of today's Sunday Times and I started reading the lead story of the Style/Travel section, which is *Garbo's Last Days*.

12:45 PM   So. Still at the same seat in Oliver's, having read through all the Sunday Times there is (less the news pages) and briefly looked at my Spanish book. I am a little-doer on a little-doing day. I feel like just sitting today – or maybe lying down. Unfortunately, I don't have a lying down place. I packed my things at the Bridleways before leaving and left my bags – one satchel and one plastic shopping bag – downstairs.

So. Tell me. What to do when one wants to do nothing and there is no place to do nothing in? What are the public nothing-doing places? Well, cafés and coffeehouses – and here I am. But this long community table makes me feel I should be actively eating or drinking or something. Somehow it has not the encouragement to do nothing of a café table; it is not my own, my private, space. The other is a movie theater. No such thing, I don't think, in Sherborne. I don't want to go to a movie anyway. I want to just sit. And write. Or read. If it were a warmer day, I could walk out to the country and sit on a rock. For all I know, in the last hour the little breeze may have died down. But I don't want to walk; I want to sit. I have come from a dizzy time in Madrid and I want tranquility.

Celso and Pepin are absolutely amazing. To be able to go on month after month so involved in the difficulties of others. But they are different kinds of people than me. Celso is always doing something. When there is nothing else, he gets a mop and a pail of water and begins mopping the floor. He is a man who always wants to be *doing*. I spend a lot of my time <u>not</u> doing – but I didn't have much chance to not do in Madrid. Except when I got sick. Who knows? – maybe that is the reason I got sick. It is something, maybe, in my very physicality – I need time doing nothing. Or maybe it is my emotional setting. <u>Doing</u>, I get tense, I worry that I am not doing it right. So doing costs me more than ordinary energy. Does that make sense?

Pepin says Celso was illiterate – though now he reads well. But I don't think reading is a thing he does a lot. For me reading – and writing –are important ways of being. And they are stationary activities. So maybe the reader has a different stance in the world – different from the doer.

Some of these thoughts come out of the first few pages of <u>La Hoja Roja</u>. Don Eloy, the main character, seems something like me. The first sentence is: "For the third time in his life, old man Eloy made himself that night the protagonist of something. The first was at his wedding; the second when he intervened in the Photographic Society in 1933." It goes on to tell how Eloy liked photography and the president of the Society asked him to give a talk (I think?) on a Sunday. And Eloy said, Oh, I don't have anything worthwhile. And the president insisted. Then there is something about Don Eloy's wife:

She never should have married him; she should have married a man a little more decorative. He had made her live on an extremely modest level. In reality, old Eloy lived 36 years together with Lucita (his wife) but he never came to totally understand her, etc.   1:14 PM
I shall pee and then go to the front and get a small salad.

1:29 PM   Still here. Now with a heaping plate of various salads before me.   News   Item: Longtime Vegetarian Returns.   Several things to note: One is that people here don't understand me when I talk. I usually have to repeat myself.   The girl at the front was very nice. She urged me to go back and heap up my plate with more salad, and after I came back she said, Oh you are missing the "_____". The "_____", she said, is a chickpea paste. And when I put some of that on the only little space remaining on the plate, she said, Oh you will want more than that. So I, being very suggestible, went back and put some more – on top of the two little boiled potatoes. And she asked, Are you writing something for your work? I said, Oh no, I'm just writing something, thereby explaining nothing but intimating that I am writing a major novel – or at least a film treatment.

The little boiled potatoes are good. I was disappointed by the cucumbers with pumpkin seeds because the cucumber turned into zucchini. I am eating rapidly although I intend to sit here for yet another 50 minutes – it now being 1:40. What shall I do after I finish eating? I'd rather do something less demanding, more somnambulant, then writing, or reading in Spanish.

I could go across the street to the news store and buy this week's Economist magazine. Although I am running out of money. I got £70 on my Visa card at the airport yesterday and it is almost gone. How did that happen? Let's see. £14 for the rail ticket, £20 for the taxi to Woking, £4 for supper, £1 for a concert program. Oh, £3 for the phone call and cab to Bridleways, and £12 for Bridleways, 85 pence to get into the old castle, 65p for tea, and £3.85 for the salad. What does that add up to? Something over £59, I think. And I have about £9.50 left. So that's about right. There are several banks in town so I should have no problem getting money tomorrow. John has a car so I should be able to get here tomorrow from Holburn. Is that the name of the village to which I am going?

So. After I had my salad in the other room and started to walk back again to this back room, there was a little brown bird on the floor ahead of me, with a bit of a crumb in its beak. I had seen it hop in through the open front door when I was heaping up my salad plate. As I advanced into this room, the bird hopped on ahead of me, until it was under this big table. One of the girls who works here came by and I said to her, There's a little bird under the table. I was afraid the bird would never find its way out the front door again. Oh, she said, he has come in before, he knows his way. She opened a back door; and the bird hopped out. Or so she told me – I didn't see him go.

But I got my answer to the question of what the weather has turned out to be. For, when she opened the door, in came uncomfortably cold air. Today is colder than yesterday. And yesterday, said John, was colder than the day before. Maybe it is the end of the world? Or the end of May? I seem to leave places just as they are turning warm, to arrive in colder places. Such was my journey from Saujon to Madrid, and perhaps from Madrid to here. I hope not. I am for warm weather now. I must get a sweater tomorrow. I noticed there is a secondhand clothing store run by Save the Children up the street a bit. Shall I get a secondhand sweater? I wouldn't have considered that a few years ago, but now I rather like the idea.

2:05 PM   I may as well sit here another 25 minutes and wait for John. The time goes quite quickly when I scribble.   A comment on pee-ing: Here, one goes through a door to the toilets; there are two lady's rooms – why, I don't know – and one men's room. You go through the door to the men's room and then there is another short hallway and another door before you reach the urinals. How different from Spain. Yesterday I went to the men's room in Madrid airport. The men's bathroom and women's bathroom were directly across from each other on a narrow hall. Both had their doors propped open. From the open door of the men's room there was almost a direct line of sight to the urinals and a woman was in the men's room, putting in more paper towels and such things. Anglo-Saxon bathroom norms are quite different from Latin norms. The sense here is retreating into impregnable (sic!) space, whereas in Spain (and France) there is no such sense of layer on layer of privacy protection. But then – I think the toilet booths in Spanish public bathrooms go all the way to the floor, so on the toilet, you have more privacy.

So. This place (the tea shop – actually it calls itself a coffee shop, and why shouldn't I?) – this place has interesting spaces. There is the front room wherein there is the display case with the salads – and other things like quiches, pies, smoked salmon, etc. This case starts right near the front door and runs into the store. Parallel is a long plank table like this one. Then, at the back of that room (placed so it is hard to make out when you enter the store) is an open doorway and a short corridor to this room. This room has this long table in the center and then around the periphery of the room are little coves with lamps placed in them and narrow shelf-tables, maybe a little over a foot wide and looking more like a library – what do you call them? – those places – oh, yes, library carrels. More like library carrels than eating places. But each of these carrels. which are arched and painted a rich rose color, has two chairs before it. Then, in the back of this room, there are two doors. One is to the kitchen. I think it is the kitchen, but what I see from here is a big stainless steel dishwashing machine. Then side by side with that door is another passageway going up two stairs to another room. In that room there are three or four tables set against the wall and separated from each other by wood and curtain partitions which go up about 4 feet.

So. Once again I am the only person at this table. There was a couple at the other end of the table, but they have now left.

2:27 PM   John should be here pretty soon. Hope so, I am ready to leave.

4:58 PM   Plush
The first Clausen/Alpert cross-England trek starts in the village of Plush in front of the Brace of Pheasants pub. The roadside flowers are magnificent – lace white, petal yellow.

7:09 PM   Middle Piccadilly Natural Healing Centre
In the yellow room. With blue trim – a grayish blue. I am

ready. Ready for the middle way, ready to pick a dilly, ready for nature and healing and centering. We did a hike of 4 or 5 miles this afternoon, arrived here about 6:45 and I am now awaiting the supper bell, which is about 7:30.

9:39 PM   And so – soon – to bed. After I read for a couple minutes. I think I will like the place – it is striving to be The Pure Land.   I think we are staying until Friday.

Middle Piccadilly   Monday, May 21, 8:01 AM

Middle Piccadilly. Isn't that great? Middle Piccadilly Natural Healing Centre. Right now I am sitting in the blue wicker chair in my yellow with blue trim room. I just finished filling out my questionnaire: Do you get headaches often? Favorite flavors? (I put down mint, melon and cucumber) et cetera et cetera.   At 9 AM I have my initial consultation and after that I get aromatherapy, which I think is a massage – but we shall see. The reason I am now sitting in the blue chair is because it is forbidden to enter the kitchen for breakfast before 8:30. So I sit here and look out the window at a gray sky and the green vine leaves trembling in the breeze. The green vine leaves hang down at the top of the window.

12:57 PM   Ah, I finally got this pen to work. My regular pen was borrowed this morning and not yet returned. I have had an "aromatherapy" – a massage with scented oil – juniper, lemon and rose for me – this morning. After, I napped. So I am newly risen.   To lunch.

2:32 PM   Sherborne

To the bank, to the laundry, to buy a sweater. That sort

of thing.

7:45 PM   Middle Piccadilly

Sitting in my room waiting for the dinner bell. The opening time for dinner – shall we say the opening of the window of opportunity? – is at 7:30. I get up to look at the notice on the inside of the door to my room; it says: "SUPPER 7:30-8:30 according to the cook. A bell will ring when ready."   Hey – this is natural? This is healing? But isn't it usually this way? In the home? The farm El Colmenar in Spain? But why doesn't the cook start earlier?   This is my stomach talking. My stomach doesn't cotton to uncertain dinner hours. In Spain I was being a Saint among Saints – here I am reverting to type. Pow Pow Pow goes the big spoon against the china bowl, I want my supper, I want my supper   Waw Waw Waw.

This has been a strangely weary day. After breakfast I had my "consultation", talking about my past health and present health, then my "aromatherapy" and then I slept. Lunch and then into town with John. But I felt vaguely ill and quite tired. The woman doing the aromatherapy said a lot of toxins would be released. Feels like it. Really Really.

7:55 Supper's window of opportunity is almost half past. The cook – a young bearded fellow – I think his name is Brian – said that the main dish tonight will be a lasagna. Ah, 7:59 The Bell.   Ask not.

9:25 PM   And so to bed.

Have I mentioned that this is the loveliest day in
England since 1607? My main occupation here
at Middle Piccadilly is sleep . . . catching up
on a month of sleep deprivation.

Middle Piccadilly   Tuesday, May 22, 7:45 AM
The cows – or is it but one cow – are/is mooing. Mooing
doesn't quite express it. It doesn't capture the essence.
For the moo is not a word but a sound. Like the chirping
of the birds. Chirp doesn't catch it either. There is a
desperation, an intensity, an emotion, an – well, it has
to be said – an animal quality – that is not a word, not
language – but is expression. Like Bam Pow Plop Pang.
These animals don't mess about – they put heart and
soul into the sounds. They don't construct anything,
they lay it all out. There. Flat. But now I hear a bird
with a melody. A pretty melody. Not a chirp. Now what
do you make of that? That is not just raw sound. That is
constructed.

I have opened the window a crisp crack to the morning
world and the cold air wafts, washes, weighs down
to the floor and circulates about my bare feet. I have
opened up to the morning, turned off the electric heater.
The window panes were all lightly fogged over, so that
through them I saw but a pale and distant world. Now
there are clearing patches in the middle of each pane and
I see the pale colors of English morning. Pale blue sky,
pale yellow sunlight on pale red brick and pale red tile.
Although the brick and tile are a ruddy pale – or, maybe,
a pale ruddy. But the sounds are not pale. The birds
have never been tamed to paleness by the climate – they
make sharp and piercing sounds. How unmannerly! How
abominably Southern!

7:57 AM　　Only a bit more than one half hour to breakfast. Middle Piccadilly is yet extreme in the breakfast hour, extremely late. The dawn here is a good deal before 5 AM; I can attest to good light at 4:42 AM this morning. That is because that is when I first looked at my watch this morning. And the next time was 5:24 – the last two numbers reversed. And then I, lying back against morning pillow, subtracted 442 from 524 and found it was 42 minutes. So there you have it: an exercise in morning numerology. Not an exact science, but that is the kind of thing one tends to at Middle Picadilly Natural Healing Centre. Then you can go up to :43 and its reversal, :34, and you find that there is 51 minutes difference and you discover that it proceeds this way – by increments or decrements of nine minutes. Now, the next question is whether the opposite of increment is decrement. I don't think so; but yet, there is increase and decrease, so perhaps it is increment and decrement. Another question peculiar to morning at Middle Piccadilly.

There is the insistent cow once again. I think there is a dairy next door. But a dairy would have more than one cow, no? Good thinking. All we can say with certainty before breakfast is that there is a cow next door. Next door is very un-Middle Piccadilly. There is a galvanized tin fence and some big galvanized tin buildings, in bad repair. Not the kind of place –　　Ah, with a grate and a rattle, the window of my bedroom throws itself wide open – the morning breeze takes command. I get up close to the window and I see there is now a crack in one of the panes of glass. I didn't notice that before; I hope it didn't just happen. I feel responsible for the crack and the wind. That comes of being a Jew. One is responsible for the wind when one is a Jew.

Anyway – what I was saying was that the great tin buildings in disrepair ill-comport to be the neighbor of a place where the bedrooms are, for example, in yellow and blue, with blue flowers on the yellow bedspread and yellow flowers on the cream wallpaper. Yes, ill-comport. And the cow is too insistent. Once in a while, well mannered, bucolic – but constant, insistent oooo ooo oooo – that, no.

So, it is now 8:16. I shall put on my socks. All in orderly procession toward breakfast at 8:30, the grand entrance to the day. Don't you think that is a bit too rigid? No breakfast before 8:30? It is not a prepared breakfast. You go in and take dry cereal and there is milk and juice. Do you think this rigidity is English? Or is it only Middle Piccadillian?   So, 8:24 – which makes it three hours from 5:24 and three hours 42 minutes from 4:42. Why, that's half a sleeptime away. For breakfast at 8:30, one should go to bed at midnight, not at 9:30.

12:43 PM   You would not believe what is happening on top of me at Middle Piccadilly. Not on top, that is just a manner of speaking. Within. This morning after breakfast – that means at 9 AM; breakfast is not allowed to proceed in a grand and leisurely manner at Middle Piccadilly. This morning after breakfast, I received a Shen Tao acupuncture treatment from Eliana. Eliana is the re-named woman of the couple who run Middle Piccadilly (before she was named Jo). Ah – I look up now – I am sitting in the blue wicker chair, facing the window in my room. The day has turned to bright blue. All haze is gone from the glass, from the sky. The red tile roof, the red brick wall, stand out sharply against the bright blue sky.

There is a remarkable pattern framed by my window:

Scribble sketch - view from Sunflower Room

So. Anyway. I received the acupuncture treatment at 9. To about 10. And, like yesterday, I fell apart, went back to bed and dozed all morning. We are all agreed that I am being liverish in consequence of my excesses of the past two months: the diet, the pollution, the stress. etc. It is as if I am finishing up my sickness of a few weeks ago. And now it is 1:02 and at any moment will come the lunch bell. Being liverish, I don't have a great appetite – but upon entering the kitchen/dining area, I believe my appetite shall revive.

    1:04   The Bell. There it is. Ask not.

3:46 PM   Our thesis – no, our topic – this afternoon is the British coinage. If I had had my writing folder with me when John and I walked down the road to Her Majesty's phone booth and while John was telephoning London, I would have written about The Green Man. The Green Man is the pub beside the phone booth. The pub sign creaked in the breeze atop a wood pole and showed the head of the Green Man – with a green leaf mustache and green leaf hair. The pub man and the pub lady were outside on the gravel forecourt painting the wooden picnic tables. The pub man was nice enough to change two £5 notes into coin for me so that that I can call Spain.

And now I am back in my room. The Sunflower Room. One of my fellow residents asked me at lunch: How do you like the Sunflower Room? Oh, is that what it is called? I asked. A question for a question – another Jewishness. Yes, she said, I think so. Oh, I like it, I like yellow, I said.

Eliana at Middle Piccadilly (left); John and two other Middle Piccadillians (right)

Have I mentioned that this is the loveliest day in England since 1607? I haven't been here all the days since 1607, but that is my judgment on the available evidence. Anyway, I am sitting in my room examining all my newly acquired money. In my wallet I have £20, £10, and £5 notes. There are no £1 notes – they are coins, fat little brass coins. I now have 10 of them. And. They differ. What a daring country – the money comes in flavors. Out of my ten £1 coins, I have five different flavors. I have four dated 1983 with a girlish-looking head of the Queen on the front and the legend Elizabeth. II D. G. REG . F . D . 1983. On the reverse is the English coat of arms, or so I take it – the unicorn and the lion rampant on the helmet, various diddle daddles and the words HONI PENSE and DIEU ET MON DROIT. Underneath the coat of arms it says, and quite rightly so: ONE POUND.   Then on the rim of the coin – or shall we say the edge? – are the words DECUS ET TUTAMEN with a cross that looks something like this: ☫ between TUTAMEN and DECUS. Translating freely from the Latin, this means Ten and Teach. Or. It could be the names of a Roman couple, familiarly known as Dec and Tut.

Moving on to £1, Type 2 (of which I have two out of my 10), it has a head of an older Elizabeth, wearing a bigger and weightier crown higher on her head, as well as a pendant earring and a necklace (the younger Elizabeth wears no jewelry, but we can see the folds of her gown over her shoulder). The older Elizabeth is cut off at the neck. The inscription is the same but reversed – the younger Elizabeth faces her name, the older the D . G . REG et cetera. And the date on the Type 2 coins is 1989. Now the reverse of the Type 2 coin shows a thistle plant growing through a crown and the words ONE POUND. On the rim are the words NEMO ME IMPUNE LACESSIT, with the cross between LACESSIT and NEMO. My understanding of this is: Never Call Me Lazy.

Okay, now Type 3, of which I have two exemplars. The front of this is the same as Type 2, except the date is 1987. Hey – maybe – the design changes every year? The reverse of Type 3, however, has a tree growing through the crown – I would take it to be an oak tree. On the rim, we go back to DECUS ET TUTAMEN. Hi Dec. Hi Tut. Now Type 4. The front of Type 4 is the same as Type 2 and 3, except the date is 1985. The back has a leek growing through the crown. The edge says PLEIDIOL WYF IN GWLAD with a plain cross between the GWALD and the PLEIDIOL. This is obviously Welsh and I take it as Pleading With Him Glad. Now, Type 5 has a front like 2, 3 and 4, except the date is 1986. The reverse has what I take to be a rose bush growing through the crown and on the rim we are back to DECUS ET TUTAMEN. So there you have it – the story of the £1 coin, delivered direct from the Sunflower Room.

The other coins. Now, sit still – this won't take long.

50 pence – the young Elizabeth. I have one of 1969 and one of 1983 and they are the same. On the reverse is Britania – is that her name? – plumed helmet and Empire gown, trident, olive branch?, a shield with St. George cross and St. Andrew? cross on one side and a lion on the other. Oh yes – the coin is silver colored and seven-sided. Now that's a nice touch – the number of sides is not even – could a democracy do that? Now, the 20 pence coins are – well, I'll be dinged – also seven-sided, with the young Elizabeth. On the back is a crowned rose. All four coins I have are dated 1982. On the bottom is the ever present D . G . REG . F . D – how about Dad Gum Regulation Fire Department? 10 pence – I have a 1968 and a 1969 – young Elizabeth and on the back a lion wearing a crown. These coins say NEW PENCE – I think the two shilling coin is the same value.

5 pence – one coin of 1970 – young Elizabeth and on the reverse a crowned thistle. 2 pence – two coins 1977 and 1988 (both double number years – significant?). These are copper coins with the young Elizabeth, on the reverse is a crown with three feathers stuck through the middle and the words ICH DIEN and a ribbon flowing to and from the crown. Hey – German? Could we guess at I Dare, in German? One penny coin – I have one dated 1988. This has the older Elizabeth, it is copper and bigger than the US penny. On the reverse is what looks like an iron portcullis – you know, the gate behind the drawbridge – with a chain hanging from either side and a crown atop. There you have it – the content of my pocket – giveth by the Green Man.   If I had the energy, I would start on the bills. They too are interesting.

Do you realize how pleasant it is to have nothing better to do than sit in a blue wicker chair in the Sunflower Room on the best day since 1607 and just natter on about nothing?

Why are you inside on the best day since 1607?   Aaaarg – always something I *should* do. Go outside. No, I don't *want* to go outside. At 5 or 5:30, according to which instruction you believe, I am to get a More Bath, which I think is some kind of mud bath. Fun, huh? The 5 PM comes on the little schedule Eliana, the head priestess, gave me yesterday. The 5:30 is on the note posted on my door, which says, This is to remind you of your 5:30 appointment. Confusing, what? So. I shall go pee in preparation and wash my hands of the money and go sit and scribble in the living room, which is the rendezvous for appointments. So I shall be there at 5 and I shall be there at 5:30. Clever, no?

4:59 PM   No, the note says, "Just double checking. Your More Bath is at 5:30." So I shall take that as the last word.

7:14 PM   Post-bath, post-nap, pre-supper. That is the status. And the place is the blue wicker chair in the Sunflower Room. Morre is with two R's and is from Austria – you not only sit in it, you also drink it. Unromantically, the bath was given in the bathroom rather than in The Bath Room. So I took my Morre Bath in the same tub in which I took my shower bath this morning. The water is supposed to be body temperature, but is made a little warmer for me and thee. Into the tub of water is poured a small canister of black liquid, the water takes on the color of mud and the bottom of the tub is gritty. You sit in the tub for a half hour, pat yourself dry, put on a terry cloth robe, drink a cupful of the black liquid – here's mud in your eye – and then you put on a cassette of bing bong ping pong soothing music and go to bed. When you wake, it is a half hour to dinner on the evening of the best day since 1607. That is the story of the Morre – maybe it is Morr – Bath, simply told.

Now it is 7:23, and 7 minutes – not before supper, but rather 7 minutes before the opening of the window of opportunity for supper. Enter John Clausen and he says, "I come here for solace".

Middle Piccadilly   Wednesday, May 23, 7:58 AM
Morning at Middle Picadilly and morning air cools my bare feet and the cow is looing – not mooing. Snorting, neighing. It is the Super-Moo. I have been up early in the morning and up late in the morning. I first got up before 6 AM to walk to the phone booth in Kingstag, about a mile away. To call Madrid. But Madrid was not home –

they must be out at the farm. And then I tried calling my sister. Not home either. I think she is in Italy. So I called TWA. Not home either. So I walked back in the morning mist, past the green fields and lacy white flowers. And back to bed. At 7:30 I rose like a rose and now I sit in the blue wicker chair.

9:55 AM   Out in the sun. Me and the birds and the motor. Very hard to be away from motors. This one is a tractor motor. The tractor is digging up the grass, I think. At least that's what it was at last night, up to 10 PM, when I passed it walking back from the telephone. But now I don't think it is doing anything – just put-a-farting idling and doing noise and fumes over the greenery. It is not a loud motor, but its noise drives all else from my mind. I think I shall have to move.

10:04   I have moved behind the house, where there is no grass, but there is a nice little murky pond set in the flagstones with bright orange goldfish swimming about, and on the far side some pots of bright geraniums. I say on the far side, but the pond is only some 6 feet by 4 feet. Now I hear the motor again because it is working now and reving and charging. And the birds, tweaking and squawking softly. There are two brilliant orange fish and one pale yellow. There is a raven calling caaw caaw caaw caw.

With a horrendous roar that fills the whole sky – splits the sky – a jet fighter screams overhead. That is the fourth or fifth such abomination I have seen and heard these last two days in Southern England. They are based here.

Now a sleek black and cream Siamese cat has walked up

and sits in front of me. And now walks away. Should I make myself a goldfish pond in Santa Cruz? Here there is a purple iris growing from the pond, other plants, round purple leaves floating flat on the water – it is all murky and quiet. Appealing qualities – quiet and murkiness. Murkiness has a tranquil property, somehow.

Ooh, there is a very large pale yellow fish, which earlier was hiding in the greenery. And another pale yellow. So I see two orange and three pale yellow. The big pale yellow is about a foot long – including his beautiful lacy tail.

The fish come up to the surface and gulp, their mouths working busily. They have the mouths and the eyes. These are early inventions, developments of life – we share a lot with these bright fish. There is a wonder about it. Makes you want to learn more anatomy and biology and such.

John comes up, holding on to his blue canvas tote bag. Writing about the left fin on the closest fish? he says – or about the pond and the motor of the bubbles that isn't working?, or about the inside of Ralph? Going into town? I ask. It is a way of being in time, he says.

That disturbs the whole thing I was beginning to write. Of how, when I was pee-ing this morning, I was thinking of how ingenious it was. The body. The elimination. The getting rid of waste products. The water coming out of the body. I looked at the sink and I thought: Well, now that is a clever device – there is someone's thought embodied in it. And the other day I was thinking that about computers and cassettes and such. There are so many new ways now of embodying ourselves. *Embody* is not the right word. Perhaps *materializing* is better.

Putting our thought processes in a material form so they are independent from us, so that they survive us. Previously there were books. And language, rituals, buildings, artifacts, customs. Now there are records and computer software, immensely complex machinery, and industrial and scientific procedures.

And so then the thought comes: Whose thought is materialized – and in this case one can say embodied – in the process of pee-ing? – this way, this ingenious way, of getting waste out of the body. And the other things – the lacy tail of the pale yellow goldfish, the eyes, all that? Since one has in mind that Joe Mifflescottle invented the piped water sink and Crapper the crapper, and so on, one formulates the idea of Super Mind who invented pee-ing and fishes' fins. It is a logical progression. But – is it too simple-minded? Certainly it is the easiest explanation. But then there is the idea of the vastness of time to allow things to develop. And it is the process – not the things – which is astounding. How did the process get going? Again, the vastness of time. Given enough time, the meshes mesh and the fits fit – things nestle down in the best way possible.

I have moved out of the sun, near the fish pond, over a few feet to the shade of the building. I am not a sun person. And by the rocks along the pond are my windbreaker, green and blue and bought in Saujon, and my sweater, dark blue and bought in Sherborne on Monday, and my blue shoulder bag. Here is the Siamese, squawking in the Siamese manner and rubbing against my leg. It is a very sleek and shiny young cat, with a sharp, all-black face. Off it goes again. I could get a cat. I don't like cats. But those are other people's cats I don't like. My cat I think I would like.

Why am I sitting here, in Sunny Southern England, on the second best day since 1607, and thinking about goldfish ponds and Siamese cats for my house in Santa Cruz? Let each country, each place, be a country, a place, onto itself. Let the birds and cats and fish of England be of England.

12:59 PM   Waiting for the lunch bell, sitting in the blue wicker chair in the Sunflower Room. There are puffy white clouds forming in the sky that exists outside the window of the Sunflower Room. English Spring, having lasted a full one and a half days, may be coming to a close. We shall see.

4:55 PM   Dorchester
Illegally parked, so I am sitting in the car. That is the logic and the illogic of it. We just walked through Puddletown Heath, near here, which is not the heath as Thomas Hardy knew it – it is part uniformly planted to conifer and only conifer, and partly clear-cut. There are gorgeous purple rhododendron bushes in full bloom.

6:54 PM   Middle Piccadilly
Feeling good to sit down, and I am sitting in the blue wicker chair. Outside, the leaves are wobbling in the evening breeze, birds are chipping cheaping. We arrived back 20 minutes ago. We stopped for 10 minutes at Minterne, where, it is written, the Churchills lived in the 17th century and now the Digbys live – maybe, once, the Digby of the monument in front of Sherborne Abbey. The grounds of Minterne are lovely, bright flowers, rolling green meadows with white sheep doing the lawn cutting, a lake, all that. And an impressive yellow stone great house which, it is written, was built in 1900 to replace

the former building.

10:08 PM   After supper, after walking to the telephone booth in Kingstag with John and Gaye, one of the four of us here right now, and trying to call Madrid and no one there. They must all be at the farm.

Green grass, golden buttercups

Middle Piccadilly   Thursday, May 24, 7:13 AM
Morning. Birds. Sunshine. All very inviting. It is the best day since Tuesday and before that since 1607. The dead Churchills will attest to that. So I shall bestir myself and without go. Bestir myself from the now familiar blue wicker chair. That involves finding socks, putting on socks and shoes, jacket, hat and scarf and opening two doors. Studies have shown it to be perfectly feasible. For a goal, I shall walk a mile to the famous telephone booth of Kingstag and try calling Spain once more. I don't

believe anyone is there – in the piso. They are all at the farm until Sunday night. But for England, for Spring, for the birds and green grass and lacy white flowers, I shall try once more.

7:57 AM   Kingstag

Standing in morning sunlight, waiting for 8 AM. For at 8 AM open the great grand offices of great grand TWA. So I stand outside the telephone booth by the side of the road and listen to morning birds and stand in morning sunlight. I just called to Spain, and – surprise – Pepin was there and we talked a while. He had been at the farm until last night, I think, and he is going back again tomorrow.

8:01   Can I trust TWA to open promptly? I shall wait another few minutes and continue scribbling in morning sunlight. There are some other people waiting here in the morning sunlight – a young man and an older man – both in shirt sleeves. They believe, it seems, that the best Thursday since 1607 will not betray them. I would guess that they are waiting for a bus to take them to work.
8:04   Now for TWA.

10:15 AM   The ravens. Caw Caw Caw. And the breeze. A cool breeze, a verging on cold breeze, against the back of my neck. The other birds – the chorus of sweet and busy singers. A bee buzzing. The sunlight on the green grass. And five-petaled yellow flowers growing in the grass – John confirms that they are the golden buttercups. The clouds – big puffy white and gray clouds drifting across the sky. Somehow, England seems to be a ship under way across the sea. There is movement, the wind, the clouds. Are they moving past us, or we past them? And doves cooing. The first time I heard them was this morning. And just now I hear them again. It is the same sound I heard in France a couple months ago when I wondered whether it came from an owl or from doves.

12:41 PM   My main occupation here at Middle Piccadilly is sleep. I just awoke from my mid-morning nap. I slept for about an hour and a half. I seem to be catching up on a month's worth of sleep deprivation, for I slept last night from just past 10 to just before six, but yet at 10:30 this morning I felt drowsy again. So. Now I am back in the blue wicker chair, and as I look out the window and up into the sky I see more gray-white than blue. The day is becoming more somber by the minute. The sounds are the tweaks of the birds – no Silent Spring here – and the drone of a motor. I think that tractor is once again working out in front of the house. This morning I had a Bach flower remedy consultation. Subtle bodies and chakras and flower and crystal essences. A poetic way of looking at physical and emotional health. The young woman made up a mixture of essences for me to take – three drops morning and night for eight weeks. I shall do it for it can do no harm and may do good – like speaking to plants, there is a quality of paying attention which is helpful, I think. Modern medicine misses magic and misses subtlety. What begins long before scientific medicine detects it and begins in the subtle interfaces of emotion and spirit and body. That I do think is correct.
So 12:52   Soon will ring the lunch bell.

6:19 PM   So. After washing some clothes, after the walk this afternoon with John down the road and across the meadows to Holwell church, I sit once again in the blue wicker chair. The meadows are full of spring flowers: the little yellow buttercups, and near the roads and hedges the tall lacy white flower, closer to the ground a fuzzy purple flower on a short stalk. Those are the flowers I noticed most among the green green meadow grasses. The grounds of the church at Holwell look rather neglected – there is no real village about the church, just one large imposing looking house, one thatched cottage and a few other houses. The church door was locked but there was a notice posted on a board outside that the key could be had at the second house up the road, which turned out to be the thatched cottage. We walked there, an elderly woman came to the door. I asked whether we could have the key to the church. She said, Well the short answer is No. We talked a bit more, we told her we were staying nearby at Middle Piccadilly and she gave us the key. John asked for a glass of water and she went back into the house, carefully shutting the door and came back with a cup of water.

The inside of the church was unexpectedly well cared for, in contrast to the outside. The main part of the church was built in the 1400s. The English village churches I have seen about here look quite different from the 12th century village churches I saw in the Charante in France. The French churches have very little light, having perhaps just two or three small windows high up in the walls. These English churches have large windows starting a few feet from the floor and thus have good light inside. Is it that the French countryside was much less secure than the English?

10:01 PM   So, having just bought three little rocks from Eliana, to bed. The rocks? Flat oval green, long amber, and an olive green pendant that you hold and it says Yes or No: mementoes of Middle Piccadilly.

Middle Piccadilly   Friday, May 25, 8:17 AM
So. It is an Extreme at the Middle and I sit here among
damp underwear. The last day at Middle Piccadilly. I sit
in the ever present blue wicker chair and look out the
window of the Sunflower Room. Alas, poor Sunflower,
you may not bloom and flourish this day. For the sky is
made up of drifting gray – it may be rain. So I went out
a few minutes ago to take my things off the clothesline.
The merely faintly dampish I brought inside and they
have a place, a warm place, a distinguished place, beside
me on the arms and back of the blue wicker chair. I lean
forward and rest my writing folder on my knee so as not
to dislodge damp socks and underpants. My two shirts
had disappeared from the line before I arrived – so I
assume some kind soul has taken them in. That, or they
have been stolen. I lean to kindness as an explanation,
for it is a far better world et cetera et cetera. So, it is now
8:25 and in five minutes it is breakfast. That is clear and
definite, for breakfast is the one meal of Middle Piccadilly
that is not Pavlovian – no bell.

10:55 AM   So. I have had my diet consultation.
More water, less citrus, no eggplant or pineapple
or peanuts. no milk, salt, red meat, sweets, alcohol,
chocolate, tea, coffee, only olive oil. All of which I agree
with except the eggplant. See a traditional Chinese
medicine acupuncturist. Take lecithin, zinc, calcium and
magnesium supplements for one or two months. Sounds
reasonable and sensible to me. So I sit again in the blue
wicker chair.

We shall leave either before or after lunch which
depends on whether we eat lunch here which depends
on whether we are here when lunch is served which
depends on whether we leave before or after lunch. The

world turns. And it may rain. Meanwhile, I shall go back to *Little Dorrit* by the good Mr. Dickens. Last night I started reading *Little Dorrit* again. Since I am once again speaking English I feel it meet and proper that I return to reading English. So I bought *Little Dorrit* on Monday in Sherborne.

4:26 PM   On the road, off the road – at a roadside rest near Honiton. This is road-world. Road-world-Britain, which is not much different from road-world-America. You can't drive away from the road-world; you can only walk away from it.

5:58 PM   Totnes
Sitting on a bench in a little square of the town by the main street. The main street runs up a hill. It is a charming town and would be much more so, of course, without the automobiles and all the accommodation made for the automobile.

9:16 PM   Ashburton
Sitting in an armchair, looking out a second-story window to green hills rolling off to blue mountains and gray dusk coming on. I like this place. We are in a bed and breakfast on the edge of Ashburton and Ashburton is on the edge of Dartmoor. The B&B is a vegetarian place and it has that down-home flavor. A nice friendly young couple who keep beehives on the moors and have their own chickens and apple trees out back. Looks like secondhand 1930s bedroom furniture, with down quilts on the beds. We had supper in a vegetarian restaurant in Totnes and across the street was a whole food (organic) store with all the Santa Cruz kind of fliers up in the windows: Feldenkrais, women's sexuality, and I don't remember the rest – but environment and new age diet

and new age psychology and all.

So. Now you take the incident of the bird shit plastic chair. At Middle Piccadilly, in the courtyard not far from the goldfish pond, are several white plastic chairs about a low round white plastic table. Now what has happened is that there are great splotches of bird shit on the plastic chairs so one doesn't want to sit in them. (Who are these formidable birds I don't know – perhaps the great black caw-caw-cawing ravens.) Anyway, a couple days ago when I wanted to sit in the courtyard I went around to the front of the house and brought a white plastic chair from there to the courtyard. For some reason, the chairs on the lawn in front of the house are not besplotched with bird shit. So this afternoon John and I were out in the courtyard.

Ah, now I no longer see the green of the hills, I only see dark land and light sky, and the potted geraniums sitting on the inside of the windowsill are reflected in the darkened glass of the window. It is 9:42.

So we walked up to the chairs to sit down and discuss something about the bill at Middle Piccadilly. And John was a little ahead of me and he took a quick step and sat down in the one chair that was not covered with bird shit and he gave a little laugh – which I caught at halfway between triumph and embarrassment. And he said, You can get a towel. That's what I did (to put over one of the other chairs).

So. There was nothing terribly unusual about that, I suppose. But it would not have happened with Pepin or Celso or the people about them. They would have insisted that I take the clean chair. They would have cleaned the other chairs.

That is the magic of what they do. They create a safe world. An environment where you feel that the people

John in the hedgerows

around you will take care of you, where you can feel good taking care of other people and not live in insecurity knowing that it is a cold hard unjust world and that if you do not take every advantage for yourself you will be left in tatters and terror at the end of the day. Making a better world, I do believe, in truth comes from the things that Pepin and Celso do. Not all the grand schemes will do any good unless we give the clean chair to the other. And it is not easy to do – it takes a great deal of will and consciousness.

Ashburton, Devon   Saturday, May 26, 8:09 AM

Fresh morning, the window open to morning. The same green hills and the darker green hedgerows snaking across them. The fields in South England are divided by hedges, some 4 feet high and some 2 or 3 feet broad. Many places the roads are sunk between the hedgerows – that is, the fields on either side are two or three or four feet higher than the road surface and then the hedges rise from the fields alongside the road so that one drives between towering hedges. I see all kinds of roads sunk below the land surface: highways to dirt lanes.

It would be a tremendous labor, without much apparent gain, to dig the roads down this way, so I assume that it happened through some sort of natural process over the centuries. But the process is not clear to me. Has the soil simply washed away, once the surface turf is taken off? Maybe.

So. Now, if I am to write what interests me at the moment, I have to write about John. And yet it is quite possible that he will read this letter or at least that those who know him well will. Well, nevertheless, I shall embark. Right now, I don't feel particularly kindly toward John. I feel resentful toward him. He has a tendency often to be rude and temperamental and inconsiderate. And I am a person who, although I may not show it, is easily offended, who resents very much slights and insults and rudeness. And I come from the School for Living of Spain, where I had before me the great examples of how to live in consideration for other people, how to think of others first. So. More later. 8:25.

9:32 AM   After breakfast. Sitting on the wood frame armchair by the side of the bed, looking out the second-story window to the green hills, the green hedgerows. Now I find myself occupied a great deal with how I relate to John. Somehow, I was with people in Spain but the focus was on doing things – the relationships never seemed to be at the center. Is that the way to say it? I thought of saying: The relationships were transparent – that is, transparent in the sense of a computer program. In a transparent computer program you don't have to concern yourself with how the program works, you proceed directly to do the work you want to accomplish. So – now we are going to walk into town.

On Dartmoor   Sunday, May 27, 12:03 PM
And Willoughby by my side. Willoughby is the dog of the establishment. The hotel. He came with us, now these several miles. Poor Willoughby, he stands and pants – Willoughby is a fat middle-aged dog. But there is no water for him – we have barely enough for the humans among us. When we go down into the valley, I think there shall be a running brook for Willoughby.

From where I lie on the grass turf near a granite rock, I look off to Hay tor. And a tiny red mite of a spider runs across this page. The third one I've seen. Now one runs across my hand – they are as common as ants. The other inhabitants of Dartmoor: young ferns, unfolding and upcurling, and dark green spiny bushes. And the sheep and cows and wild ponies. There are very few trees – none close by. Although on the hillside across the valley I see some of the white flowering trees. These are medium-sized deciduous trees covered now with little white four-petaled flowers. They look like miniature apple blossoms and completely cover the tree. The leaves of the trees look like Oak leaves, lobed and indented.

Oh, here is Willoughby again, panting and slobbering. Down Willoughby. Willoughby seems old by the way he moves, but his coat is still a lustrous rich chocolate brown. I wish I had brought my *Little Dorrit.*

My God, there is a plethora of miniature insects. Here is a fly no bigger than a pinhead. I am reading *Little Dorrit* again and I am in the *Rich* section – where all the Dorrits are fabulously wealthy, up from Marshalsea Debtors Prison, where Little Dorrit was born some 20 odd years earlier.

Dartmoor's white flowering trees

Dickens opens the second half of the book, the *Rich* section, at a monastery at the top of the pass between Italy and Switzerland. This is a parallel to the beginning of the book, which opens at a quarantine station in the Port of Marseille.

Willoughby is a great nuisance. He refuses to lie down. I think he wants something to eat – as befits the house dog of a gourmet hotel. I think he regrets having strayed so far from the fleshpots. Ah – there he goes after two little fox terriers and their master. We may have lost Willoughby.

So. The moor. What is a moor? Well, maybe it doesn't mean much more then unused land. There are the rough and rolling hills, the granite outcrops, the stony eminences, which are called tors.

4:04 PM   So. On high – highest of the high. I am sitting on top of Hay tor, warm in the afternoon sun, looking out over miles of rolling greenery. Down below are the many colored cars, parked and rolling and roiling, and the people lying about on green turf. John is clambering about on the tor over there, which looks like a giant stone sculpture of a brain or an intestine – something like that.   Stone   Sky   and   Grass.   Ah – here arrives a rock climber who came up the sheer face of Hay tor. I came up the easy clamber side. Well, down I go.

Above my head on the white plastered wall is the head of a long-gone stag and off to my right are a helmet and breastplate and a fearsome looking broadsword

Ilsington   Monday, May 28, 4:24 PM
In the church yard. Ilsington is a village about a mile or two from our hotel at Haytor Vale. We see the church tower from the window of our room and we decided to walk over. It is an old village with a 13th to 15th century church and several thatched houses, peaceful, surrounded by the green rolling hedge-rowed hills. And it is not charming. Why? Because, I think, it doesn't

want to be charming, the inhabitants don't want to be charming. The little touches are lacking. Plain Jane working people in a Plain Jane village. There are not, I think, many outsiders in Ilsington.

6:28 PM   Haytor Vale
In the Rock Inn – the pub of Haytor Vale. We walked back here on a rather longer route of 2 1/2 miles. We have a dinner reservation for 7 PM at the bar. John walked on

back to the hotel and I am sitting in a Victorian pow-wow circle made up of five stuffed armchairs covered in the same antique floral pattern cloth. This circle is in a small room a half flight of stairs down from the bar level. Right above my head on the white plastered wall is the head of a long gone stag and off to my right on the wall is a helmet and breastplate from, say, the 16th century and next

Churchyard at Ilsington

to them hangs a fearsome looking broadsword. No – I look again – the walls are not plastered, they are stone and they are whitewashed or white painted. (I don't know the difference between whitewash and white paint.) The walls are over a foot thick, as I can see in the opening of a small window on the wall to my left.

So. John and I had a good talk in the graveyard. The graveyard of the church at Ilsington. I find that I have glitches of irritation and resentment at things he does. And he also has glitches with me. Traveling together is never easy. Particularly, probably, for me – since I am accustomed to being by myself, doing exactly what I want to do when I want to do it, and not having to accommodate other people. So it is necessary, I think, to keep talking, keep talking to keep being friends as well as fellow travelers. The difficult thing is that I invariably find that these momentary and daily glitches of relationship go all the way down and all the way back to the bedrock of being. So, this could be a voyage across the briny deep as well as a trip across the moors and headlands.

So. Now appetite is stirring. I had a light lunch – a cup of stewed fruit and a slice of bread and several crackers with tahini. The great culinary event of today, thus far, occurred at breakfast, for at breakfast at the hotel I had a real English kippered herring. For the last time. As Mr. F used to say (this from Flora Casby, the character in *Little Dorrit*. Flora always quotes her dead husband, Mr. F.) – Mr. F said something like: Nothing in life repeats itself, except the kippered herring you had for breakfast. That has been my experience – once I had kippered herring at 8:30 AM, I had it again all morning and into the afternoon. Actually, Mr. F. may have mentioned another food. I will look it up in *Little Dorrit* – if I remember and if I can find it – and duly record the word for word in these pages. The kippers I have been familiar with in the

United States come in a long flat can and are little strips of rather moist smoked fish. The one at breakfast this morning was the whole fish, strong, dry and bony.

6:57   Another few minutes and dinner will be on – we have a 7 PM reservation. We also ate here last night. I think I shall look about for John. He may not find me here midst the armor in the Victorian pow-wow circle.

8:51 PM   At Room 1, Hotel Bel Alp

Yes. Here is the quotation from Mr. F (according to Flora in *Little Dorrit*). It is at page 463 (Part 1, Chapter 35). Flora says (and it wouldn't do any good to quote the preceding part of her declaration, for Flora talks in a wholly disconnected way: "... but that is past and what is past can never be recalled except in his own case as poor Mr. F. said when he was in spirit, cucumber and therefore never ate it." Amen, Mr. F – but in *my* own case it is kippered herring.

Launceston, Cornwall   Tuesday, May 29 1:44 PM

Just a word. In the rain in the restaurant – the Greenhouse, a vegetarian restaurant. We are driving to the coast of Cornwall and Launceston is just inside Cornwall from Devon. A town in the rain, with stone town gate and stone castle remains.

3:40 PM   Tintagel

Cold. Oh oh, why did I leave my long underwear in Madrid? I sit in the car and the cold wind whistles without. The car is parked in the yard of LUXURY FLATS FOR SALE, STARTING AT £39,950. At one side King Arthur's Bookstore and across the street is King Arthur's Tea Shop. The rain comes pelting down on the car roof now.

5 PM Tintagel

Hey, it is interesting. Rose is the color, outside is the Rock. Also outside is white mist, a small black bird, feathers ruffled and rumpled, sitting atop the chimney, and, beyond the Rock, the Sea. I sneeze mightily three times; something in the room irritates my nose. Rose is the color of the carpet, the drapes are blood red, the wallpaper is rose on white and tan, the bedspread is rose and yellow-tan. Two heaters are going. Ah, there goes the Workman, carrying his tools. The Workmen, an elderly fellow, has been, as we say in the vernacular, potchking about the house all afternoon, blocking doorways with battered aluminum ladders and that sort of thing.

I have set my chair in front of the big plate glass window and I look out, first at the black tarpaper and gravel surface of the deck, with the pools of rain water and the raindrops shivering into the pools, then at the wood plank fence about the deck, and then, through the horizontal spaces between the planks, at the Rock. The Rock is where the Castle was – the castle reputed to be that of King Arthur.

And now I wish I had bought the used paperback of Spencer's *Faerie Queene* when I saw it on Saturday at the used bookstore in Totnes. For that is the thing to read while looking at the Rock. Tintagel is sort of Coney Island At The Castle. Although I have never been to Coney Island so perhaps I am not qualified to compare. The King Arthur Bookshop, which sells trinkets and trash and a few books, the King Arthur Tea Shop, fish and chips – all that kind of thing, and on the Tuesday after the bank holiday weekend and in the cold rain, still the streets are crowded with aimless and bored people.

Mr. Guest and me – note the plank fence about the second story deck

The house I am in is on the last street running parallel to the sea. It is a vegetarian bed and breakfast run by Mr. Guest. But Mr. Guests's métier is more buying and selling; he showed us the three flats on the main street which he has for sale. The bed and breakfast is a hobby of his wife. But. His wife is now in Canada so the bed and breakfast is more or less shut down and the Workman is potchking through it and the breakfast table is covered with flashlight, dishtowel, cellophane tape, thumbtacks, bottle lids, rubber bands and several dozen other unremembered miscellaneous objects. The same miscellany is spread across all the surfaces in the kitchen. I helped John for 40 minutes putting away things and clearing away the surfaces of the kitchen. John is soul-bent on cooking macrobiotic. For, of the 100,000 things that humankind has found to eat, John eats only 14. And so, since it is nigh impossible for him to find food that agrees with him in restaurants, he wants to cook for himself.

Actually, although I was mildly appalled when we first arrived, I like this place more with each passing minute. Mr. Guest, though not much of a housekeeper, is a friendly and interesting fellow. He lived in Canada near Toronto for many years and will probably return there. He competed for England as a shot putter in the Rome Olympics but, as he says, he is just too little. I was only 200 pounds at the time, he says. And he has M.E., which I just heard of a few days ago – I think at the Natural Healing Centre at Middle Piccadilly. It is, apparently, some kind of flu-like virus which you never get rid of.

Anyway. I have to go back and elucidate on John's food. He is quite sensitive to food and wants to eat very sensibly – no spices or fats or sugar. Which is hard to do, even in vegetarian restaurants. There are white pigeons on the deck outside – and coveys of dove-ys float in the wind above. A further word about the heaters. There is one heater in each of the bedrooms. But, says Mr. Guest, they are – what did he call them? – stationary heaters, I think. Stationary heaters, he said, you must turn on the night before. They have bricks inside, he said, and the electric coils heat the bricks which stay hot. So he brought up another heater, a radiant heater, which is providing the now-time heat. But there is only one, which is in John's bedroom, which is the Rose Room, so it is here that I sit scribbling. Our landlord is seeking, he said, to borrow another one for my bedroom.

Tintagel   Wednesday, May 30, 11:32 AM
Almost ready – to hike.

1:50 PM   Trebarwith Strand
On the rocks by the sea – a rocky cove, an opening in
the cliffs where a little stream comes to the sea – much
like places near Santa Cruz. But this is a much-visited
place. There is a pub on the other side of the stream and
sunbathers on the narrow strip of sand. We walked here
about 2 miles up from the south. Our friendly landlord,
Mr. Guest, drove us to the starting place and we are
walking back to Tintagel.

Tintagel   Thursday, May 31, 8:13 AM
I already walked into the village this morning – the
tourist tattered village of Tintagel. My hope was to buy
the morning newspaper, but the news agent doesn't open
until 8:30. So said the young man in the butcher's shop
across the street. The butcher and a tea shop were the
only places open shortly after 7:30 AM. Also, in a nearby
parking lot, the Thursday market was setting up. I saw
only one table – of clothing – already set up. No fruits
and vegetables. Tintagel is the kind of place where I
would expect the major stalls of the weekly market to
be selling ashtrays made in Taiwan saying "Souvenir of
Tintagel, King Arthur's Castle". I came back in one-third
of the distance by climbing a fence and cutting across a
meadow. Strangely I came back to the same place that
puzzled me yesterday when I returned from our walk
along the coast. I was not feeling too good at that time.
I had eaten a lot of cherries and the result was an upset
stomach. Ah – the porridge is ready.

8:57 AM   After breakfast. A pigeon is cooing outside.
The pigeon is not a natural here. Mr. Guest's son keeps
them. And thus the circling white doves about the place.

11:17 AM   Sitting on top. It is said to be the highest

cliff in England. Some 3 miles north of Boscastle. The sea far below is glassy gray blue and breathing. Up and down, swell and wane. The only white is where the swells strike the rocky shore. Here, in this microplace, microclimate, it is a balmy day. A few feet landward. over the little ridge. there is a smart little breeze blowing. Overhead the sky is blue, but out to sea, it frays into gathering thin gray-white clouds. The woman at the National Trust Farmhouse, where we started a mile back, said it would rain later today

John and the Cornwall sea

4:44 PM   Boscastle

Sitting in the afternoon sunlight on a curbboard in Boscastle – warm and unbalanced, mildly weary and my stomach saying who? wha?. I just ate a quarter of a pastie and a modicum of a Cornish cream tea. You have to work 16 hours a day in the slate quarries to appreciate those. Me – I'm still tofu and grains.

~

Leaving England

The one-car yellow train rolls through the evergreen fields of Somerset. It is exciting to be setting out, slowly and orderly, on a long journey. I wouldn't mind going at this speed all the way to Santa Cruz.

Castle Cary, Somerset   Saturday, June 2, 6:42 PM
Away away. The one-car yellow train rolls through the evergreen fields of Somerset – away, away. Away to Westbury, Reading and Heathrow. In an orderly genteel kind of way. Dark trees and a stone tunnel, a stone shell of a tower on a hill. Next town. 6:45. Stop. Wild pink roses alongside the track. It is flower time, rose time, writing time. It is exciting to be setting out, slowly and orderly, on a long journey. Hey, I wouldn't mind going at this speed all the way to Santa Cruz. (Here is the conductor – white hair, rosy red, bulging blue-shirt belly.) Oh, I'd say 20 miles per hour. Leisurely, sedately, stopping the night in inns spaced across the sea. Fish dinners and a swim in the sea water pool. 200 miles a day. Ten days to New York. Or it could be a ship.

It is a shame – there are only four of us venturers, voyagers, on the yellow car from Castle Cary and points beyond.   Black and white and green all under: cows

on the meadow.   So. Here is a point: there are no
hedgerows alongside the rail line. Now. is that because
the railroads have only been about for 150 years?

Flower time in Somerset

7 PM   Fromme.   We are not going to get to Westbury
much before my 7:20 train from there to Reading. Yes
– and 150 years is not enough time for a hedgerow to
develop? Or, is it that this is now out of the hedgerow
country? I don't think so – there were hedgerows in
Dorset and Devon.   Next stop Westbury – I shall
gather myself together.

7:12 PM   Westbury

On Platform 3, waiting for the 7:20. It is a blessing to
understand the announcement. Westbury, it must be
told, smells. Like cow shit. Fact. Can't change facts. To
what do we attribute this? Fertilizer factory? Cows?

Could be cows. So. The 7:20 arrives at Reading at 8:11. But I don't get to Heathrow until 9:50. That is by bus. Maybe it is not cow shit. It is more a chemical smell and it begins to burn my throat. In the modern world there are things distinctly worse than cow shit. Distinctly. A chill wind blows down the tracks. I sneeze. I shall recover my faithful cashmere scarf from my blue shoulder bag.

7:23 PM   Gliding out of Westbury, silken smooth, rolling, rolling. This is the train of trains – the InterCity to London town. Actually this is the line of my old friend – what was his name? The builder of the Great Western Railroad to Bristol and the Atlantic sea? He had a name to conjure with. Can't remember it. Something like Ichabod Kingdom Somebody. Paddington Station and the Great Western Hotel and the great iron paddle-wheel steamers to America. [2016 Note: Isambard Kingdom Brunel, 1806-1859.]

7:43 PM   Say Hey – alongside the track is a canal, locks and all. And riverboats on it.

Heathrow   Sunday, June 3, 9:53 AM
At the Berkeley Arms – not a bad airport hotel – £31, neat room and buffet breakfast, which I liked not, for there was no porridge. I have a willy-wobbly stomach yet. It is a cool overcast morning. I wait for the 10 AM hotel bus to the airport, standing in front of the Berkeley Arms, leaning against the glassed-in entrance. Across the street there is Ace Motor Spares, Tote Bookmakers, Heathrow D.I.Y. Hardware: "Timber and Glass cut to size – Tool Hire – Lawn Mower". England is still a nation of shopkeepers. The Berkeley Arms has a low plastered wall about its asphalted precincts and at the driveway entrance, the wall ends in two pillars. The pillars come to

a point with a roll below it, like the hat of a medieval lady and then below the roll there is a cone covered with small slabs of green-gray slate – a bad architect's evocation of the tone and timbre of Berkeley Arms.

10:04 AM   On the bus and away – on the road, past the plastered low wall, past the shops. Chemist, grocer, gas station – yes, the stuff of daily life at Heathrow. Now, the road borders the airfield – airplanes, autos, a miscellany of buildings and dark green bushes. On the other side of the road are the airport hotels, now a large new Texaco gasoline station. We pass among the big black square and solid London taxicabs. Now we pause at a light. The overpass has a sign: "British Steel. A Great British Company". Now through a long tunnel, I suppose it goes under the runway. There, to the right, is a great tall tower with a large radar screen, going round and round, atop.

10:12 AM   We stop at Terminal 2 – this is where I came in last night on the bus from Reading. The gray-haired English couple, who are going to Austrian Airlines, get off. My my – I fear I will carry back half a dozen unwritten postcards.

10:22 AM   Terminal 3
In the terminal. There is a great confused crowd of people and luggage in one corner of the terminal. Over the heads of those that go before me I see red signs which say "TWA SECURITY – STOP HERE". The fellow in front of me says that the papers have said that security is going to be much tighter – they are going to open one bag in ten – so it is said.

10:30 AM   We inch and push and gradually gradually

approach the red signs. It looks like this is a preliminary line. After this line, you get in the regular ticket line. So it goes in Airport Land. I now doubt I will have a chance to buy the Sunday paper – this looks like a full time, two hour job – standing in various lines.

10:39 AM   The rate is about a foot every three minutes.

10:42 AM   Now fourth or fifth from the desk with an Airport Personage at it.

10:56 AM   Now in the Next Line. In Line #1, a bright young woman asked me some searching questions. Where have I been in Europe? What part of Madrid did I stay in? When I said Vallecas, she said, Oh, in the Southwest part, it's rather a poor neighborhood, isn't it? I told her of my friends. She asked in some detail what I had in my bags – battery operated devices? gifts given to me? did I pack it myself? The process is, at the same time, scary and reassuring. The airlines have turned serious about security.

11:29 AM   Still waiting in lines. Checked and re-checked and checked again. Through the x-ray machines a second time. The fellow in front of me was completely patted down in a weapons search. Now the final line at the boarding gate. My God, boarding an airplane is a deadly serious business. The only thing I had time to do, other then wait in lines, since my departure from the hotel at 10 AM was to buy the Sunday newspaper. Had I a free half hour I would have spent my remaining £60 on something.

11:39 AM   In the lounge – finally. We are boarding.

12:01 PM   On the plane – and have been for 20 minutes. The plane is full. I have a window seat, but no window.

12:52 PM   Up and off – white mist curling fiercely over the wing. Through drifting white shreds of cloud. Maybe we will reach sunshine? Not yet.

10:12 PM (New York time)   New York
3:13 AM in England. Happenstance took me to New York.

~

New York City

It cost $3.19 and I got a straw. An orange juice at the Fountain Cafe in Lincoln Center – out in the open air, umbrella overhead and blooming impatiens in the flower box at my elbow.

New York   Monday, June 4, 7:27 AM
New York is Summer. That is what drove the search for a New World – the search for warmth. Spices and Summer. Maybe because New York is closer to the Sun, it becomes Summer here suddenly. Now, I am 40 stories closer to the sun, sitting on the futon in the spare bedroom of Ron Goldsand's apartment on East 72nd St. From below, far away muffled, comes the sustained mechanical roar of a bus motor.

5:12 PM $3.19 and I got a straw. That is the Fountain Café at Lincoln Center and an orange juice. Out in the open air, umbrella overhead and blooming impatiens in the flower box at my elbow. Pink and paler pink and red and redder.

I have been living a New York kind of day today. I walked down Third Avenue from 72nd St. to 32nd St.

and then went to a French restaurant around 29th St. for lunch with Janet Ashe. The restaurant was small and noisy, the food was excellent – I had a green salad and roasted monkfish. Then I started walking back up Third Avenue, but around 50th, I took a bus. As I got off the bus, there was Ron jogging by. New York is actually a small town; yesterday evening, I was walking towards Central Park with Ron and, Hello, there was Janet walking with a friend. So – Ron showed me a ticket for tonight's ballet (standing room – $11) he had bought. So I came here to Lincoln Center to buy one for myself. Ron said, It's a short way – just through Central Park. But I am walked out for this Monday, so I took a cab – $4. So, between orange juice and cabs, it will cost me more to buy the ticket then to pay for the ticket, if you follow me.

Otherwise, it is no longer summer in New York. Autumn approaches with a shifting bit of breeze and gray clouds overhead.

New York – Grand Central Station
Wednesday, June 6, 10:12 AM

On the train – the choo-choo train to Saratoga Springs. I am going for the waters and I feel much in need of the waters cure. I feel mildly trembly within after going to bed near 1 AM last night and up at 6:30 and carrying my bags through the streets of New York and the precincts of Grand Central Station. This is a grand railway car – large and solid, rich red and brown, velveteen and the New York Times. Backward in time we will roll – to solid times and solid places in solid rail cars. The years will roll away and when I arrive in Saratoga Springs, it will be 1880 – a solid gentleman arrives for the water cure. I have the touches and the forethought. The New York Times, a copy of Mr. Dickens book, The Pickwick

<u>Papers</u>, a roast breast of turkey sandwich and a green salad. Aha – the gentleman in the navy-blue blazer and the lady are speaking Russian as they sit in the seats behind me. A merchant of Petersburg or a minor noble in the Tsar's Russia, no doubt. The wheel goes round and round and there are Tsarists at Saratoga Springs. The Old Order is flickering on once again, Winston. Too bad you are not here – you now could go back to Africa and once again conquer the unruly Boers. Yes yes – and of course, we must recognize that the turkey sandwich is in an orange and white paper bag, the green salad in a clear plastic carton. The Tsar can be restored and the Boers conquered – plastic will take longer.

1:33 PM   Leaving Albany. We are now on a bridge crossing a wide river. Is it yet the Hudson? Now we are on the same side as the tall buildings of central Albany. In between Grand Central Station and Albany, I have eaten the turkey sandwich and the salad. Read through half the New York Times, talked to Margery Wolfe, who sat down next to me, read the proposals of the Social Justice Committee, and occasionally looked out at the broad blue-gray Hudson flowing. So now I feel stuffed in body mind and spirit. If I sufficiently digest the turkey, I would dearly love a hot bath and a massage this afternoon. Possible?

Albany airport   Thursday, June 14, 5:52 AM
Homeward, Homeward.   Albany   to JFK
to SF0   to Home.

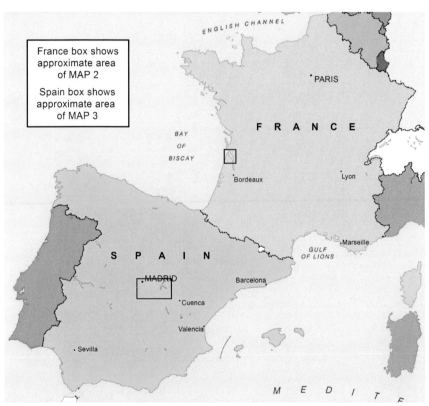

Map 1: Locations in France and Spain

(➡ points to La Petite Eguille)

1 cm = 2 km

1 inch = 3.16 miles

Map 2: Countryside around La Petite Eguille

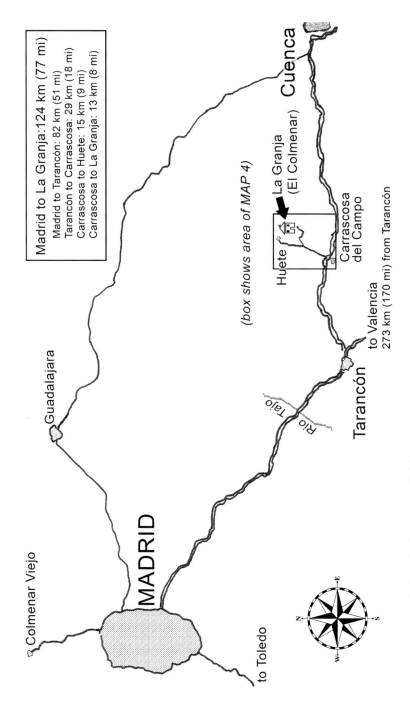

Madrid to La Granja:124 km (77 mi)
Madrid to Tarancón: 82 km (51 mi)
Tarancón to Carrascosa: 29 km (18 mi)
Carrascosa to Huete: 15 km (9 mi)
Carrascosa to La Granja: 13 km (8 mi)

Cuenca

La Granja
(El Colmenar)

Huete

Carrascosa
del Campo

(box shows area of MAP 4)

to Valencia
273 km (170 mi) from Tarancón

Tarancón

Río Tajo

Guadalajara

MADRID

Colmenar Viejo

to Toledo

Map 3: La Granja in relation to Madrid

320

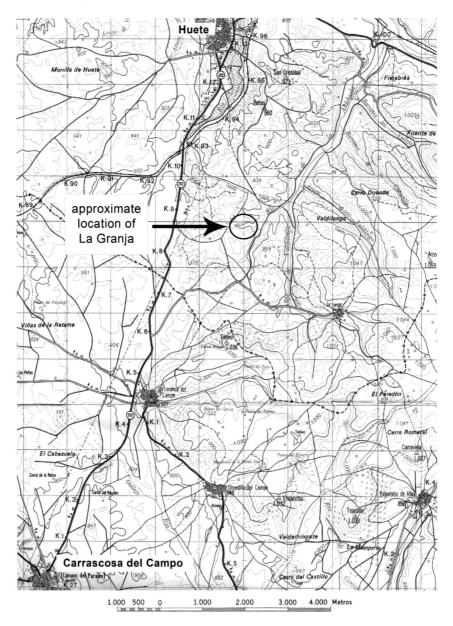

Map 4: Countryside around La Granja

List of photos and scribble sketches

Made in the USA
Middletown, DE
04 February 2017